Praise for *Creep*

"Brilliant . . . [Gurba] skins the myth of California as a progressive playground. In its place, she offers a blistering portrait of life in the golden state . . . Despite the degradations and horrors *Creep* chronicles, it's a hopeful book. A hopefulness shot through with anger, awareness, and unrest. A hope rooted in the steadfast belief other worlds are possible."

—*The New York Observer*

"Personal, incisive, and comprehensive . . . Gurba delivers a brilliant critique that looks at history, racism, misogyny, the carceral state, modern heroes, and her own identity while exploring how to defy the oppressive actions of creeps."

—Alta

"A emotional firestorm of a memoir that reaches deep into the toxic traditions that run rampant in the U.S. This book helps readers connect the dots around collective oppression and find our way out."

—KCUR's Up to Date

"Truly exceptional . . . Gurba's lyrical prose forces us to face the sexism, racism, homophobia, and other systems of oppression that allow some Americans to get away with murder while the rest of us live in constant fear. Every piece is rife with well-timed humor and surprising conclusions, many of which come from the author's staggering command of history. Profoundly insightful, thoroughly researched, incredibly inventive, and laugh-out-loud funny, this book is a masterpiece of wit and vulnerability."

—*Kirkus Reviews* (starred review)

"A truly distinctive, authentic, and dynamic literary voice . . . Without a doubt, *Creep* confirms that Myriam Gurba is one of our great American intellectuals, one who expertly utilizes a rapier wit to slice away the façade of hypocrisy, bigotry, bullying, and crime that marks our contemporary moment. She speaks truth to power with panache and lawyer-like logic, producing eloquent and vital essays that simultaneously provoke and entertain."

—*Los Angeles Review of Books*

"[With] sharp wit, keen observations, literary stylings and wrath . . . *Creep* [is] a tender and beautiful ode to [Gurba's] Mexican and Mexican-American heritage, the powerful men and women in her family, and how this identity is a strength and a source of art inextricable from who they are in the world . . . Gurba is fearless and unrelenting, sharing her own stories and threading them with history, literature and cultural criticism . . . Each piece is layered and rich. Gurba skillfully captures how all the concerns she examines here intersect. It will challenge readers in all the right ways . . . Gurba is a force to be reckoned with, and *Creep* is mighty powerful—a terrifying, even humorous, masterful ode to place and self."

—*BookReporter*

"Gurba's writing . . . has the intensity of making plain what you likely have felt or experienced, but not put language to."

—Diana Arterian, *LitHub*

"Powerful . . . Full of lean prose and biting commentary, [*Creep*] is as emotionally heavy as it is hard to put down."

—*Publishers Weekly*

"Fierce and engaging cultural criticism."

—*Library Journal*

"As insightful as it is poetic, [*Creep*] explores the knife's edge between sanity and madness."

—*Bay Area Reporter*

"Gurba's ability to deftly connect cultural and personal histories with heartbreaking poeticism and laugh-out-loud wit is often dazzling. A profound collection of essays on the ways violence seeps into the lives of the marginalized."

—Electric Literature

"[A] wide-ranging collection of memories . . . Gurba [. . .] vividly dissects the insidious toll of sexual violence and racism through firsthand experience [and] unsparingly challenges us to confront the many ways those who prey on others are obscured and even protected by our society."

—*Booklist*

"Brilliant."

—*The San Francisco Chronicle*'s
"Most Anticipated Books of Fall 2023"

"Gurba goes for the jugular."

—*Bustle*'s "Best New Books for Fall"

"In *Creep*, Gurba stitches together a no-holds-barred analysis of violence in and out of national borders, interpersonal relationships, and literature. It is a testament to Gurba's dexterity as a writer but also her courage to embark upon the expedition of her own memories."

—Morgan Jerkins, *New York Times*
bestselling author of *This Will Be My Undoing*

"Boom! Myriam Gurba's writing is a nuclear explosion."

—Silvia Moreno-Garcia, bestselling author of *Mexican Gothic*

"Myriam Gurba is not someone you want to make mad. Her writing makes me feel like I have a far cooler, smarter big sister standing up to familiar monsters: bad men, our deepest fears, Joan Didion, our stolen girlhoods. Myriam makes me think and feel but, most importantly, Myriam's writing makes me feel like writing because her fire is contagious."

—Karla Cornejo Villavicencio, author of *The Undocumented Americans*

"With its powerful voice and truth-telling, Creep will help cement Myriam Gurba's reputation as a singular and essential voice in American literature. Again and again, the tales in this book reveal the strength of a woman joyfully and relentlessly defending her dignity against those who would demean her."

—Héctor Tobar, author of National Book Critics Circle award finalist *Deep Down Dark*

"Myriam Gurba is the most fearless writer in America. And is most generous and kind to those who have no champion, while setting fire to the towers of the villainous. *Creep* is another beautifully daring book. Long may she reign."

—Luis Alberto Urrea, Pulitzer Prize finalist and author of *Good Night, Irene*

"The poetic wit, humor, and brutal brilliance of Myriam Gurba's *Creep* make for unforgettable reading."

—Lisa Teasley, author of award-winning *Glow in the Dark* and *Fluid*

"With deadpan humor and devastating wit, Myriam Gurba creeps through the hypocrisies of rape culture, patriarchal violence, anti-Mexican racism, and familial trauma to expose the brutality in everyday life. Who else could take on Joan Didion's racial grammar while demolishing Barbies and extolling the integrity of sluts? 'Humor can only go so far,' Gurba writes, and when she drops the mic on her own survival the text shimmers. Meticulously researched and boldly articulated, *Creep* dares us all to stop pretending."

—Mattilda Bernstein Sycamore, author of *The Freezer Door*

"Myriam Gurba, in her fiercest and most original work yet, reminds us that our personal and familial histories are inextricably linked to the violences of historical memory; that no amount of silencing of our language and literatures can undo the shameful legacies of dispossession and dehumanization. *Creep* is a powerful work that narrates the trajectory of one Mexican family and the feminist geographies of both self-making and self-destruction against the backdrop of a violently misogynist twentieth century. Necessary and unsettling, Gurba's razor-sharp insights puts us all in touch with the insidiously toxic and systematic demand for our complacency and compliance. A masterful writer, Gurba graces our collective rage with a finely crafted prose more dangerous than any arsenal."

—Raquel Gutiérrez, critic and academic

"'Kids in California inherit a macabre history,' Gurba writes, and, as a trans queer person who grew up in California, *Creep* attends to questions within me whose answers, until this moment, only rumbled beneath the surface. Decolonizing with exactitude, deep intelligence, extensive research, embodied knowledge, family history, and memoir, *Creep* ingeniously spans an immense range of subjects, interrogating the archives of history that exist within and without us, painting it all with masterfully complex and colorful poetic strokes—and with depth and humor. This is the best book I have read in years, the LGBTQIA+2 anthem I have been waiting for. Myriam Gurba is a genius and the voice of our generation. *Creep* has liberated me."

—Daniel Sea, filmmaker and actor

ALSO BY MYRIAM GURBA

Mean

Painting Their Portraits in Winter

Dahlia Season

CREEP

ACCUSATIONS AND CONFESSIONS

MYRIAM GURBA

Avid Reader Press
NEW YORK LONDON TORONTO
SYDNEY NEW DELHI

Avid Reader Press
An Imprint of Simon & Schuster, LLC
1230 Avenue of the Americas
New York, NY 10020

Creep is based on my recollection and interpretation of many moments that made me. I expect that some people may remember these events differently. I have changed certain names and identifying details while remaining faithful to core truths. Dialogue, conversations, and other instances of speech have been reconstructed to the best of my ability.

First Avid Reader Press trade paperback edition September 2024

AVID READER PRESS and colophon are trademarks of Simon & Schuster, LLC

Simon & Schuster: Celebrating 100 Years of Publishing in 2024

Manufactured in the United States of America

1 3 5 7 9 10 8 6 4 2

Library of Congress Control Number: 2023936256

ISBN 978-1-9821-8647-0
ISBN 978-1-9821-8648-7 (pbk)
ISBN 978-1-9821-8649-4 (ebook)

Ya mataron a la perra,
pero quedan los perritos.

—A popular corrido

CONTENTS

CREEP

TELL

It's easy to get sucked into playing morbid games. When I was little, I happily went along with a few.

I played one with Renee Jr., the daughter of the woman who gave me my second perm. She and Renee Sr. lived in a tall apartment building across the street from the used bookstore where I sometimes spent my allowance. Sycamore trees towered in a nearby park, and when their leaves turned penny-colored and crunchy, falling and carpeting the grass, they created the illusion that we lived somewhere that experienced passionate seasons. Santa Maria's seasons could be hard to detect. The closest we came to getting snow were whispers of frost that half dusted our station wagon's windshield, hardly enough to write your name in.

Renee Sr.'s face was as gorgeous as my mother's. The scar above her lip accented her beauty. Above her living room TV hung a framed cross-stitch, *God Bless Our Pad*. I sat on a black dining room chair in the kitchen, trying to look out the window above the sink. The sky was a boring blue. Cars chugged along Main Street. A gust of wind sent sycamore leaves scattering. Renee Sr. gathered my hair in her hands, winding it around rollers. The ragged cash my mother had paid her was stacked on the kitchen counter. Beside the money, chicken thighs defrosted.

My feet rubbed the spotless linoleum floor. I liked the sensation of my tight socks gliding against it.

"Hold still," said Renee Sr. "Quit squirming." Renee Sr. had a perm and an odd, impatient voice. She sounded how I imagined an ant would. Dangerously high-pitched. Venomous.

Once her mother was done setting my hair, a grinning Renee Jr. waved at me, inviting me to her bedroom. I accepted. Renee Jr. had inherited her mother's beauty, accented by long teeth instead of a knotty scar.

Renee Jr. and I knelt on her chocolate-colored carpet. The apartment, including her room, smelled of buttered flour tortillas and fabric softener. The scent made me feel held, safe, and I couldn't wait to rinse the perm solution out of my hair so that I could sniff that fragrance again. The stuff Renee Sr. had squirted on me made my head stink and my scalp burn.

Renee Jr. dumped a pile of Barbie dolls between us. Lifting one by her asymmetrical pageboy, I asked, "You're allowed to cut their hair?"

Renee Jr. petted a blonde and nodded.

"They're mine," she said. "I can do whatever I want to them."

I tried not to act envious. I wasn't allowed to cut my dolls' hair or my own. My mother had put that rule in place after I tried giving myself Cleopatra bangs.

With the bedroom door closed, Renee Jr.'s dolls enacted scenes inspired by US and Latin-American soap operas. They yelled, wept, shook, and made murderous threats. They lied and broke promises. They trembled, got naked, and banged stiff pubic areas. Clack, clack, clack. They slapped and bit. They hurt one another on purpose and laughed instead of apologizing. They cheated, broke up, got back together, and cheated again.

They were lesbians.

They had no choice.

Renee Jr. had no male dolls.

Renee Jr. carried a distraught lesbian to the open window. I hurried after her.

She shrieked, "I can't take it anymore! I'm gonna jump!"

Silhouetted against the boring blue, we watched the doll go up, pause, and then plummet. Face-first, she smacked the ground unceremoniously.

She's dead, I thought.

Renee Jr. and I looked at each other. Smiled. We had discovered something fun. Throwing dolls out the window and watching them fall ten stories was something we probably weren't supposed to be doing. Soon, all of Renee Jr.'s dolls were scattered along the sidewalk beneath her window, contorted in death poses, and we had nothing left to play with but ourselves.

My parents owned a book with glossy reproductions of paintings and drawings by Frida Kahlo. One of the paintings, *The Suicide of Dorothy Hale*, looked like the game invented by Renee Jr.

I was growing out my perm. I liked the one Renee Sr. had given me better than the first one I'd gotten, but I didn't plan on getting a third.

Gilda's mother and mine were downstairs drinking coffee and gossiping in Spanish. Gilda's mother spoke Spanish Spanish. She was Spanish and had a challenging nickname. In Spanish Spanish, the nickname didn't mean anything. It was cute gibberish. In Mexican Spanish, it meant underwear.

Regina, Gilda's across-the-cul-de-sac neighbor, was with us. We were gathered in Gilda's bedroom, and I was wearing a shawl, white wig, and granny glasses. Gilda had told me to put these things on. She said it would make the ghost stories I wanted to tell more realistic.

I rocked in the corner rocking chair, reciting ghost stories until I ran out.

We shared some silence.

I continued to rock.

Regina said, "We should play a game."

I was hesitant. Regina's games usually led to sudden humping, and I didn't want to be humped by Regina.

"What game?" asked Gilda.

"Delivery room," answered Regina.

"How do you play?" asked Gilda.

Regina said, "Well, there's three of us, so one of us can be the doctor, one of us can be the pregnant lady, and one of us can be the husband!"

"Okay!" we said.

Regina told Gilda to get a pillow or stuffed animal and stick it under her sweater. Gilda chose a pair of lace-edged pillows and followed instructions, creating a lumpy bulge.

"Looks like twins!" said Regina. She ordered Gilda onto her bed and said, "Spread your legs." Regina rolled up her sleeves and said, "Ma'am, you're gonna have to push." Looking at me, she said, "Sir, you have to support your wife. This is one of the hardest moments of her life. It could kill her."

I composed myself and fell into my role. I was a married man. I had to support my wife. She could die. The twins could kill her. I hadn't considered this when I'd gotten her pregnant.

After five minutes of huffing, groaning, panting, and pushing, Gilda gave birth to fat, healthy twins. We rotated roles, quickly realizing that the best role was pregnant lady. The worst was husband. All he did was cheerlead. I gave birth five times. The first two times, my babies survived. The third time, my baby died. We made the corner where the rocking chair stood the cemetery. We had funerals for babies and women who died in childbirth. I died twice.

When was the last time you played a death game?

Were you alone or did you play with others?

How much did you trust them?

In *Philosophical Investigations*, Ludwig Wittgenstein postulates that "'games' form a family." To that I would add that players form a family.

The game I played with Renee Jr. is related to the game I played with Gilda and Regina. I mostly trusted the kids I played with, but my guard stayed up around Regina, especially when she was doctor, and I was pregnant lady. Pregnant lady is vulnerable. Doctor is powerful. Danger breathes in the space between them.

My father tells stories about growing up in Norwalk, California. Celebrities sometimes visited. In 1955, Bela Lugosi came to town. Known the world over for his portrayals of Dracula, the Hungarian actor was admitted to Metropolitan State Hospital, formerly Norwalk State Hospital, for treatment of his morphine addiction. During his stay, the vampire read scripts. He would later star in B moviemaker Ed Wood's science-fiction film *Plan 9 from Outer Space*.

My father lived in a tract home next door to a Mexican family with five or so kids. One of the kids accidentally killed her sister by sticking her fingers in the baby's fontanel.

Can you imagine?

The oldest boy in the family was named Zippy. Zippy was bright and gangly and mostly wore shorts and T-shirts. He invented a game. By Orr and Day Road grew a eucalyptus tree whose trunk could hide several boys. Zippy and his friends would cluster behind it and wait. Neighborhood kids would come out to watch.

My father hid behind a juniper with other little observers.

They were tense with excitement.

A Buick began making its way through the intersection.

Zippy released the tricycle. It sped into the street. A realistic child mannequin wearing overalls was loosely tied to its handlebars, and the Buick collided with it, loosening the rope and sending the "child" sailing through the air. When the mannequin hit the asphalt, its limbs contorted. Its head rolled off.

"Aaaaaaaaaaaaaaaaah!" screamed the old white lady who'd left her Buick running in the middle of the intersection. She ran in zigzags with her hands on her head.

"I killed him! I killed him! I killed him!" she shrieked. "I killed the baby!"

A curbside bush filled with children shook with laughter.

When my father took us to Norwalk to visit my uncle Henry, we would drive through Zippy's intersection. I half expected to see his tricycle and mannequin roll into the street until I remembered that Zippy was now an adult and that Zippy was in prison. I never met Zippy. I knew him only as a character from Dad's Norwalk stories. When telling Zippy tales, my father would insist that the stuff his neighbor had done was terrible, just sadistic, except Dad didn't look or sound horrified. The corners of his lips turned up and I could hear nostalgia. His voice told on him. He recalled those death games fondly.

My father was four years old when he left Mexico and arrived in California. It was 1951. That same year, *Excélsior*, a Mexico City newspaper, published this headline:

WHILE PLAYING WAR THREE LITTLE BOYS "EXECUTED" A MAID BY FIRING SQUAD

Beneath the headline appeared three candid photos of three big-eared kids, Carlos and Raúl Salinas, ages four and five, and Gustavo Rodolfo Zapata, age eight. According to the article, the trio was in police custody but didn't understand why.

The shooting had happened the day before, December 17, around noon, at 425 Palenque, the mansion where brothers Carlos and Raúl shared a bedroom. Their mother, Mrs. Margarita de Gortari de Salinas, had gone shopping at around eleven o'clock. Her sons and their friend were left in the care of two staff members. One was the cook, María Torres Garrido. The other was Manuela, a twelve-year-old

Indigenous girl from San Pedro Azcapotzaltongo. María usually kept an eye on Manuela. The girl had been working at 425 Palenque for a month and a half.

When Margarita returned home an hour and a half later, she was met by police, who told her what her children had done. Margarita told them that the boys must've found the loaded rifle that her husband, the economist Raúl Salinas Lozano, kept hidden in a closet. Pretending to be at war, the boys had needed a weapon and an enemy. They'd cast Manuela in that role when they came upon her sweeping.

Aiming his father's .22 at her face, Carlos fired.

Manuela and her broom fell.

María was the first to find her, and when she asked the boys what they'd done, they triumphantly chorused, "We have killed Manuela!"

Carlos squealed, "I killed her with one shot! I'm a hero!"

A reporter visited the boys and spoke with them. He wrote that they seemed slightly agitated but mostly calm. With their mother minding them, they sprinted up and down police corridors. She'd told them that while they were with the police, no more games. They'd played enough.

Four months before the murder at 425 Palenque, another killing had taken place at a rowdier address, 122 Monterrey.

On September 7, *La Prensa*, another Mexico City newspaper, published this headline:

HE WANTED TO DEMONSTRATE HIS MARKSMANSHIP AND KILLED HIS WIFE.

CRIME COMMITTED BY AN AMERICAN DURING A SCANDALOUS SPREE

By the eighth, the news had reached the United States.

HEIR'S PISTOL KILLS HIS WIFE;
HE DENIES PLAYING WM. TELL

The accused was the broke-ish grandson of William Seward Burroughs, the bank clerk who invented the first commercially practical calculator. Unlike his grandfather, thirty-seven-year-old William Seward Burroughs II was an aspiring writer, gun enthusiast, narcotics connoisseur, and queer nihilist who had yet to do anything notable except father a child. An outlaw, he'd fled to Mexico City and was soon joined by his twenty-eight-year-old wife, Joan Vollmer, their son, William Seward Burroughs III, and Julie, a daughter from Joan's second marriage.

William ended Joan's life ten days before Mexican Independence Day.

It was storming. Black water flooded parts of Mexico City.

William had recently returned from a South American vision quest that would later be aestheticized in the novel *Queer*. In need of cash, he made an appointment to sell one of his guns to a Mexico City College student, Robert Addison.

At the Bounty Bar and Grill, where William wrote parts of what would become *Naked Lunch*, Joan bought a lime soft drink with a splash of gin. The dark green cocktail sloshed as she limped upstairs to John Healy's apartment. John bartended downstairs and had met William through Spanish classes.

William carried his valise into the apartment. Joan brought her glass and cane. She sat on a stuffed living room chair across from Eddie Woods and Lewis Marker, William's vision quest partner. Both were on the sofa. Both heard William say, "Put the glass on your head, Joanie! Let me show the boys what a great shot Bill is!"

I've listened to men explain what Joan felt in the seconds before her husband shot her. One of these explainers was Matt, someone I "dated" when I was fifteen. I met Matt at the Catholic Charities thrift store where he worked. He was a haggard twentysomething with a greasy pompadour and stringy sideburns. He played drums in a band

and had written a novel in ink by longhand. He read Beat poets. He lectured me about things I already knew, like that Andy Warhol was a homosexual from Pittsburgh.

After taking me to eat dinner at a Chinese restaurant where fish swam laps in a long aquarium, Matt drove me to the house he shared with an alcoholic surfer, Corey.

"Sit," he told me.

I sat on the living room couch and watched Matt stuff a video into the VCR's rectangular mouth.

Naked Lunch played.

The critic Gary Indiana describes this movie as "an amalgam of several Burroughs texts, not just *Naked Lunch*." The film also draws from the writer's life but takes liberties with details. The actress Judy Davis plays Joan Vollmer, one of two female characters whose voices the audience gets to hear. The actor Peter Weller plays William Burroughs. We hear his voice a lot. In the scene inspired by the events that took place at 122 Monterrey, William Burroughs's alter ego, Bill Lee, sits at a cluttered vanity table. Opening a drawer, he pulls out a sleek handgun.

He announces, "I guess it's time for our William Tell routine."

Facing the bedroom window, Joan turns around. Her blue dress hangs open and reveals a lacy white slip. She plucks an empty drinking glass from the cluttered dresser, sits on the windowsill, and balances it on her head. Bill smiles and cocks his pistol. He looks at Joan and takes aim. She returns a stoic stare.

Matt said, "See, Joan wasn't scared. She trusted him."

He squeezed my leg.

Was he going to ask me to balance something on my head?

In real life, Joan giggled after placing the glass on her head. Then she said, "I can't watch this. You know I can't stand the sight of blood."

William took aim with his Star .38 and fired.

The glass hit the floor, rolling in circles.

Joan's tired head slumped to one side.

William's tiny audience thought Joan was kidding.

Finally, Lewis said, "I think you hit her."

Everyone rushed to her.

When William noticed a small blue hole in Joan's head, he screamed, "No!" He jumped into her lap and chanted, "Joan! Joan! Joan!"

Maybe he wanted to be consoled by her.

The living expect a lot from dead women.

After watching *Naked Lunch* with Matt, I bought a copy of the book from the used bookstore.

I went through a whole bottle of Advil trying to finish it.

When I did, I was even more confused.

It wasn't a novel.

It was chaos.

I didn't admit that to anyone. Instead, I told people I loved it. I told people Uncle Bill was a genius. Brilliant. I pretended to get it. This impressed Matt's friends. It made me likable.

During a press conference held to promote *Naked Lunch* the movie, a reporter asked William Burroughs, "Do you regret the period in your life when you were addicted?"

He answered, "The point is a writer can profit by experiences which would not be advantageous or profitable to others. Because he's a writer, he can write about it."

William Burroughs could just as easily have been talking about shooting his wife in the head. That's what people looked forward to seeing when they watched *Naked Lunch*. That hole he made in her brain.

Courtney Love and Amy Adams have also played Joan Vollmer on-screen, but my favorite portrayal remains Judy Davis's.

She brought something achingly queer to the role.

Watching her open her pink mouth and exhale onto the cockroaches climbing the wallpaper made girls like me swoon.

William Burroughs was held at Cellblock H of el Palacio de Lecumberri, a prison. He stayed for thirteen days, and after his release, he reunited with his brother, a snob named Mortimer. They decided that Julie and William Jr. would be sent to live with relatives. Arrangements for Joan's burial at Panteón Americano were made.

In exchange for 320 pesos, she came to occupy grave 1018.

In 1952, William Burroughs returned to Texas.

In 1953, a Mexican judge found him guilty in absentia. Eduardo Urzaiz Jiménez ordered the gringo to serve two years in prison, but his sentence was suspended.

Ace Books published his first novel, *Junky*, that same year.

It makes mention of his time in Mexico.

Six years later, *Naked Lunch* made William Burroughs famous.

Joan Vollmer is still in Mexico. I imagine her grave is less visited than Frida Kahlo's blue house.

I have looked for more information about Manuela, the girl killed during the war game. I can't even locate her last name. Manuela is derived from Emmanuel, Greek for the Hebrew Imanu'el. The name means "God is with us."

Would Joan Vollmer have been friends with me? Maybe.

Joan was a slut.

According to my middle school classmates, so was I.

Joan was raised somewhere with passionate seasons, Loudonville, New York. Her mother was named Dorothy, and her father and brother shared a name, David. David Sr., a chemist, worked at the Gevaert photographic film factory. Since it was owned by Germans, the federal government seized the factory during World War II and gave it to David Sr. to manage.

When Joan would step outside, David Sr. would follow her in his car. She got no privacy and dreamt of escaping to Manhattan. Until then she was stuck at Saint Agnes, an Episcopalian school. She listened to Beethoven and loved her hands. She thought they were her most beautiful feature, better than her legs. Her classmates voted her "Most Intellectual." She wrote fancy essays for her French class.

> The psyche of the Fascist ideology of the Nazis reveals itself in the music of Wagner. It's not by chance that this music is Hitler's favorite. When Hitler was rising to power/would be present, the orchestra played La Course des Valkyries. This music, with its almost hysteric heroism and its theatrical and pretentious grandeur, represents, in a symbolic way the spirit of the Fuehrer . . .

In her yearbook photo, Joan is a delicate Atlas, a pretty girl with the world on her mind. Her high cheekbones curve sharply. Her thin lips frown. The drape of her dress reveals a bit of back, her spine. Under her name appears a list of her accomplishments.

Cum Laude
Gold Medal
Bleatings Board '37, '38, '39
Silver Cross and Bar '36, '37, '38, '39
Secretary of Freshman Class
Barnard College

After winning a three-hundred-dollar scholarship, Joan left to study journalism in New York. At seventeen, she married. She regretted the decision, dumped her husband, and got married again, this time to a Columbia law student. When she started to regret her second marriage, she got lucky. Her husband got drafted, and during his absence, Joan got pregnant with Julie.

Joan's parents sent her an allowance. Combined with the military money she got from her second husband, she was able to subsidize a bohemian life at several New York addresses.

One was 420 West 119th Street.

Another was 419 West 115th Street.

The writer Joyce Johnson describes Joan's Upper West Side homes as early prototypes of what a later generation would call "pads." At Joan's, an artist, intellectual, swindler, drifter, mystic, or whore could make herself at home. She could cry into the greasy sofa. She could annotate Marx in the bathtub. She could vomit in the closet. She could pluck her eyebrows until they were crooked. She could heave a sigh of relief when blood reddened her underwear. She could burn toast and eat it in bed.

Joan's second husband divorced her.

Joan met Edie Parker, an art student, at the West End Bar. The girls became friends and Edie mentored Joan in the art of the blow job. Edie's boyfriend Jack thought Joan might hit it off with his friend William, a Harvard graduate from St. Louis, Missouri, who was working as an exterminator in Chicago. Jack foretold an "affinity between Joan's sharp, glittering wittiness," and William's cuntiness. When introduced, Joan matched the exterminator wit for wit.

"You're supposed to be a faggot," Joan told William. "But you're as good as a pimp in bed."

William moved into Joan's and got his own room. Their sex didn't always go as planned. Joan would burst into William's room, ready for fun. The exterminator would cough up classic excuses. My foot hurts. I have a headache.

William fell in love with narcotics. He and Joan fooled around with inhalers, huffing Benzedrine. They experimented with amphetamine and caffeine and stayed up for two weeks.

Joan erupted in sores. She saw and heard things that only she could see and hear. She woke up in Bellevue's mental ward and worked for a week and half to convince doctors that she was sane. Her dad came and got Julie. William came and got her.

Joan and William's friends kept going to jail. Worried about what might happen to them, they plotted their escape from the city that Joan had once idealized.

Before leaving, the couple booked a room at a Times Square hotel.

After knocking her up, William took Joan west.

William sank family money into a broken-down ninety-nine-acre property north of Houston. Julie and William Jr. crawled the land. Neither William nor Joan was in any condition to maintain a ranch. They were addicts and the law kept buzzing around them.

They invited their friend Herbert to come down from New York and work as their farmhand. He became their courier, commuting back and forth between the farm and Houston, wrangling their supply of Benzedrine, marijuana, and liquor. Herbert noticed that Joan and William slept in separate rooms. He also noticed that William always seemed annoyed with Joan.

As Herbert, Joan, and William walked through the woods, Joan struggled to carry Julie. She asked, "Can you help me?"

William said nothing.

Herbert snapped, "Why don't you fucking help her?"

William answered, "The Spartans knew how to manage the weight of female infants. They threw them from cliffs."

William had planted marijuana. The crop turned out miserable. Finding someone to unload it on was challenging. William was relieved when a sucker finally came along.

He tried quitting narcotics and did for a short while, but in Beeville, police arrested him for having sex with Joan on the side of the road while the kids sat in the car. The whole family got locked up. Authorities revoked William's driver's license.

"May buy a house in New Orleans," William wrote to a friend. "I must have someplace to stash the brats."

In New Orleans, William left Joan at home with the kids. She knew it was a matter of time before he'd be arrested again, and when he was, the police raided their home, confiscating marijuana and guns. They threw William in jail.

After his release, William was admitted to the De Paul Sanitarium. A staff member interviewed Joan, asking her for her husband's history. The interviewer jotted notes on Joan.

> Patient's wife appeared to be an attractive woman . . . She was expensively dressed . . . She was restless, spoke with a fixed, forced smile throughout the interview, smoked one cigarette after the other. She was admittedly "nervous," ducked or raised her head to the ceiling when speaking, but seldom met interviewers' eyes . . . There were several bruises on her arms for which she declined to give an explanation other than words to the effect that she "bruised easily." On the surface she was friendly.

William signed himself out of De Paul and took the family back to Texas. He was nervous about appearing before a New Orleanian judge; he worried he'd be sentenced to Angola, a plantation turned prison.

William scouted for a place to live in Mexico.

Joan and the kids soon joined him in Colonia Roma, at 210 Orizaba.

In Mexico City, Joan consoled herself with tequila.

William spent their money on narcotics and men.

"I'm personally fine," Joan wrote to a friend. "Although somewhat drunk from 8 a.m. on."

William became a client of Lola la Chata, a chicharrón vendor turned narcotraficante. When Joan found William cooking at home, she grabbed his spoon and threw it in the toilet.

William smacked her. He smacked her again.

Joan wanted a divorce.

William took Lewis, a gringo he had a crush on, on a trip to Ecuador. They hunted for hallucinogens. William paid for everything. Meanwhile, Joan took the kids on a drunken road trip to my mother's hometown, Guadalajara. On their way back, they stopped in Parangaricutirimícuaro, a town in Michoacán that really fills the mouth. They visited the volcano, Paricutín.

Days before climbing the stairs to 122 Monterrey, Joan met up with a friend.

Her skin was covered in sores. Her smile was missing half its teeth. Her scalp peeked through bald patches.

"I'm not going to make it," she said.

Headlines play language games. The headline "Heir's Pistol Kills Wife; He Denies Playing Wm. Tell" hides the murderer behind a gun, making it seem that a pistol, and not a man, did the dirty work. The headline "He Wanted to Demonstrate His Marksmanship and Killed His Wife. Crime Committed by an American During a Scandalous Spree" conjures playful intent. The American didn't mean to kill his wife. He only meant to show off. If I could've written a headline for what happened that night, it would read "To Impress Two Men, One That He Was Sleeping with, Man Plays Russian Roulette with Head of Smart Wife Who Wanted Divorce."

After school, Matt picked me up in his van. As I buckled my seat belt, he asked, "How's it going?"

I took this as an invitation to tell him about my day, and I launched into a play-by-play, going period by period.

When I got to lunch, Matt interrupted me.

"Do you have to talk about high school so much?" he whined.

I turned to look at his twentysomething-year-old face. It was already pruning.

"Matt," I answered, "I'm a sophomore."

Matt was on his back. His Levis and boxer shorts were wrapped around his ankles.

It wasn't a good look.

His penis had a troubling mole.

Fully dressed, I sat on the edge of the bed, trying to avoid his genitals. I didn't want to take off my clothes. I was wearing too cute of an outfit. A black blouse with black butterflies under a black V-neck dress. Black-on-black striped stockings. Black pointy-toed shoes.

"Touch it," Matt snapped.

I didn't know what to do with it. I'd never interacted with one while sober and I had no desire to grip Matt's little pink monster.

I shook my head.

"Touch it!" he repeated.

I froze.

Matt exhaled through gritted teeth, sat up, and faced his nightstand. He pushed the pump on a bottle of lotion, squirting white goo into his palm. Then he lunged, grabbed my hand, slathered it, and jerked it onto his penis. While Matt moved my hand up and down, I stared at a Gauguin postcard tacked to the wall. I focused on the faces of Tahitian women.

Matt told me that we were dating but not girlfriend and boyfriend.

I told people he was my boyfriend anyways.

After Matt, I dated a woman who later became my wife. I didn't have another boyfriend until I was in my thirties. That guy tricked me into playing William Tell–ish games with him, hazing me into them with an innocuous instruction: "Toss me my boots." He'd left them by the futon, and I lifted them off the tile floor by the heels, gingerly lobbing them in his direction. As the boots landed near his feet, he looked at me with theatrical disgust.

"Babe," he said. "That's not a throw. I want you to *throw* them at me. Throw them as hard as you can."

My boyfriend's instructions confused me.

"Why?"

"Because. Because I want to see how well you can throw. I want to see how much power you have."

I shrugged and said, "I can't throw that hard. I have, like, no power in my arms. They're noodles."

"Try."

I sighed, walked to his boots, picked them up, and carried them back to the futon. He stood arms akimbo by the kitchen table. "Ready," he said.

I pretended to wind up a pitch and then chucked his shoes as gingerly as I'd tossed them the first time. They landed with a gentle clatter.

He shook his head.

"You didn't follow instructions. I'm going to have to teach you how to throw. Go stand against the wall."

He'd already critiqued and corrected my running style, but I felt anxious about having to stand against the wall for this new lesson. It had a firing squad feeling.

"Keep your arms down. Don't move. I want you to feel a good pitch. I want you to feel it in your body."

I was about to answer that I didn't want to feel a good pitch, but the shoes were already hurtling at my head.

I ducked and ka-pow; they smacked the wall, leaving a gray mark.

"We're gonna have to do it again."

"Why?!"

"Because you moved!"

We repeated the game until I didn't flinch. One boot nailed me in the tit, causing searing pain—tits are the testicles of the chest—but I did as I was told because I was scared. I obeyed my boyfriend because I didn't trust him.

William got used to hurting Joan. Joan thought she'd gotten used to it but hadn't.

She wanted a divorce. William gave her a permanent one.

I hope people bring her flowers in Mexico City.

She deserves them.

So does Manuela.

In 1986, when I was nine, I learned about a man who claimed to have killed a girl by accident.

Her story was on the news a lot.

The victim was eighteen-year-old Jennifer Levin.

A cyclist was taking her usual morning bike ride through Central Park when she spotted Jennifer's half-dressed remains behind the Metropolitan Museum of Art. She found a pay phone, dialed 911, and reported the body. Police gathered around it and gawked. One found her underwear about fifty feet away. Someone had cut, bruised, and bitten Jennifer. They had also twisted her bra around her neck. A medical examiner determined that she'd been strangled.

The last person Jennifer was seen with was twenty-year-old Robert Chambers.

Robert told the police that Jennifer had made him go to the park and made him participate in what sounded like a sex game. He said that Jennifer got aggressive, that she overwhelmed him. He couldn't take it, and once he managed to get one of his hands free, he sat up, grabbed her neck as hard as he could, and flipped her over. She landed next to a tree and didn't move.

I didn't know what rough sex games were, but I was pretty sure that Robert Chambers was lying. Others believed him. Why would somebody with such a patrician jawline lie?

I spent part of the summer that Jennifer Levin was murdered at my grandparents' house.

They lived in Guadalajara and all of Mexico was vibrating with enthusiasm. The epicenter of this excitement was Azteca Stadium in Mexico City. The country had been chosen to host the World Cup and it was here. It was happening. Walking through Guadalajara with my grandmother, we saw soccer posters pasted against cemetery walls and TVs broadcasting games in butcher shop windows. Peddlers sold every conceivable form of soccer merchandise on street corners, at tianguis, and in the sharp shadow of the cathedral. Men in cowboy boots shrieked and danced in place when their teams won, and men in cowboy boots wailed and sank to their knees when their teams lost. During the World Cup, Mexican masculinity seemed dynamic. Nuanced. Expansive.

To get into the spirit, I wore soccer cleats as everyday shoes and clacked across my grandparents' tile floor, unable to sneak up on anyone. My footwear led my uncle Álvaro to believe that I was a big soccer fan (I wasn't; I preferred kickball), and he came home one day with a white plastic bag that he handed me. I pulled out a commemorative World Cup doll, a mustached jalapeño wearing a straw sombrero and red soccer jersey. The mascot's name was el Pique, and at night, I cuddled with my vegetable, clutching him to my chest. After caressing his facial hair, I pressed my fingertips into his green skin to feel what he was stuffed with. Beans. Maybe beads. Oddly, he smelled of incense. Had he been blessed at church?

When Argentina played England in the quarterfinals, Argentine player Diego Maradona scored a legendary first goal by punching the ball with his left hand. Despite this illegal touch, referee Ali

Bennaceur awarded it. After the match, journalists probed Maradona, trying to get him to confess to how he'd scored that first goal.

"A little with the head of Maradona," he replied, "and a little with Hand of God."

I watched a crowd watch this historic game at my grandparents' house. One of my uncles had invited some of his guy friends and a woman who'd been introduced to me as Lola, his secretary. While the men crowded around the TV, drinking beer, whistling, clapping, and smoking cigarettes, my uncle placed his hand on his secretary's hip. The hand moved, sliding between Lola's legs. I was intrigued by this touching. My uncle had a wife and Maradona had given him a great alibi.

"It wasn't me," I imagined him sputtering to my aunt. "It was the Hand of God!"

My grandfather wasn't around that day. He'd become a busy man. Earlier that year, one of his former classmates, the celebrated writer Juan Rulfo, had died, and my grandfather was now on a mission to establish himself as a premier Rulfista, an expert on his departed friend's life and oeuvre. In his essay "The Persona of Rulfo," the writer Antonio Alatorre illustrates how my grandfather resolved unknowns about the acclaimed but enigmatic Rulfo.

> Juan had engineered his life story to create a two-year hole, a perfectly empty space, a zero. The truth about those two years came to light some days after Rulfo's death thanks to Ricardo Serrano, one of his classmates, who published the piece "The Seminarian Rulfo" in the January 29, 1986, edition of *Excélsior*. The article was illustrated by various photographs, one of them a group of seminarians. In it, both men appear looking very serious. If you haven't heard of Serrano's essay, it wouldn't surprise me. Nobody is obligated to know everything. A newspaper article, by definition, is ephemeral anyway. I learned about the essay by Serrano nearly two years after it was published because he gave me a photocopy of it.

My grandfather loved newspapers.

He especially loved those with his name printed in them and kept a stash of those in a special room.

At the time of Rulfo's death, Miguel de la Madrid governed Mexico. Carlos Salinas de Gortari, de la Madrid's minister of planning and budget, succeeded him. It is widely believed that President Salinas came to power through electoral fraud, and his family certainly had a lot of practice shaping fate, forcing it to do their bidding. President Salinas was the same little boy who shot Manuela while playing a war game, and though he'd confessed to the killing, evidence of the murder had largely disappeared. Newspapers memorializing the murder had vanished from libraries.

The censors working on behalf of the Salinas family did a pretty good job of rewriting history, but they failed at purging the truth completely. A few old newspapers resurfaced, and there he was, big-eared, goofy, and four years old, proudly shouting, "I killed her with one shot! I'm a hero!"

President Salinas has been able to hide a lot. It's never been proven that he rigged the 1988 election; the ballots were burned. It's never been proven that he had anything to do with the assassination of his successor, Luis Donaldo Colosio, who was shot point-blank in the back of the head as he moved through a crowd during a campaign rally in Tijuana. It's never been proven that Carlos had anything to do with the assassination of Jose Francisco Ruiz Massieu, his brother-in-law, whose neck was struck by machine gunfire as he was leaving the White House Hotel. When authorities implicated the president's older brother Raúl as the mastermind behind the Ruiz Massieu assassination, Carlos told the press, "I am completely convinced of his innocence!"

There are many things we'll never know about Carlos Salinas de Gortari.

That he shot a girl when he was a child isn't one of them.

The truth is in print, and some people, like my grandfather, hoard the printed word. They understand the power of ephemera.

• • •

In *Queer*, William Burroughs writes that "Mexico City is a terminal of space-time travel, a waiting room where you grab a quick drink while you wait for your train."

I've experienced Mexico City this way and this way only.

When my aunt Nena, who was also my godmother, was dying, my mother and I rushed to the airport. We boarded a plane to Mexico with the hopes of being able to say goodbye to Nena while she could still hear us. My mother and I didn't say so, but we were both worried that we wouldn't make it in time.

I'd never rehearsed death with my godmother. We'd played zero morbid games together. Instead, Nena was someone who modeled confronting mortality for real. Muscular dystrophy took her youngest daughter, my cousin Pollito, and Nena took charge of Pollito's legacy, writing and self-publishing a book about her. Nena became the boss at deathbeds and funerals, and she was so strong-willed that I couldn't imagine anyone but her directing her funeral. I pictured her doing this from the comfort of her coffin, insisting on shutting the lid herself and smacking away anyone who tried to fix her hair.

Nena was the boss of my grandmother's death. As her body had cooled, my godmother, my uncles, my parents, and my cousins gathered around the bed where our matriarch had stared at the ceiling for more than a decade. With a rosary threaded through her fingers, Nena muttered Hail Marys and Our Fathers. She aimed her face at the ceiling because beyond it was God, and she told the Almighty that it was time to receive her mother's spirit. She explained to the divine what her mother had suffered on earth. She sounded angry about it. Addressing the sky, my godmother wailed. Her wails grew birdlike and took flight. We wailed with Nena. We'd wanted my grandmother to be free from pain, but now we were in pain. Spirit inhabited Nena's wailing and ours. The spirit moved throughout the room, encouraging us to release our pain. An icon of la Virgen de Guadalupe, that hung from a nail a few feet above my grandmother's bed, looked shyly away.

After the men from the mortuary wheeled my grandmother to a van, loaded her up, and drove off, Nena told me, "Get your purse. We have a lot to do."

We drove to the busy flower shops by the cemetery and ordered several large arrangements. We drove to a women's clothing store and chose a white dress for my grandmother to be buried in. We drove to the mortuary, where we handed documents, a crystal rosary, and the white dress to a funeral director. These mortal chores were a lesson. My godmother was showing me how much work death really is. Death doesn't end with a gunshot. The bullet is a starting point, and there are many administrative steps that the living must complete before the deceased can heave a sigh of relief. The dead depend on us. Without us, they don't sleep well.

To get to Nena, my mother and I had flown out of LA and touched down in Mexico City for a layover. We never left the airport. I wanted to but it wasn't feasible. We didn't have enough time to do anything but wait.

I tried to relax. Breathe stale airport air.

We bought coffee and sat at a bistro table.

I people watched.

My mother's phone rang. She spoke little. Listened mostly. When her short conversation ended, she told me that her little sister had called. Not only was Nena gone, but my uncle had already cremated her. It bothered my mother a lot that Nena's husband had turned her to ash so fast. My mother felt robbed of her sister's body. It's awkward to say goodbye to an urn. A face, even if its wrecked, is still a face.

It was pushing midnight when we arrived in Los Mochis. I'd never been, and I didn't know anything about the city except that it was coastal, that my aunt had lived there, and that it was where police re-re-recaptured the famous narcotraficante Joaquín "El Chapo" Guzmán, leader of the Sinaloa drug cartel and talented prison escapee.

At the Mochis airport, a driver met us and helped us with our bags. I felt like I was wearing a suit of filth. We drove through the darkest night and stopped at a restaurant. We dragged our suitcases inside and found Nena's husband in a wood-paneled room with four tables arranged in a square. I recognized two cousins. The others were strangers.

"Well, well, well!" screamed my uncle. He looked ready to spit. "The Americans are here!"

My uncle and my mother have been feuding since they met. That happened the night that he took Nena on their first date, and my grandfather appointed my mother their chaperone. My mother ordered the most expensive dinner on the menu and made sure to get dessert.

After our rude welcoming, we went to my uncle's house and slept for a few hours. When I woke up, my left eye was swollen. I don't know why it chose to puff up. By breakfast, the swelling had subsided.

At the high-ceilinged church where we held Nena's funeral, I kept expecting for my aunt to pop out from behind a religious statue and yell, "Surprise!" Instead, an urn held her ashes. It sat on a short table near the altar. From a framed portrait beside the urn, Nena's brown eyes stared. Several flower bouquets surrounded her.

The church felt as stuffy as the airport. Most everything in it was off-white. My mother grabbed one of the fans tucked into the wooden slot attached to the pew in front of her, using it to cool herself. She looked elegant and so I snapped her picture. She smiled and tapped the fan against her chin.

Grandchildren and friends eulogized Nena. I didn't speak. Had I spoken I would've rambled about four experiences. One, the time she took me ice-skating in a hotel shaped like an ancient pyramid. Two, the time we bumbled into a kidnapping in progress, and she got us away safely. Three, the time I went with her to a chiropractor and he grabbed her by the ears and adjusted her. I heard a cracking sound and thought he'd killed her. Four, my grandmother's funeral, when Nena became the boss of death.

An archway beside the altar fed into an alcove. After the service, mariachis in skintight pants played their instruments and sang by this entrance. We sang with them. My cousin picked up the urn containing his mom and we paraded to the archway. The mariachis led us. We stepped inside a small mausoleum where music echoed off walls, vases, and bones.

Violins played as the priest opened a small door. That would be my aunt's drawer for eternity. Another priest swung a censer back and forth. The smell of frankincense and myrrh filled the space. Smoke curled in ghostly shapes. The priest placed the urn inside and shut the door.

We dispersed, wandering into the church and then out into the sun. I had my suitcase with me. I had to leave Mexico fast. I was due in domestic violence court in California, supposed to testify at a hearing where I'd face the ex-boyfriend who'd used me for target practice, nailing me with shoes, books, bottles, you name it. I'd managed to leave him before he could give me archery lessons, and I was nauseous about having to see him again, make my case for a restraining order. Getting a man who resents you to leave you alone can be a lot of work. Almost as much work as dying.

I began asking funeral goers if they could shuttle me to the airport. An elderly couple agreed to. I rode through the emerald countryside with them, and when I got to the airport, I darted to my gate.

"Step aside," said a guard.

Another guard took my suitcase and made a spectacle of unzipping it, rifling through my underwear, dresses, and books.

"Stand with your legs apart. Spread your arms."

I held my breath as she frisked me.

Once the guards were done humiliating me, they let me proceed to my plane.

I'd been unable to get a direct flight to LA, so I landed in Tijuana. I figured I could walk back to the United States from there.

I took a taxi from the airport to the Otay Mesa Port of Entry. More than a million trucks cross through the port each year. I'd crossed it by station wagon, suburban, and van but never by foot. I wobbled in my clogs and dragged my pink suitcase along the stone path to the inspection station, bump thump, bump thump, bump thump, muddling past vendors selling balloons, gum, puppets, soccer balls, and salvation. At the inspection station, I showed an official my passport and placed my suitcase on a conveyor belt. An X-ray machine looked inside and spat it free. I retrieved it, wheeled it outside, took a deep breath, and walked for about a hundred feet.

I looked left.

I looked right.

Things seemed to be happening to the left.

I went left.

In a daze, I dragged my suitcase and stared at my phone, texting with a friend. I texted as I crossed a bridge. I texted as I walked down stairs. I texted as I pushed through a turnstile. I texted, heard traffic, and smelled mangos, diesel, and tar.

I stopped texting.

I looked up.

Waving at the top of a tall flagpole was a red, white, and green flag.

My eyes scanned the cityscape.

A uniformed woman holding a machine gun nodded at me.

I speed walked to the nearest building.

I approached the counter.

In Spanish, a young man wearing a vest said, "Hello. Welcome to Mexico!"

"No!"

"What?"

"I'm in Mexico?"

"Yes!"

"But I just left!"

"Welcome back!"

"I don't understand. Did I just walk out of Mexico and accidentally . . . walk back in?"

He slowly nodded. Smiled.

My left eyelid twitched.

I turned and dragged my pink suitcase back outside, sprinting across what must have been twenty lanes of traffic. My armpits reeked of tabasco sauce. The pink dress I was wearing flapped in the light breeze stirred by passing cars.

At a broken sidewalk, I looked left. I looked right. Last time I chose left, I wound up in Mexico. I decided to go straight.

I focused all my mental energy on visualizing the path leading to the Otay Mesa Port of Entry, hoping that by willpower I could make it reappear. As I concentrated, I walked deep into the belly of a gray neighborhood without sidewalks. Some streets were paved. Others weren't. I needed water badly. One stray dog after another followed me. Crows looked down from homemade roofs and laughed at me. I saw no other pedestrians. My arm burned from dragging my pink suitcase. I considered abandoning it. Maybe the dogs could use it.

Accepting that I was lost, I promised myself that I would not be like my father. I would ask the first person that I saw for directions back to the United States.

I spotted a man seated beneath an awning made of corrugated steel. Shade covered him. He wore a dingy pair of tight underwear. I felt sorry for his chair.

"Excuse me," I said. "How do I get to the United States?"

The oracle hugged himself and laughed in a way that made me feel like maybe he was the wrong person to ask. Once he settled down, he said, "Not by going in the direction you're headed."

"Which way do I go?"

He pointed.

"Thank you," I said.

I turned and walked in the direction that I'd come from, stray dogs scampering after me. I needed at least five tacos. And a 7UP. *Nobody is going to believe me when I tell them*, I thought. Mexico wanted me to stay, but I couldn't. I was due in domestic violence court.

CUCUY

I used to introduce a certain civics lesson with a mug shot. The last time I taught the class, I projected this sad photo onto a screen mounted at the front of my classroom. A tired Mexican, his upper lip lightly shadowed, gazed upon us. Leaving my podium, I approached the screen, pointing at the mug shot with my yardstick.

"Check it out," I said. "This picture was taken by Phoenix police in 1963. You can see the guy's booking number on the sign he's holding up. We're going to talk to our neighbors for a moment about who we think this man is, and we've got a little while to discuss the following questions: Why was this mug shot taken? What did this guy do to become famous?"

A football player growled, "Give us a clue, Gurba!"

"Okay. I bet you already know this guy's name. There's a speech named after him that I bet a lot of you have memorized."

My high schoolers, especially those who looked like the tired Mexican, took their instructions seriously. I roamed, listening to them improvise his identity, history, and significance. Shy boys huddled, discussing the possibility that the guy in the mug shot had immigration-related problems. A few steps away, girls vigorously argued. One faction believed that the tired Mexican was caught driving without car insurance. Another faction believed that he'd hit an old lady with his car. Turning to a girl with braids, a girl with braces said, "I think he got busted stealing food to feed his family."

"Aw," said the girl with braids. "That's so sweet. I vote for stealing food."

Once five minutes had passed, I announced, "We have some time to talk as a whole class now. Anyone who wants to can share who they think this man is, why he's famous, and why the cops took his picture."

Since it wasn't every day that a Mexican appeared in our curriculum, the kids were itching to connect with the man in the mug shot. One boy shouted, "That's my uncle Edgar!" Another yelled, "No way! That's my cousin Hector!" Other students compared the mug shot to friends and classmates, pointing out similarities between eyes, noses, lips, hair, and ears.

A boy named Freddy blurted, "That nerd was late returning books to the library!"

Everyone laughed.

"How come you think that?" I asked.

"Cuz that fool looks like Kevin Ortega!"

I tried not to laugh. The mug shot did resemble Kevin Ortega, a nerd I'd be teaching next period.

Once every kid who wanted to speak had gotten their turn, I said, "All of your theories were interesting to hear. Now I'll tell you who this guy is and what he got accused of. This guy's name is Ernesto Miranda. He didn't get in trouble for jaywalking or stealing milk or running people over with his car or for keeping his library books too long. In 1963, Ernesto Miranda was charged with kidnapping and rape."

Kids gasped.

"That guy?! Rape?!"

"Yup!"

"But he looks . . . normal!"

I said, "I agree. Perfectly normal. So normal, in fact, that he looks like many people we know."

Everyone was sitting up straight.

"You guys wanna hear the story of what happened to him?"

"YES!"

"Okay, its March 1963. The setting is Phoenix, Arizona. Think cacti. Lizards. Sand. Tumbleweeds. An unforgiving sun. Have any of us been to Arizona?"

A girl waved and shouted, "Yuma! I've been to Yuma!"

I said, "Excellent! That's near where Cesar Chavez died! So detectives knock at the front door of the home of Ernesto Miranda, a dockworker who loads fruits and vegetables by night. Holding their baby, Ernesto's common-law wife, Twila, answers and—"

"Wait, WHAT?" screamed a girl. "This motherfucker has a CHILD? And a WIFE? I thought you said he was a rapist!"

"I said that he was charged with rape. And why wouldn't a rapist have a wife?"

In a tone suggesting that he was stating the obvious, a short boy answered, "Miss Gurba, if a guy has a wife, he shouldn't have to rape nobody."

I took a deep breath, pointed to the mug shot, and said, "This is what a rapist can look like. They're normal, everyday people, and we've probably had moments in our lives when we've associated with rapists and didn't know it. You know, no one walks around saying, 'Nice to meet you. I'm a rapist! Wanna hang out?' And rape has nothing to do with a husband or anyone else not getting enough sex. You hear me? Instead, rape has to do with geography, with putting a victim in her place and making her stay there. Got it?"

Most of the girls in class nodded.

Returning to our story, I told everyone that detectives took Ernesto to a police station, where he was handed a numbered placard and ordered to stand in a lineup with three other men. A two-way mirror reflected their unsmiling faces. On its other side stood a nervous eighteen-year-old girl. She'd reported to police that during her walk home from work, a Mexican man wearing glasses and a white T-shirt had kidnapped her. After tying her up, he drove her to the desert and did her dirty. Only one man in the lineup, Ernesto, wore glasses and a white T-shirt. Still, the girl wasn't sure that he was her attacker.

Cops marched Ernesto to an interrogation room. They sat him

down and lied to him, telling him that he was in big trouble; several women had positively identified him as their attacker. A detective handed Ernesto a copy of a standard statement form. Ernesto scrawled his name on it. In the spaces provided for age and education level, he wrote twenty-three and eighth grade. He filled the rest of the page with a plain yet anatomically graphic confession that ended with him driving his victim home. His last words to her were "Pray for me."

Girls gasped.

"The nerve!" one shouted.

"I know!" I shouted back.

The confession led to Ernesto's conviction and a judge sentencing him to twenty-to-thirty years on each count. Ernesto's lawyers appealed his case, and *Miranda v. Arizona* was eventually argued before the Supreme Court. The question before the justices was this: Can the confession of someone like Ernesto—a modestly educated poor person who doesn't know that they're entitled to have a lawyer help them with the police—be admitted into evidence?

The Supreme Court's answer to this question was no. Ernesto had been coerced, cheated out of specific protections. Had he known about the Fifth Amendment, the law that gives us the freedom to keep our mouths shut when cops try to make us say what they want to hear, Ernesto might've kept the knowledge of his dirty deeds to himself. Had someone told Ernesto about the Sixth Amendment, the law that's supposed to guarantee us access to an attorney, he might've gotten decent representation, a lawyer who could've advised him to save his confessions for church.

The lunch bell was set to ring in a few minutes. I scooped a small stack of papers off a table and walked from group to group, distributing them. I said, "Next time we meet, I'll finish telling you the story of Ernesto Miranda. And I'm passing out the little speech I was telling you about. It's called the Miranda warning. Like I said, you probably have it memorized. If you don't, practice it. Read it to the mirror. Read it to your dog. Read it to your mom. Mirandize your grandma if you have to. I'm gonna ask someone to recite the Miranda warning next class. That'll be your quiz."

"I can recite it right now!" Freddy yelled. He made a fist and thumped his chest.

The bell rang.

"I appreciate your enthusiasm, Freddy. Maybe next time."

Most kids scooped up their backpacks, purses, or bags and shuffled out of the room. A few stayed. Two Mexican girls sat in the corner by the thermostat, eating sandwiches and mumbling, "You have the right to remain silent. Anything you say can and will be used against you in a court of law . . ."

Two other Mexican kids, Paul and Daniela, sat at the table by the radiator. A plastic bag filled with baby carrots rested between them. They took turns fishing nubs out and dunking them into a small plastic container of ranch dressing.

Watching them was making me hungry.

"Can I have a carrot?" I asked Daniela.

"Did you forget your lunch again, Miss Gurba?"

"Maybe."

She laughed and said, "I like this class."

Paul said, "So do I."

"What do you like about it?" I asked.

Paul said, "I don't know. It's chill."

Daniela said, "I like learning about crime! The only other class where we learn about crime is forensic science."

"What do you do in forensic science?"

Beaming the way sports fans do when asked about their favorite team, Daniela answered, "Oh my God, we had a unit on serial killers! It was so fun! We got to pick our favorite and do a presentation on him. My favorites are Jeffrey Dahmer and Richard Ramirez."

"Hey, I like Richard Ramirez too!" said Paul.

Daniela asked, "Who's your favorite serial killer, Miss Gurba?"

My mouth went dry. My palms began to sweat. I sat on my hands. In a small voice, I answered, "I don't have one."

"Really?!"

"Really."

"Why not?"

Rather than explain that I had my own Richard Ramirez, I said, "I just don't."

Daniela shrugged and ate another carrot.

The thing I never wanted to be was a teacher.

What boring lives those people led.

My mom was a teacher. My dad was a teacher. Most of their friends were teachers. At the dinner table, we never heard any good gossip. Only teacher talk.

I wanted to be something fun. An archeologist. A painter. An architect. If I couldn't make any of those happen, I'd settle for being tall.

I practiced being an archeologist whenever I could. Summer vacation allowed me to dig full-time. I'd hop on my bike and sail down sidewalks, ready to break my father's rule. My brother, my sister, and I weren't allowed to leave our neighborhood alone. I left all the time.

I opened my mouth, tasted the country air, and pedaled toward what hadn't been a river in years. I intended to sift through the trash scattered along its thirsty bed. A rusty spade rattled in my bike basket. I'd found the tool in an empty lot and considered it a good omen. I was meant to excavate, to inspect ruins, to court decay.

Perched on shale, alligator lizards napped in the August sun. Tumbleweeds tangled in barbed wire fencing shivered as pickup trucks roared past. I huffed and puffed. Sweat matted my tomboy sideburns, a bead of it sliding down my golden neck. I breathed through my mouth. Someone had run over a skunk. Its bisected remains oozed on the warm asphalt.

Before the freeway came into view, the liquor store appeared. My feet pulled back on my pedals. I hopped off my bike and cautiously walked it into the parking lot. I circled the store, looking for signs of . . . him.

They say he hitchhikes, I thought. *And evil has to eat and drink too. He could be in there, buying Twinkies.*

I didn't know his name yet. None of us did.

We'd glimpsed a rough police sketch of him. San Francisco's first female mayor, Dianne Feinstein, had flashed it at us on TV. During a late-summer news conference, she'd announced, "Somewhere in the Bay Area, someone is renting a room, an apartment, or a home to this vicious serial killer. I'm hoping that people will look at this composite drawing."

After looking at it, anxious Mexicans made jokes.

Too many of us knew someone, an uncle, brother, cousin, or friend, who resembled the police drawing of the Night Stalker. That's what the tabloids had dubbed him. He'd terrorized Southern California for weeks, invading homes, torturing victims, and murdering them. Now he was doing the same up north. We lived along the Central Coast, near the 101 freeway, a road the Night Stalker might've used to get to San Francisco. Our town, Santa Maria, was a convenient place for travelers to get out of their cars, stretch their legs, and refuel with a snack.

"The Night Stalker drawing looks like a watercolor by Picasso," Dad had said during dinner.

"Which one?" I asked.

"El Loco."

After shoveling everything on my plate into my mouth, I sprang out of my seat and sprinted to the bookshelf holding our encyclopedia set.

Grabbing the *P* volume, I flipped to "Picasso."

No locos.

Only *Guernica.*

I completed my inspection of the liquor store parking lot and decided that the coast was clear. The only other people in the lot were a trucker eating a hot dog and a woman sobbing into the wheel of her

Pinto. The Night Stalker was still on the loose, but he hadn't made a pit stop here. I hopped back on my bike and sailed north, toward the county line, toward the riverbed.

The Night Stalker had struck in a scattershot pattern.

Glassell Park.

Rosemead.

Monterey Park.

Whittier.

Monterey Park.

Monrovia.

Burbank.

Arcadia.

Sierra Madre.

Monterey Park.

Glendale.

Sun Valley.

Northridge.

After exhausting the southland, he'd turned his attentions north. Once he murdered in Lake Merced, taking the life of Peter Pan, a sixty-six-year-old accountant, it seemed that all of California belonged to him.

Like the night, he could materialize anywhere.

Homeowners installed window security bars. Handymen crouched, boarding up cat and doggie doors. Mexican grandmothers snuck into the bedrooms of grandchildren who worshipped Ozzy Osbourne and sprinkled holy water in the four corners. At swap meets, kids were told that if they strayed from their mother's sight, they'd get smacked with a shoe. Calloused hands locked dead bolts and we prayed that if you-know-who wandered onto our street, he'd scurry past our mailbox and oil-stained driveway.

If the Night Stalker had to take lives, I hoped he'd pay a visit to my enemies.

I was old enough to have a few. I was eight.

Some Mexicans murmured that the Night Stalker and el Cucuy, a bogeyman who kidnaps and dines on naughty children, were one and the same. Because Mexicans compulsively assign nicknames, many of our families have a Cucuy. Mine does. Ours is a güero to be avoided. To call someone a Cucuy is a public service, a warning. A Cucuy is a person who should under no circumstances babysit.

Some theorize that the legend of el Cucuy was spawned by an Iberian superstition, el Coco. "Duérmete, niña," goes the monster's macabre lullaby, "duérmete ya . . . que viene el Coco y te llevará. Duérmete, niña, duérmete ya . . . que viene el Coco y te comerá."*

In 1799, the Spanish painter Francisco Goya self-published *Los Caprichos*, an album featuring impressions of eighty etchings and aquatints. Goya's forty-third capricho, *Que viene el Coco*, depicts the backside of a shrouded figured approaching a bed. A seated woman stares at his face, transfixed as she clutches a frightened girl. Beside her huddles another scared child. The sheet draping Goya's Coco hints that he might not be supernatural. The artist's caprichos were, after all, satire. Maybe el Coco is Mommy's special friend in disguise, the one who comes to keep her company at night when Daddy is away. If the children can be convinced that a bogeyman roams their house at night, they'll be less tempted to spy.

Our parents used neither el Coco nor el Cucuy to prevent my brother, my sister, and me from wandering at night. They relied on a soggy murderer, la Llorona.

There are countless versions of her legend, but one ingredient always stays the same. Water. The story has to have water. One retelling of it goes like this. In a Mexican village, a married man takes a smitten girl as his lover. He enjoys getting her pregnant and leaves her with a big litter of kids that she has a difficult time feeding. Every

---

* Go to sleep, little girl. Go to sleep now . . . the monster is coming and he will take you. Go to sleep, little girl. Go to sleep now . . . the monster is coming and he will eat you.

time the husband comes to see her, he promises to leave his wife, swearing that soon, they'll be a proper family. Years pass. Her beauty withers. So does her faith. She accepts that her man is someone else's. He'll never leave his old, balding wife. She's an amazing cook.

With nothing left to do but make the unfaithful husband pay, the sancha walks her bastards to the river and feeds them to it, holding them down until the bubbles stop. She lets out an ungodly moan and wades into the freshwater grave, joining her bobbing children.

In death, the sancha grows a conscience that dooms her sobbing ghost to slog through mud. She wanders riverbanks, looking for children. Short or tall, plump or scrawny, freckled or bucktoothed, any child will satisfy her. She wants to be a mother again, wants to press kids close to her bony breast, sniff their fontanels, cover them with fleshless kisses. At this moment, along a deserted riverbank, she's weeping and begging, "Where are my children? Where are my children? Have you seen my children?"

When Dad recited this tale at bedtime, he imitated la Llorona's screeching groans.

He sounded like Liberace.

Grandma loved Bob Hope, Tongolele, and Liberace. She lived by a billiards hall in Whittier, in a one-story house that smelled like pets lived in it. In December, Mom and Dad took us there to eat prime rib, unwrap Christmas presents, and tell Grandma that we loved the polyester sweatsuits she gave us every year, thank you so much for them, we can't wait to put them on and avoid standing close to the heater. A few months after our visit to Whittier, the Night Stalker came. He chose a house by the 605 freeway and crept through its flower bed, placing an upside-down bucket in the soil.

The window he climbed through belonged to Maxine and Vincent Zazzara. Maxine was a gregarious lawyer who sang in a church choir in Downey. Vincent, a retired investment counselor, loved planting trees so much that he surrounded his house with about seventy-five of them. He also owned two restaurants. It took two days for Vincent's employee, a pizzeria manager named Bruno, to find his remains.

Bruno stood on the doorstep of his boss's ranch-style house, ringing the doorbell.

"Vincent!"

The Zazzaras' screen door was unlocked. The front door was ajar.

Bruno slid some receipts through the mail slot and took off.

The next morning, Bruno arrived with another employee. They found the front door still ajar. They decided to go in.

Their boss was on the couch in the den. He'd been shot.

Maxine was in the bedroom. Her eyes were gone.

In the early morning of May 14, my birthday, the Night Stalker struck again, in Monterey Park. Bill Doi, a World War II combat veteran, dialed 911.

He wheezed, "Help me."

Firefighters found books and papers strewn about his den. In the middle of the mess sat Bill, struggling to breathe. Like Vincent, he'd been shot in the head. Firefighters tried resuscitating Bill after he stopped breathing, but he was dead by the time they reached the hospital.

While flipping through a *National Geographic* in my pediatrician's waiting room, I overheard two secretaries speculating that the Night Stalker worshipped the devil. They poured sugar into their coffee mugs, stirred it, and spoke in low tones about the murders, agreeing with each other that the "Prince of Darkness" had to be involved. The devil seemed everywhere and nowhere during my childhood, and no one was more determined to find evidence of his handiwork than reporters. One place they sought evidence was a Manhattan Beach preschool. Virginia McMartin ran it as a family business, and according to reporters, the McMartins forced children to participate in Satanic rituals. One little one said he'd seen cats be stabbed to death at preschool. Another said that he was driven to a "circus house" and molested after seeing someone romping in an elephant costume.

Yet another kid said that he was driven to a cemetery to unearth a coffin and watch a corpse be ravaged by knives. Soon, similar complaints mushroomed across the country. Dropping kids off at day care became a high-stakes game. Who knew what might happen to them. They might be forced to eat each other's liver while pledging allegiance to Satan.

It was rumored that pentagrams drawn in both blood and lipstick had been found on the bodies of Night Stalker victims, and his emergence in Northern California provided more fodder for Satanic gossip. The Church of Satan was headquartered in San Francisco at 6114 California Street, and its founder, Anton LaVey, had performed at least one Satanic baptism in the black Victorian house. Archival footage shows LaVey ringing a bell at his audience. Dressed like a dime-store devil, he exchanges the bell for a sword. He chants, "In the name of our great God, Satan, Lucifer, I command thee to come forth and bestow these blessings upon us . . ."

At the altar, a naked woman rests on a table. Behind her hangs the horned Sigil of Baphomet, a goat's head in the middle of a pentagram, the official insignia of the Church of Satan. Wearing a robe with the sigil, Zeena, Anton LaVey's three-year-old daughter, obediently waits at the woman's feet.

This is the kind of stuff people were panicked was happening at childcare centers across North America.

After Mayor Feinstein's press conference, the Night Stalker ditched Northern California. He headed south again, reemerging in Mission Viejo, and it was an hour and a half past midnight when he tiptoed into the Romero family's backyard. James, a thirteen-year-old motorcycle enthusiast, had stepped outside. He was having trouble sleeping, and he wanted a pillow he'd left in the truck his family had taken to Rosarito Beach. They'd returned from their trip to Baja California a few hours earlier. They were all asleep.

James pulled the door handle. The truck was locked. He headed back to the house and heard rustling.

Probably a cat. Or a possum.

James wandered to the garage.

He tinkered with his minibike.

Through the ventilation grate came a scuttling sound.

Footsteps.

Someone glided past the window screen.

James crouched behind his parents' car, then sprinted into the house, to his bedroom. Peeking through the window, he saw a man wearing a black baseball cap, black jacket, and jeans cross the lawn.

"James!" screamed his dad. "Why are you up?"

"There's a prowler!"

James ran outside and watched the man hop into an orange Toyota. He glared at James before speeding away. James memorized part of the license plate: 482 T.

His dad called 911.

Cops walked the perimeter of the house.

At the base of the door where the Night Stalker had stood, a lifeless bird.

The winged thing found outside the Romero home signaled the presence of Ricardo Leyva Muñoz Ramirez, an AC/DC fan who believed himself the right hand of an infamous angel.

"You don't understand me," he would tell authorities. "You are not expected to. You are not capable of it. I am beyond your experience. I am beyond good and evil. Legions of the night—night breed—repeat not the errors of night prowler and show no mercy. I will be avenged. Lucifer dwells within us all."

Richard was born near the witching hour on February 29, 1960, a Monday. All seven members of this leap year baby's family were present at his birth, Richard becoming the fifth and final child of Mercedes Muñoz and Julian Tapia Ramirez. Mercedes worked at a boot factory. Julian laid track for the Santa Fe Railroad. They called the family's newest member Richie and raised him in El Paso, a Texas town made wet by the Rio Grande.

Accounts of Richard's childhood tend to emphasize his sweetness, beauty, and ominous peculiarity. When Mercedes and Julian brought him home from the hospital, Ruth, Richard's only sister, treated him like a living doll, dressing him up and parading him around. Richard was uninterested in sleep, instead rocking to the sour hum of the refrigerator, the meows of stray cats, and gunfire echoing from the TV. Once he learned to walk, Richard amused himself with an all-American death game, playing cowboys and Indians in the hot dirt outside. Groggy after so many sleepless nights, he parked himself in front of the TV and watched a cartoon coyote try to squash a roadrunner with a boulder.

He guzzled Coca-Cola and burped the alphabet.

Soft drinks were Richard's hydration.

His smile rotted. That was the only part of him that was not good-looking.

At school, Richard goofed off during class. After school, he held hands with a neighbor girl, Nancy, and led her to the cemetery for some fooling around. Having outgrown cowboys and Indians, he pursued live game. After choking the life out of a rabbit, he slit open its stomach, scooped out the entrails, and fed them to his dog. Richard played middle school football until his coach learned he had epilepsy, and a few of his biographers magnify this detail, implying that getting cut from the team may have been what set Richard on the path to channeling Lucifer.

I hate football so much that I've been kicked out of a Super Bowl party for jeering at both teams and I didn't go disembowel anyone. Instead, I laughed it off. I was forced to go to that party anyway. Men pushing the football theory would rather not reckon with certain influences in Richard's life. These influences introduced him to the sadistic pleasures of authoritarianism and empire; they molded his manhood.

In Chihuahua, Richard's father, Julian, had taught Mexicans to kill. He'd been a police firearms trainer but didn't want his kids growing up to be cops. Drunk on the American dream, Julian believed his sons and daughter could realize his fantasies through public education. He didn't get that Texas schools weren't built to serve his kids. Teachers treated Mexican students like a pestilence, and the Ramirez kids brought home unimpressive report cards. This hurt Julian. So that they might feel his disappointment, he beat his children with a hose.

When Julian was humiliated by non-sentient things, his rage had nowhere to go. He couldn't make objects feel his pain and so it flowed out of him and back. He exploded and yelled, thumping his head against the garage door until blood ran down his face. When Julian couldn't get a drainpipe to fit in the kitchen, he grabbed a hammer and pounded his head.

To escape, Richard crept along sidewalks, sand, and dandelions. He stopped at windows and spied on people undressing, eating, watching TV, and generally not terrorizing each other. Rounding a corner, he stepped through the gates of Concordia Cemetery, drifting along its fifty-two dry and dusty acres. Wandering its mausoleums, cacti, headstones, and mesquite trees was better than running from his father. The graveyard was the resting place of more than sixty thousand souls and Richard trusted that none of them was going to chase him, tie him to a tree, and tenderize him.

Curling up on the dirt, he shut his eyes.

Below pulsed Texas's underworld.

Settler priests.

Chinese railroad workers.

Victorian stillborns.

Freemasons.

Cowboys.

Catholics.

Kit Carson.

Mormons.

Buffalo soldiers.

Richard slept on the grave of the outlaw John Wesley Hardin, a gunslinger who committed his first murder at age fifteen. Hardin proceeded to take thirty-nine more lives and perhaps his spirit slithered into Richard, intoxicating him with frontier poison.

To commune with a living serial killer (they're not rare when you consider how many people cops, soldiers, prisons, and insurance companies kill), Richard headed to the Truth Apartments, to drop in on his cousin Mike. Tattooed and muscular, the former GI had joined the army in 1965. A Green Beret and decorated war hero, he completed two tours of duty in Vietnam and returned with medals, as well as some unconventional trophies.

Mike passed a joint to Richard. Lifting it to his gray smile, Richard inhaled. With the radio playing, they cruised Alameda Street. The cousins talked in figure eights for hours, hotboxing in parking lots. They felt big when they were together. An important pair of men.

Jessie, Mike's wife, was tired. She and Mike had two kids, Paul and Orado. Jessie supported all three of them and she prayed someone would give Mike a job. Any job. She also prayed that Mike would stop disappearing with Richard. What kind of man spent his days getting stoned with a twelve-year-old boy? It was weird. And embarrassing.

When Jessie complained, Mike saw her brains on the wall. Gooey spaghetti. Why couldn't the bitch be more like his little cousin? He should be worshipped for every breath he took, and he basked in the boy's admiration, returning the affection by sharing secrets with him, regaling Richard with stories set on and off the battlefield. The Green Beret gave his shaggy-haired protégé lessons in irregular warfare, modeling cunning, stealth, and invisibility. He taught him that the key to a successful attack is the element of surprise.

"It's us," Mike told Richard, "the poor and downtrodden, against them, the rich and influential." Women were their enemies too, and Mike confessed that in Vietnam, he'd held women captive and done anything he wanted to them. GIs were encouraged to rape prisoners, and Mike kept a shoebox archive documenting his military atrocities.

Fetching the box from the closet, Mike scooped out its well-worn treasures, placing them in Richard's hands. The boy's fingers traced the violent images. The photographs proved Mike's stories were true. The rapes, mutilations, and decapitations he'd raved about were all there. Mike's bond with Richard was erotic, triangulated by contraband snuff.

Mike was proud he'd killed twenty-nine people. He slept above his trophies: eight shrunken heads that he hid in a battered suitcase beneath his bed. In Vietnam, he'd used the heads as pillows, pressing his face to his victims'. Those that the US Army had sent Mike to kill believed that for their souls to enter heaven, their bodies must remain intact. By snatching their heads, Mike waged spiritual warfare, reaching into his victims' afterlives, attempting to control their souls.

Mike executed more victims than Richard, making him more Night Stalker than the Night Stalker, but the soldier was never found responsible for anyone's murder, not even the one he would later commit in front of three kids.

It was springtime. Richard was at the Truth Apartments playing mini-billiards. Feeling parched, he headed to the kitchen. He opened the fridge and noticed Mike's gun on the shelf.

"What's that doing there?" he called out.

"I may be using it," Mike answered. "I want it to be cool."

Richard grabbed a drink and returned to his game.

Jessie arrived carrying groceries. She struggled. Worried she'd drop the eggs, she cried, "Hey! I'm dying over here! Get off your asses and help!"

Mike screamed, "Shut up!" walked to the fridge, and grabbed his gun.

Weapon in hand, he faced her.

"What are you going to do with that?"

"If you don't shut up, I'll kill you."

Jessie said, "I dare you."

A bullet tore through her head. Thump.

Shrieks from Paul and Orado.

"You don't ever say you saw this. Understand?"

Richard nodded, hurried past the dead wife, and left.

A few days after, Richard, Julian, and Mercedes went back to the Truth Apartments. Mike had called them from jail, asking them to fetch some of Jessie's jewelry. Mercedes waited in the car.

Father and son entered the apartment. It was nothing like the other day. It was quiet and still.

Hot.

Dried blood made the air savory. Dust particles hovered in the light.

Violence haunted the place.

Richard looked at the spot where Jessie had fallen.

A sense of mastery crept over him.

"Get her pocketbook," said Julian. "Find the jewelry."

Richard turned Jessie's purse upside down, dumping the contents on the bed. He slid his fingers through, across and into her stuff.

Touching her things was touching her.

Julian saw the slug that had killed her. He stooped and picked it up.

The ex-cop marveled at it, then put it in his pocket.

When they left the apartment, Richard was different.

Reborn.

A Texas jury sympathized with Mike. They found him innocent by reason of insanity and sentenced him to four and a half years at a state mental hospital.

In 1977, authorities freed him.

The cousins reunited.

Remember what my student said during the Ernesto Miranda story? That if a guy has a wife, he shouldn't have to rape anybody? After Vietnam, Mike lived according to that creed. A wife is all a man should need. With a wife, a man shouldn't have to hurt strangers.

What kind of bird was left on the Romeros' doorstep?

I want to know.

Hummingbirds, robins, swallows.
Whip-poor-wills, crows, blackbirds.
Ravens, cranes, herons.
Cuckoos, roosters, gulls.
Eagles, vultures, turkeys.
Nightjars, puffins, nighthawks.
Owls.

Richard went west. That's what you do to Manifest Destiny.

Violets for Mei Leung.
Lilies for Jennie Vincow.
Lilies for Dayle Okazaki.
Lilies for Tsai-Lian Yu.
Gardenias for Maxine Zazzara.
Gardenias for Vincent Zazzara.
Gardenias for Bill Doi.
Daffodils for Mable Bell.
Daffodils for Mary Louise Cannon.
Daffodils for Joyce Nelson.
Hydrangeas for Lela Kneiding.

Hydrangeas for Maxson Kneiding.
Hydrangeas for Chainarong Khovananth.
Violets for Elyas Abowath.
Violets for Peter Pan.

MAN FOUND GUILTY OF 13 "NIGHT STALKER" MURDERS

LOS ANGELES, Sept 20 (AP)—A man was convicted of 13 murders and 30 other felonies today by a jury that decided he was the Night Stalker whose attacks terrified Southern California in 1985.

In addition, the jurors found 18 special circumstances existed, making the man, Richard Ramirez, eligible for the death penalty.

The defendant, convicted of all counts against him, demanded to be absent from court when the 63 separate verdict forms were read by Superior Court Judge Michael Tynan.

Judge Tynan granted his request, saying a recent appeals court decision gave him no choice. Mr. Ramirez, who left the courtroom with shackles rattling around his ankles, heard the verdicts from loudspeaker in a nearby holding cell.

Asked what he thought about the verdicts, the 29-year-old El Paso native said only, "Evil."

When I first began teaching, I worked night school.

I taught adult ed and many of my students were immigrants. A few were retired gang members.

Our school occupied a building that still looked like a bank. It had been one until it got robbed. The old vault housed the teacher's lounge. My classroom was on the second floor, right above it.

The whiteboard wobbled as I wrote, "Prompt: Fill a page writing about HOME. Use the five senses in your description. Give home a spirit. Make it so real that place feels like person."

The students put pen and pencil to paper and wrote.

When everyone seemed finished, I asked, "Would any of us care to share?"

An OG wearing Dickies with razor-sharp creases cleared his throat. He volunteered, "Um, I'll go."

His bald head bobbed as he read his description of the place where he'd grown up, the place that had made him. East Los Angeles. He said that his neighborhood is a place where the food tastes good, the girls are smart and pretty, and people look out for each other. He said that there was a summer that a man tried to test his neighborhood. This man was a "psycho"; he'd been sneaking into people's houses and doing bad shit, evil shit, and he'd picked the wrong neighborhood to fuck with. The psycho came to hide in East LA, but the neighborhood wasn't going to let him. The psycho's picture was on the front page of the *LA Times*, and nobody felt sorry for him. Everyone was willing to beat his ass, rip him apart, and redeem his carnitas for a reward. A mob chased him. One homeboy beat him with a tire iron. The police intervened and saved the psycho's life. If they hadn't shown up, the neighborhood would've played soccer with his head.

The OG proudly looked up from his page.

I wanted to shake his hand. Reverentially, I asked, "Is that about the Night Stalker?"

He slowly nodded.

I said, "I remember watching the trial. That shit was spooky. Ramirez would flash the pentagram he'd drawn on his hand at the news cameras."

"Yeah," said the student. "He'd shout, 'Hail, Satan!' If it wasn't for the police, there would've been no trial. The neighborhood would've taken care of him."

I said, "I know why they saved him. Like recognizes like."

The OG's lips curled, giving me a smile.

• • •

IN THE SUPREME COURT OF CALIFORNIA
THE PEOPLE,
Plaintiff and Respondent,
S012944
v.
Los Angeles County
RICHARD RAMIREZ,
Super. Ct. No. A771272
Defendant and Appellant.

On November 7, 1989, defendant Richard Ramirez was sentenced to death for the so-called Night Stalker murders following his convictions of 12 counts of first degree murder (Pen. Code, § 187, subd. (a)), 1 one count of second degree murder (§ 187, subd. (a)), five counts of attempted murder (§§ 187/664), four counts of rape (§ 261, former subd. (2)), three counts of forcible oral copulation (§ 288a, former subd. (c)), four counts of forcible sodomy (§ 286, former subd. (c)), and 14 counts of first degree burglary (§ 459). The jury found true allegations of multiple-murder, burglary, rape, forcible sodomy, and, forcible-oral-copulation special circumstances. (§ 190.2.) The court imposed a sentence of death.

After receiving his sentence, Richard said, "Big deal. Death always went with the territory. See you in Disneyland."

I've always wondered, did Richard's words have any influence on ticket sales at Disneyland?

One of my PTSD symptoms is insomnia.

I can't defend myself if I'm unconscious.

This symptom developed after a man who could pass for Ernesto Miranda's cousin decided to follow me down a residential sidewalk one summer afternoon. I was close to the age of Ernesto's victim, nineteen years old. For years, the phantom sensation of what the guy did (he shoved his face between my legs, nose to my pussy) would ambush me as I tried drifting to sleep. I pictured his head, just his head, floating between my legs, taunting me with a smile.

As a tomboy, I'd had a crush on a disembodied head. She lived in Disneyland, inside of a crystal ball at the Haunted Mansion. Her name was Madame Leota. She conducted séances, chanting, "Serpents and spiders, tail of rat, call in the spirits, wherever they're at . . ." I liked Madame Leota's blue makeup. Her cheekbones.

I sometimes think of the man who raped me with his face as my Richard Ramirez. Richard randomly let some people live. Obviously, my Richard let me go. He killed Sophia, another woman he stalked, in Night Stalker style. For what he did to Sophia and others, my Richard Ramirez was sent to San Quentin State Prison. On death row, Richard Ramirez became his neighbor.

In 2003, Metallica shot the music video for "St. Anger" at San Quentin. They played before hundreds of men, but Richard wasn't allowed to see them. Still, he found a way to connect. Through a guard, he smuggled a memento to guitarist Kirk Hammett.

"It was a magazine with us on the cover!" Hammett told a reporter. "And the subscription tag said, 'Richard Ramirez' . . . He was a Metallica fan . . . I still have the magazine. It's a nice little novelty item."

At school, Ernesto's mug shot is back on-screen.

I stand near it as I finish telling his story.

In 1967, during his retrial, Ernesto's common-law wife, Twila, testified against him. She said that three days after his arrest, she'd visited Ernesto in jail. They discussed his written confession and he admitted to the rape. Ernesto gave Twila an errand. She was to find his victim and relay a message, that Ernesto would marry her if she dropped the charges against him.

With Twila's help, Ernesto was again convicted of rape.

"Disloyal!" a boy shouted from the back of the class.

I straightened my spine and said, "Explain."

He said, "That's his wife!"

A girl shouted, "So his wife should be loyal to him even though he's a rapist?"

The boy said neither yes nor no. Instead, he mumbled, "If that was my wife . . ."

I went on. I said that Ernesto was released from Arizona State Penitentiary in 1972. In Phoenix, he became a local celebrity. On-screen, I displayed a copy of an autographed, printed Miranda warning card, the kind Ernesto sold for $1.50. In January 1975, Ernesto was hanging out in a neighborhood called "the Deuce." He wandered into a bar and spent the afternoon drinking and playing cards there. An argument broke out. Ernesto went to the bathroom. When he returned to the table, one of the men he'd been playing cards with brandished a knife. He stabbed Ernesto in the neck and chest. Ernesto died and nobody was charged with his murder.

The class burst into applause.

My grandmother is buried beside her second husband in Whittier, at Rose Hills Memorial Park.

Her little sister, my great-aunt, is buried within spitting distance.

Rose Hills is divided into gardens and gets traffic jams on the weekends. Some refer to it as the Disneyland of death. The rapper Eazy-E is buried in the Lupine Lawn. Jaime Escalante, the East LA math teacher who inspired the movie *Stand and Deliver*, a calculus drama, is buried in the Lakeside Gardens. Grandma rests in the Garden of Solace. Last year, my cousin and I went to decorate Grandma's grave on her birthday, but we couldn't get into the cemetery. The gates were locked. Police surrounded it. Apparently, a man in an RV had been spotted waving a gun in the Garden of Tranquility.

Down the knoll from Grandma rest Maxine and Vincent Zazzara. They're buried side by side, at the foot of a thick pine tree, in the Garden of Commemoration. "Nothing has ever been said about God," wrote Thomas Merton, "that hasn't already been better said by the wind in the trees." I visit the Zazzaras when I visit Grandma. I take them money. Coins. Everybody needs money, the dead too, and California is an especially expensive state to die in. Sap rains on the Zazzaras' headstones. The coins on their headstones catch the sunlight. Glint. The garden smells like Christmas. And the cemetery feels like an amusement park.

LOCAS

My cousin Desiree and I never played house. Pretending to be a mom who hits her kids with anything in reach or a dad who forgets to pay his child support didn't interest us. Instead, we played at being female gangsters, cholas, young women with big hairdos and tattooed hands that could apply eyeliner as deftly as they could aim a shotgun at an enemy's head. Our gang had two members, us, and we planned on recruiting no one else, not our siblings, not our parents, and definitely not our grandma. We called ourselves Pocas Pero Locas and we practiced throwing gang signs, curling our small fingers into PPL.

Desiree and I were fourteen and thirteen when we created our two-girl crime family. We needed this little organization badly. There were things Desiree couldn't tell her parents and there were things I couldn't tell mine. Turning away from grown-ups, we created a tiny Cosa Nostra for protection, affection, and fun. Pledging our allegiance to PPL, we helped each other to carry our burdens as best as we could. Committed to what we've built, Desiree and I remain as loyal to our childhood enterprise as the Pope is to gold.

The day Desiree appointed me to tell her story, I started sketching it in my head. I knew it would begin with our hands. Hands are what we use to beautify ourselves. Hands are what we use to turn the volume up on the radio. Hands are what we use to commit facts to paper. Hands are what we use to caress lovers, fold letters, poke holes, and kill.

My hands will show you why two California girls dreamt up a make-believe mafia and why one of us gravitated to a real one. My hands have permission to describe the romance and seduction of hustling. My hands will demonstrate that my cousin is living proof of the high cost some girls are expected to pay for surviving the United States of America, the country with the world's highest incarceration rate.

Crime reporters have covered bleak moments in Desiree's life. What they've written about her is true but recklessly incomplete. Published by the *San Gabriel Valley Tribune*, one of their articles begins, "Police arrested four people Thursday for using fraudulent gift cards to make hundreds of dollars worth of purchases at Walmart." Desiree was this group's only woman. At age thirty-six, she was also its oldest member and its only "wanted parolee." Before the reporter reveals that my cousin surrendered without a fight, he raises the stakes, writing that "two loaded handguns were recovered from inside the suspects' car."

The *San Gabriel Valley Tribune* names no eyewitnesses. None of the arrested are heard from either. The only person quoted by the newspaper is Glendora police lieutenant Rob Lamborghini. He likely fed every detail about my cousin's supposed activities to the reporter, and the article's tone is sympathetic to Walmart, as if the US multinational corporation were a helpless woman whose purse was nearly snatched by four degenerates. If you ask me, we should all rob Walmart. There are a million reasons why. Here's one. In 2003, lawyers working on behalf of the company paid a $52,000 bribe to Mexican officials. This money bought them permission to build a store one mile from Teotihuacán's pyramids, and construction workers broke ground in an alfalfa field, digging and digging, churning soil. A crew of archeologists overseeing the project soon unearthed evidence that Walmart was messing with ancient ruins. Along with a seven-hundred-year-old wall and altar, the company also disturbed nine graves.

When fans of *Law & Order* hear the word *criminal*, I doubt that Walmart comes to mind. Instead, the people Rob Lamborghini gets paid to talk about do. Most police departments staff someone like him, a representative whose job it is to speak to reporters about how cops keep us safe, a spokesman who convinces taxpayers that the police are here to catch bad guys, bad guys like my cousin.

At her mother's ramshackle house in Riverside is a box filled with Desiree's faded school assignments. The first is dated January 8, 1980. On its slightly rumpled paper appear two red handprints. Beneath these hands, which look like a child's bloody palm prints pressed against a foggy windowpane, someone, probably the teacher, neatly wrote, "Fingerpainting is fun!" A slightly smeared family portrait drawn in primary colors is dated six days later. A large blue circle with wide eyes and a big mouth dominates the center. Under this face, in an adult's crisp penmanship, the words "This is my grandma." To the right floats a small blue circle, its mouth open in a scream. Worried eyes glance back at Grandma. Beneath it, in the same adult's crisp penmanship, "This is my mommy." To the right of these faces, a faceless yet ferocious red scribble.

"This is my Daddy."

Desiree's own writing appears in pencil against a lined sheet of paper dated April 18, 1983. Over the top of the sheet peeks a self-portrait drawn in crayon, a smiling face with green eyes framed by brown hair. Underneath its chin, the words "When I grow up, I will be a teacher because I want to help children do work and read."

My cousin has no recollection of writing this. She can't imagine her seven-year-old self at a classroom desk, dreaming about a cheerful future. Instead, she remembers things she was supposed to keep secret, things that we're now going to set free.

For all of this to make sense, we need to talk about the big blue face in the middle.

We need to talk about Grandma.

Our grandmother was a vain woman who believed that her children and her children's children and her children's children's children were born for one reason, to carry on her legacy as a great beauty.

Each of us was her mirror, duty bound to reflect her former physical glory. Though she was withered by the time we met her, Grandma believed that her eyes still elevated her, making her superior, aristocratic. Unlike her mother's brown eyes, Grandma's glowed green, a decadent color that Desiree and I inherited. Our eyes pleased Grandma, but she wanted more from us. Grandma had been a lanky kid and she expected the same from her granddaughters. We loved food too much for that to happen. We packed away ice cream sandwiches and mashed potatoes, roast beef and tamales, petit fours and pastrami, Cream of Wheat and refried beans, ketchup and eggs, hash browns and gravy. Eating turned us sturdy and gave us hamster cheeks. Our lips blew up too.

Nothing could be done about our thick lips, but Grandma had a fix for our stomachs and noses. To get our waistlines under control, we needed to go on diets. Everybody at Grandma's was always on a diet so we had a variety of examples to choose from. We could use Dexatrim. We could drink SlimFast. We could join WeightWatchers. We could try the grapefruit diet or the cottage cheese diet or an all-juice diet. We could follow the Elizabeth Taylor diet. It seemed to be working for her. She had eight husbands.

To make our noses skinnier, Grandma encouraged us to pinch them, guaranteeing us that if we squeezed our noses long enough, they'd shrink. Sitting in front of the TV, absorbing reruns, Desiree and I held our noses and breathed through our mouths. We hoped these efforts would make us worthy of Grandma's love.

Our grandmother was named after the one thing that didn't escape Pandora's box, Hope, and she bragged that her special eyes were the result of a French soldier who'd sailed to Mexico to fight on behalf of Emperor Napoleon III. This French soldier was a mask. There was nothing French about our grandmother or her parents or her parents' parents. Grandma was like Pío Pico. He'd been the last governor of Mexican California, and his ranch sprawled about five miles from Grandma's one-story ranch-style house in Whittier. Pico's grandmother had been a Black woman. So had Grandma's.

Grandma was sitting in the armchair by the fridge when she pulled her pant leg up and tugged her knee-high stocking down. She displayed her calf and smacked it twice. In her mysterious accent, one that sounded more Transylvanian than Mexican, she boomed, "Look at these legs! I had the most beautiful legs in all of Guadalajara! I also had the fastest legs. I was such a beautiful girl that men chased me. They chased me! And the more I ran from them, the more beautiful my legs became."

I looked at Desiree. We wanted to laugh so bad.

Grandma's leg looked grandmotherly. All of her did.

Grandma's favorite subject was her beauty though she sometimes discussed her other gifts. She claimed to be the seventh son of a seventh son and said that her unique position in the birth order blessed her with psychic abilities. Without invitation, she shared her powers with the public. At a pharmacy, my father and I nervously watched her make a beeline for a very pregnant chola with swollen ankles. Standing before the long-haired girl, Grandma rubbed her hands together and raised them, letting them hover near the baby bump, which was more of a baby boulder. She closed her eyes and, in record speed, slid into a trance.

"A girl!" Grandma shouted into the antacid aisle. "You will be the mother of a baby girl!"

Grandma opened her eyes. She waited to be shown some gratitude.

In a singsong voice, the chola said, "Nope! I'm having a boy. The doctor already told me. We have a picture of Mikey Jr. hanging on the fridge."

Grandma glared.

How dare this flip-flop-wearing bitch reject her prophecy.

Turning around, Grandma stomped away. I could almost hear Mikey snickering.

Grandma was telling the truth about having been a twiggy kid. A picture taken on the day of her first Holy Communion shows her bony legs kneeling on a prayer bench. Her palms are pressed together in a semblance of prayer, and a white veil covers half her head. Her glossy black hair shines. She looks icy, saintly, and ready for Jesus. In a picture taken about seven or eight years later, Grandma's iciness has temporarily melted. Her hair is swept away from her face and held in place by barrettes. With her arms behind her back, she sticks her chest out. One hip is cocked. As Grandma shoots the photographer a honey of a smile, her skirt hides Guadalajara's most beautiful legs. Someone took this snapshot in the place where she met our grandpa.

In 1843, a friar donated a stretch of land, which had belonged to a Carmelite convent, to the state of Jalisco. From its grounds sprang Mexico's first panopticon-inspired prison. Named after Jalisco's governor, la Penitenciaría de Escobedo was nicknamed the Red House for its color. This neoclassical fortress could jail up to fifteen hundred Mexicans, and during the Cristero War, the government used it to lock up Catholic fighters. When the conflict ended in 1929, la Escobedo was torn to rubble.

Revolution Park replaced the penitentiary. It was designed by the architect Luis Barrágan, and expatriates gathered beneath its shade trees to gossip, swap war stories, and girl watch. Our Yankee grandfather sat among these men, his eyes following our grandmother's legs as she strolled the park's redbrick path with her sisters. Our aunts say that Hope was taken by Peter's Slavic good looks, but I think that that story comes from the same place as Grandma's French soldier. I believe Grandma wanted to escape from her family. A family can be a hole, and to crawl out of one, girls need help. They need rope.

After a two-year courtship, our grandparents married.

Hope was seventeen.

Peter, thirty-four.

Nine months after their wedding, Enrique was born. Gloria was next and then Roberto, my dad. In 1952, my grandmother kissed her mom goodbye. After my grandparents and their children climbed aboard a northbound train, they stuck their arms out the windows and waved. Bracelets jangled. Several hours into their journey, my uncle and father devised a way to entertain themselves. Cheering, they leapt from train car to train car, watching the tracks blur beneath their bodies. Had their ankles twisted or their feet missed the railing, they would've fallen and been instantly ground into chorizo. When risking their lives got old, the brothers went back inside and stared out the windows. Iguanas lazing on tree branches flicked their tongues and stared back.

After three days of travel, a sharp whistle blew. Passengers stood. The five migrants disembarked, stepping onto solid earth at Los Angeles' Union Station before squishing into a taxi that zipped them downtown. Grandpa checked the family into the Gates Hotel. Stomachs rumbled so he herded everyone to the hotel diner. At the counter, my dad twirled on a chrome stool, feet dangling. Grandpa ordered breakfast. In minutes, a waitress in a white uniform set a plate of steaming waffles smothered in butter and maple syrup under my dad's chin. With a cloth napkin tucked into his shirt, he scooped the goodness into his mouth and groaned.

Ecstasy.

Glimpsing LA City Hall through the diner window, my four-year-old dad confused the white tower, which would be made world-famous by the TV show *Dragnet*, for the Empire State Building. Dad was in awe. He was now a New Yorker.

The family settled in Estrada Courts, a public housing project in Boyle Heights. Grandpa found work welding in Santa Monica but hated the commute to the west side and back. Forty miles? On a crowded bus? With innumerable stops? Five days a week? Forget it. LA was a city where every man was encouraged to rely on his own automobile and Grandpa would become self-reliant. On a Monday morning, he slipped his checkbook into his back pocket, put on his gray fedora, and hollered at my dad, his only kid not yet in school.

"C'mon, Butch! We're buying a car!"

Hand in hand, they walked to a gas station on Soto Street. Outside of a mechanic's garage, recently hosed jalopies for sale glistened in the sunlight. Grandpa wrote a three-hundred-dollar check for a 1940

Studebaker Commander. Father and son proudly drove the beauty home. Estrada Courts didn't have garages, so they parked the blue car about half a block away, on the street. The Studebaker ferried our grandpa to a Douglas Aircraft plant where he worked swing shift. A bench mechanic, he crafted parts out of sheet metal. He soldered the aircraft's most important piece, the toilet.

Grandma gave birth to another girl, Veronica, and at Echo Park's Queen of Angels Hospital, Grandma pushed out her final kid, Petra, Desiree's mom. Lured by freeway billboards that advertised cheap suburban homes, Grandpa moved the family southeast, to a three-bedroom tract house in Norwalk. He got a discount, opting to buy the model home near the train tracks that hordes of potential buyers, busybodies, and lookie-loos had toured, kicked, and shrugged at. The new place had a garage for the Studebaker, which got replaced by a Chevrolet. Grandpa and my father drove the Chevy to a Polish butcher shop in Culver City to buy the tastiest kielbasa in LA County. Back in Norwalk, my grandfather stood at his stove, frying this sausage until its skin snapped and crackled. Plating the meat alongside kapusta, he sat cross-legged at the kitchen table, dipped his kielbasa in mustard, and downed it with ice-cold beer.

Fifteen years after their arrival in California, Grandma found Grandpa in the driveway. While working on his Chevy after Thanksgiving dinner, his heart had stopped. My father still jokes that the dinner was *that good*, and because Desiree and I weren't born yet, we mostly know Grandpa through jokes like that one.

Once Grandpa was gone, Dad grew his hair out and split. With money he'd saved from flipping burgers, he drifted the world, a hippie vagabond sleeping beneath the Greek moon, aboard Turkish trains, and in Bedouin tents. Enrique, who became Henry in California, went to Vietnam. Gloria got married. Veronica went to college. Petra got pregnant.

Desiree was born in Whittier, the town where Richard Nixon, the only US president to resign, ran for high school class president and lost. Desiree would briefly go to Nixon's high school, but first she went to Ocean View Elementary, a place from which you absolutely could not see the sea. Desiree lived with her mom and Grandma and Grandma's second husband, a cranky furniture store owner named Bob. Their home sat on a spacious lot. It was roomier than the Norwalk place, with avocado trees in the backyard, more than one bathroom, and a baby grand piano in the living room. Grandma, Aunt Petra, and Desiree piled into the Cadillac to come celebrate my first birthday in Santa Maria, but we mostly drove down to Whittier to see them. Going to Whittier was exciting. It gave us a chance to get away from our cow town and learn about big-city problems like rush hour traffic, smog, and road rage. All the cuss words came out as navigating the 101 upped Dad's blood pressure.

To get to Grandma's, we had to drive past the Fred C. Nelles Youth Correctional Facility, a reform school for boys. As we got close, Dad said, "Look. Kid jail."

Trees and a hedge blocked our view, so I relied on my imagination. Behind the vegetation, I pictured a short prison with kids wearing striped pajamas. They held small sledgehammers and smashed small rocks. Everything I knew about jail came from cartoons and I couldn't imagine why kids would need to go to jail. Why not just send us to our rooms? Wasn't that our version of jail?

At Grandma's, there was always new profanity to learn from Petra. She strung four-letter words together in mind-altering ways and when she couldn't find a word to express herself, artistic frustration inspired her to invent a new one. A box of candy usually sat on Petra's dresser, and Desiree and I were often huddled near her chocolate-covered macadamia nuts, trying to sneak one. Slowly, I'd swivel my head back and forth, up and down, and back and forth again.

Tall shelves lined Petra's bedroom walls, and on the shelves were dozens of Barbie dolls gripped by metal stands. The stony dolls stood on their tiptoes, staring straight ahead, low blond ponytails gathered tightly at the napes of their long, thin necks. Repeated over and over, this was who Grandma wanted us to be, a beige and blue-eyed creature with nostrils narrow enough to make sneezing dangerous.

A woman named Ruth Handler had created the Barbie, naming her after her own daughter. The doll had debuted the year Petra turned one, 1959, and became such a hit that she needed her own press secretary; fans bombarded her with twenty thousand letters a week. Adventurous little girls were Barbie's intended market. Noticing that they had only baby dolls to play with, Handler wanted little girls to rehearse being all types of women, not just moms.

Barbie had a Dreamhouse, a Corvette, and a handsome boyfriend who could never get her pregnant. Petra was a single mom who waitressed at Sir George's Smorgasbord and worked as a bill collector. Dolls and food filled her up. Dolls were great company. They were silent, posable, and safe. So was a box of cookies. The worst cookies might do was choke you, but family could do the same. Petra once told Desiree and me that anyone who'd grown up in Norwalk in the 1950s had gotten their ass beat as a child and that anyone who said different was a liar; kids wandered up and down Imperial Highway wounded. Yeah, Petra had been lifted off the ground by her blond ponytail, dangled, and smacked across her face, but at least Grandma hadn't put cigarettes out on her. That was white trash, and our family wasn't Okie. Being used as a human ashtray, now that would've crossed the line into child abuse.

Petra owned every Barbie released between 1959 and 1970 and then some. My aunt allowed me to touch her plastic women, but I had to handle them like religious relics. Petra found a lot of her collection on the weekends. She spent Saturdays and Sundays digging through dead people's stuff at estate sales, rummage sales, yard sales, and flea markets, and she traded doll-hunting tips with other fanatic collectors, men she called "fags." The community of Barbie freaks my aunt belonged to met at conventions where fans dressed like their favorite dolls.

Fashion Queen Barbie.

Color Magic Barbie.

American Airlines Stewardess Barbie.

When Desiree turned eight, Petra took her to one of these

conventions. Before they went inside, Desiree got the crap beaten out of her in her mom's VW. You'd have no idea that this happened from looking at the glowing picture of my cousin that appeared later in the *Los Angeles Times*. A photographer made her briefly famous; the caption beneath Desiree's convention photo states that my eight-year-old cousin was introducing "Beth, her Cabbage Patch doll, to a Barbie outfitted in a pageboy hairdo and sunsuit."

Though she often looked weary, my cousin was a beautiful child. She sparkled with mischievous charisma, the type of troublemaker you wanted to get in trouble with and who you wanted to take the heat for. Her cinnamon-brown hair reached to her waist, and she had our grandfather's broad, high forehead, a feature Dad said was a sign of maximal intelligence. Barbie had this same high forehead. Desiree swung back and forth between fearlessness, rage, and glee, a cyclone of a girl who loved Smurfs, Barbies, Strawberry Shortcake, and her Cabbage Patch doll, Beth. Desiree had appointed herself Beth's protector and she guarded her carefully, stashing her birth certificate in an undisclosed location. She didn't want anyone stealing it, and she knew that family stole from family. Desiree had watched one of our older cousins, who was also one of her babysitters, ferret into her parents' wallets looking for cash.

The December before Desiree began running away, my dad took me and my siblings to Knott's Berry Farm, a frontier-themed amusement park. Desiree came with us. It was such a great day. Like Christmas times ten. We watched gunslingers duel near the saloon and got whiplash from being jerked around by roller coasters. We petted and rode depressed ponies. For lunch, we bit into fried chicken, biscuits, stewed rhubarb, and boysenberry pie. Standing next to the cigar store Indian, Desiree looked marvelous. Her outfit was way cooler than mine. She listened to Wham!, the English pop duo whose slogan was "CHOOSE LIFE," and she was wearing one of their T-shirts with patchwork jeans and high-topped sneakers. I was wearing a white V-neck sweater, a collared chambray shirt, and dad jeans. Next to my cousin, I looked like a gay librarian.

My dad was obsessed with riding the stagecoach, so we waited in line for a turn. Once we were on board, and the horses picked up the pace, Desiree tapped my leg and we stood, sticking our heads out the window and flinging our arms in the air, squealing like Mardi Gras revelers.

"Get your heads back in the stagecoach!" Dad yelled.

It was safer for us to be daredevils in public.

We were less likely to get hit if there were eyewitnesses.

We toured the park's ghost town, sprinting from the blacksmith to the jail to the one-room schoolhouse and to the theater that staged melodramas. An empty coffin stood on the wooden veranda outside the undertaker's office, and Dad called out, "Desi! Myriam! Pretend you're dead!"

We got inside the casket, and when Dad snapped our picture, instead of being dead, we came very, very alive, laughing and waving so fast our hands blurred. Nearby was a man-made stream where we submerged pans underwater, lifting sand and swirling it, looking for gold. A man dressed like a forty-niner took our pans and poured our yellow flakes into small glass vials. He handed them to us, and we held them up to the sunlight, watching our precious metal shine.

"Don't open them," Dad warned.

Back in her bedroom, Desiree and I knelt on her carpet. She held her vial and twisted the top, unscrewing the lid. "I want to touch it," she said. She slowly tipped the glass. It slipped. In a flash, the water and gold vanished. It felt sickening to watch my cousin lose her meager riches, to watch her poke the carpet with her finger, hoping to salvage a gold fleck or two. The plush fabric had drunk the beauty of our day.

When Desiree outgrew Cabbage Patch dolls, she took up collecting Garbage Pail Kids. She dumped these trading cards out of their wooden box and onto the floor, spreading them across her carpet. We sat cross-legged, sifting through her collection. Garbage Pail Kids were unwelcome in our house—my mother said they were vulgar and offensive—so looking at Desiree's was a treat. The series was a satirical fad, spoofing the Cabbage Patch Kids. A trend that swept the eighties, Garbage Pail Kids reimagined the popular talcum-scented dolls that Coleco Industries advertised as being harvested from a magical field. The dolls came with certificates of adoption, like Beth had, and a few had health problems from premature harvesting. The Garbage Pail Kids corrupted these pretty fables. The weirdos depicted on the trading cards were Cabbage Patch Kids nurtured by toxic waste, acid rain, and frog urine. There was Adam Bomb, whose head was an explosion. There was Corroded Carl, covered in cysts. There was two-headed Schizo Fran punching herselves.

After sorting the cards, Desiree put them back. We jumped on her bed and pillow fought until we were breathless. Although I liked learning new cuss words at Grandma's, Desiree and I cocooned ourselves in her room to avoid the casual verbal cruelty we could be subjected to at any time. For leaving the fridge open or making a mess in the microwave, you could be told to go to hell. You could use up the last of the Tylenol and be told that you should never have been born. To drown out the voices that might say these things, Desiree kept the radio tuned to an oldies station. Rosie Hamlin crooned our feelings, "It's just like heaven being here with you . . ."

Before going to work, Petra dropped Desiree off at the babysitters' house. From the outside, it looked normal. Inside, it was *Hell* by Hieronymus Bosch. The babysitters were distant cousins, and once we were grown women, my cousin told me about the things that they did to her as a child. I believe my cousin. She said that it was so bad that they sometimes sent her home with blood in her calzones. Desiree wanted the touching to stop but didn't know how to make that happen. She told me that the babysitters told her, "If you tell anyone, your mom will die." They added that if she blabbed, no one would believe her anyway.

Who'd believe a no-good little girl like her?

The same year that Desiree wrote, "When I grow up, I will be a teacher . . ." she prepared to stop the incest. She placed an overturned trash can in her closet and tossed her jump rope over the rod. Grabbing the ends, she tied a noose. She climbed onto the can, slid the rope over her head, and jumped, expecting the lights to go out. Hitting the floor with a thud, Desiree shook with rage. On television, dying looked so easy.

Whether we were at Grandma's house or mine, Desiree and I emerged from our rooms to watch reruns of *The Twilight Zone* and *The Munsters.* Despite being science fiction, some *Twilight Zone* episodes, like the classic "Nightmare at 20,000 Feet," had terrifyingly relatable plots.

Accompanied by his wife, Julia, Robert Wilson, a psych patient recovering from a nervous breakdown, boards an airliner bound for home. As Robert shuffles his newspaper, Julia drifts off to sleep. He glances out the window. Heavy rains smack the plane. Lightning flickers, revealing an apelike creature ambling along the wing. Inches from Robert's face, the wooly gremlin peers through the glass. It vandalizes wires beneath an engine cowling.

Panicked that it's going to cause a plane crash, Robert tells the crew about the monster. When they look outside, all they see is rain. Once the plane lands, nurses strap Robert into a straitjacket and wheel him away on a gurney. The closing shot confirms that Robert was the sanest passenger on board; the aircraft engine has been badly damaged.

Desiree knew what it was like to say something that threatened the comfort of the people around her. When she finally got the courage to speak up about what was happening at her babysitters', she was told to shut her mouth, to swallow the monstrous truth. She did and the truth ate away at her, giving her heartburn.

The Munsters was a comfort show. To us, they were the only Mexican family on TV, and they refused to assimilate into the bland suburban community where they lived, Mockingbird Heights. Technically, Herman Munster was created in a German laboratory, but he walked like one of my uncles, a tall, stiff Mexican who wore shoes that made him even taller. Herman's wife, Lily, wore witchy makeup like my mom, and their son, Eddie, a werewolf, had a widow's peak as sharp as any cholo's. Rounding out the family was Grandpa Munster, a vampire, and Marilyn, a white non-monster niece. The Munster Koach, their customized car, was the family's most Mexican member. It took three chopped Ford Model Ts to build this hot-rod hearse.

Desiree would have run away to our house if she could have, but we lived too far. Not knowing where else to go, she hid in Whittier's Michigan Park. After learning the hard way that the slide freezes at night, she curled up on a bench, shoved her fists in her pockets, and slept. Once she got hungry, she slunk back home. When her mom found her in the kitchen, she welcomed her back with an ass whooping. Desiree ran away again and again and again and the afternoon that she slung a bag of clothes and a few cassette tapes over her shoulder, a homegirl picked her up from Michigan Park and gave her a lift back to where Grandpa had bought the blue Studebaker, East LA.

Desiree was welcomed into a gangsters' pad. These homies recognized the fire in her and decided to keep it alive. They fed her bowls of homemade chicken soup and offered her a warm couch to sleep on.

"A lot of people say that gangs are disgusting," laments Desiree. "That they're trouble. That everyone in them is a lowlife. But when I got in, I found a lot of other lost souls. I knew my homeboys, my brothers, weren't going to let anyone put a hand on me ever again. I knew the women were going to protect me as well. I was down for whatever. I was down to handle things. They took me to the streets where I could take out all of my pent-up frustration and anger."

Various older cats and homegirls, including a hood mom, mentored Desiree, teaching her street values and ethics. "What they taught me molded me. You don't let anybody punk you, and I took their lessons with me to jail and used them to survive. We were a family, and we didn't let people disrespect us. I wish somebody in our family would have done the same for me. In the neighborhood, there are forms of respect. You get hugs. You get handshakes. It's very disrespectful if you walk into a homie's house and you don't say hi to him. You'd think that you'd get more respect at home than on the streets and that part was confusing. I'd think, *Wow. The homies respect me more than I'm respected at home*."

Desiree's defiance made her glamorous to me. So did her maturity. She started middle school before I did and got cleavage before I did and wore lipstick before I did. Whenever she dared me to take a risk, I did it in the hopes of earning her admiration. If she'd dared me to smoke an exploding cigar with her, I probably would've gone and fetched a box of matches. I was that committed.

I heard Petra joke that she was going to put bars on Desiree's windows to keep her from running away again, and after my aunt spoke to my parents, the three of them decided that country air might do my cousin some good. Desiree would be banished to Santa Maria for the summer. It might seem like the threat of spending summer in a cow town would have been enough to prompt Desiree to bolt again. It didn't. Not at all. Desiree wasn't running away to East LA in search of thrills. She was seeking safety. Because my family could give her that, she agreed to pack her bags and stay with us.

As Desiree boarded a coach that would lumber up the 101, Petra peeled away from the bus station with smoke practically billowing from her tires. LA's smog went from thick to gone. In place of strip malls, freeway overpasses, helicopters, and crowds rolled hills blanketed by grass and wildflowers. Hawks sailed overhead, waiting for gophers to pop out of holes. Cows sniffed at clover. Llamas grazed.

Not a gangster in sight.

As the bus lurched north, the Pacific Ocean stretched to Desiree's left.

Looking away from the water, her angry green eyes wandered a landscape that droughts had turned crunchy.

Dad and I sat in the station wagon, waiting. When I saw my cousin step off the bus, my heart turned cartwheels. Desiree! She was mine for the summer! Distance from the homies was supposed to set my cousin straight, criminally detoxify her, but Desiree would not be outwitted. She'd thought of a way around Petra's plan. She would mold me into her substitute homie.

Though we were sisters from another mister, it would be decades until Desiree would tell me about what had happened at the babysitters'. She felt too ashamed. She did trust me enough to talk to me about the path she'd begun walking, her vida loca. She'd already been jumped into a gang but was shy about telling me how she got initiated. She worried that I might tell my mom and that my mom would rat her out to Petra.

"I did think about convincing you to get jumped in too," Desiree has teased. "But I'm glad I didn't. I'm glad you didn't become my cellmate."

I soon noticed that Desiree avoided small talk with my friends and looked at strangers with suspicion. If she'd been a waifish white girl, her aloofness would've earned her a charming label, shy. Since Desiree had a womanly figure and now groomed herself chola-style—hair teased into a peacock fan, eyebrows plucked gone and replaced by sharp apostrophes, lips accentuated by dark eyeliner, a rosary dangling against a white T-shirt, baggy khaki pants ironed with sharp creases, and a tattoo of Saint Teresa—people accused my cousin of being intimidating and rude. This toughness masked her fear and discomfort, two feelings she couldn't shake. I would say she had post-traumatic stress disorder, but the *post* part would be wrong. Desiree was still living through trauma, and it was going to get exponentially worse.

Just as a hood mom had begun to mentor her, Desiree took up mentoring me. Shut away in my bedroom, she spent hours instructing me in penmanship. I practiced in a sketchpad until I mastered the elaborate lettering we used to inscribe keepsakes like photos, envelopes, and prayer cards. Sitting on a Louis XVI–style armchair from Grandma's furniture store, I listened to my cousin tell stories about the homegirls she sometimes went joyriding with in a stolen red station wagon. It sounded fun, like something I could be easily talked into doing. The most outlaw thing I'd done was sneak out with a group of girls to go toilet paper some stuck-up bitch's house. A sheriff caught us hiding in the bushes and made us sit in his car for a lecture. He told us that we were pretty and that we were lucky we'd been found by him. Otherwise, we probably would've gotten raped by cowboys.

When I told Desiree that some girls who I'd thought were my friends had made fun of me for being queer, telling me that I was "pretty . . . for a lesbian," my cousin soothed me with homosexual hood stories, describing a butch homegirl who hooked up with only the finest hynas. The neighborhood honored her with maximum respect. Liking females was nothing to be ashamed of. Being a homophobic bitch? Now, that was wrong. That deserved to be met with violence.

Desiree explained that it was a homegirl's duty to pen pal with homeboys who'd been locked up. They missed their freedom. They got lonely and needed support. Mail was like sunshine for them.

"Can I write to you?" I asked her.

"Of course!"

Desiree opened her purse and pulled out glossy pictures of homeboys and homegirls whose government names I never learned. Bandit. Sad Girl. Payasa. These homies wore rosaries, sometimes several, and this fashion choice seemed wise. Given how dangerous their world was, they needed heavy spiritual armor.

One afternoon, I said, "We should make our own gang!"

Desiree looked like she'd hit the jackpot. "Okay! What should we call it?"

"Pocas Pero Locas!"

We cracked up and threw PPL with our fingers. Then, I said, "Wait here." I ran to the blue bathroom and locked the door. My cousin's makeup bag was on the counter, and I reached into it and pulled out her tools. Face-to-face with myself, I mimicked the steps I'd seen my cousin take to cholafy herself. First, I outlined and colored my lips brown. Then I plugged in her curling iron and wound my bangs around its hot metal. After freeing my steaming curl, I ratted it with a hairbrush. I aimed a can of Aqua Net at my head, pushed the valve. Aerosol hissed. A shellac coated my work. My claw froze. I was ready.

I knew that my mother would hate the new me reflected by the bathroom mirror.

I looked like DJ, Desiree Jr.

When I leapt back into my bedroom, Desiree shrieked with surprise.

"You look MAHVELOUS!" she declared and handed my little sister her camera.

Desiree's birth as a loca had already happened in East LA, during the only beating that she ever looked forward to. The initiation occurred on the back patio of a small apartment located off McBride Avenue and Whittier Boulevard, a street synonymous with lowriding.

Desiree didn't ask to be jumped in. The homegirls came to her. They understood she was down, and they first brought up talk of her becoming one of them as they kicked back at a pad, listening to oldies and drinking beer. Days later, a homie mentioned that she should "get into the neighborhood," and his suggestion touched Desiree. It meant that a small local army would forever have her back.

Wow, she thought. *They really want me!*

She waited for the others to suggest that she become one of them. She wanted the consensus to grow. The more the homies expressed their desire for her to become part of "the neighborhood," the more wanted Desiree felt.

Finally, the hood mom announced, "I'm jumping you in."

On the evening of her entry into the neighborhood, Desiree braided her long brown hair. She dressed comfortably in a T-shirt, sweatpants, and tennis shoes. Six homegirls stood ready. Most came in jeans. One wore shorts. Desiree and another excited initiate waited on the dim patio from which there was no easy exit.

A homegirl called out, "All right, who wants to go first?"

"I do!" yelled Desiree.

Plywood sectioned the space off from an alley. Benches offered seating. There wasn't much room but there was enough to fight and dance, and after Desiree offered herself, the six homegirls pounced.

They weren't trying to kill her. The point was to see how well she could fight, and she gave them an excellent fight. The homeboys cheered. They shouted, "That's right! That's right, homegirl!"

After the beating, the homegirls embraced her. Each one kissed Desiree.

"Welcome to the neighborhood," they said. "This is for life."

As usual, the owner of the red station wagon couldn't find his car. As usual, Desiree and her homegirls had taken it joyriding. This time, the owner had reported it missing. The hooptie was easy to steal—all you needed was a nail file and some determination to start it—and Desiree was cruising around East LA with the homegirls when a dark car pulled up behind them and flashed its lights.

The cops who stopped her that night belonged to a gang unit. Father Gregory Boyle, the Jesuit priest who founded Homeboy Industries, one of the world's largest gang-intervention and rehabilitation programs, has described these units as behaving like colonial armies, occupying forces. In a *Los Angeles Times* editorial that slammed the city's anti-gang policing, Boyle pointed out that the acronym for the unit's original name, Total Resources Against Street Hoodlums, spelled TRASH. After some pressure, the police swapped the word *total* for *community*.

LAPD chief Daryl Gates praised CRASH. He described the unit as manned by "the very best." In interviews, he said that gang members didn't intimidate his officers. It's easy to see why. Desiree was a fourteen-year-old gang member who still drove the way Grandma had taught her to, with both feet on the pedals. The cops hauled her to Eastlake Juvenile Hall, and Desiree called her mom. She wanted to come home.

"I'm done," said Petra. "I'm gonna let the system take care of you."

Desiree has shown me a picture of her taken at Eastlake. Wearing orange pants and a gray sweatshirt, she squats in front of a white wall, throwing a gang sign. Kids weren't allowed to take pictures in Eastlake, but one of the staff was using my cousin for sex. In return, she got "favors," like the photo. Desiree describes juvenile hall as "that type of playground."

When she arrived at Eastlake, authorities processed Desiree and then stuck her in a cage. Guards replaced her clothes with what the homegirls called a muumuu, and they confiscated everyone's shoes, setting them outside the door until breakfast time. Shoelaces were a no-no. A girl could use those to put herself out of her misery.

Desiree played cards with herself and played cards with herself and played cards with herself. Guards occasionally released her to make phone calls or hang out in the dayroom. The dayroom was where Desiree came face-to-face with her rivals. Because she was using violence to make a name for herself, fighting anyone who even glanced at her the wrong way, Desiree was forced to stay in her cage most of the time.

When she was good, they let her go to school. Or church.

Church was where girls got to see guys.

Sometimes, they hosted dances.

Bathrooms were communal, and stepping inside, Desiree was startled to see a boy carrying a towel.

Dude asked, "Whassup, mija?"

Desiree answered, "What are you doing in the girls' shower?"

"I'm a girl."

To prove it, the G dropped her clothes.

Great, thought Desiree. *Now I'm gonna have to fight this bitch in the shower.*

Instead of fighting her, the butch befriended my cousin.

Speakers belonging to Narcotics Anonymous visited and shared stories. Desiree didn't want to hear it. She thought, *Man, I wanna go back to my room! This is stupid.*

She wasn't ready to hear survival stories yet. She just wanted to get numb and fight. She believed that no one could hurt her more than her abusers already had. She believed that because of them, she was ruined.

The gang paranoia fired up by Chief Daryl Gates wasn't new. Still, I learned nothing about its anti-Mexican roots until I got to college. From kindergarten to high school, the main thing I was taught about Mexicans was that the righteous US Army had kicked our asses, forcing Mexico to cede half its land. To fill in the gaps left by my teachers, I majored in history. I wanted to understand how being young and Mexican had become equivalent to being a criminal. More to the point, I wanted to understand what made it so easy for this country to fuck my cousin.

I couldn't discuss any of this with Desiree. After the summer that we created Pocas Pero Locas, we saw each other less and less. She called occasionally from pay phones in East LA, but those calls dried up. We'd ask Petra how Desiree was doing, and she'd answer, "I don't know." Grandma eventually confirmed that my cousin was on drugs and kept getting locked up. I wanted to write to her, but I didn't know where to send the letters. Sometimes I wondered if my cousin was even alive. When exposés on California jails and prisons came on TV, I'd watch, hoping to catch her green eyes.

My family's first California home, Estrada Courts, was completed in 1942, the same year that Angelenos incited a panic that would be used to terrorize Mexican kids. It was World War II, and employers were suddenly desperate to hire people they had been discriminating against forever. Mexicans and women were in demand, and this need stirred anxiety. Were white men going to get their jobs back when the war ended? Who was taking care of the kids? Moms were busy building tanks and planes! Instead of addressing LA's social problems, local politicians and leaders shifted attention away from themselves and onto Mexican youngsters, the barrio's "juvenile delinquents."

Enter José Diaz. On August 1, José, a twenty-two-year-old farmworker born in Durango, Mexico, got all gussied up to go to Eleanor

Delgadillo Coronado's birthday party. She lived with her parents on a ranch near Sleepy Lagoon, a local reservoir that teenagers used as a lover's lane. At Eleanor's party, a small orchestra played. Kids danced, fought, and drank. José usually didn't drink but he was convinced to sip a little. He'd just enlisted and would be shipping out. Slightly tipsy, he left Eleanor's at one o'clock in the morning. A short while later, Eleanor found José lying on his back in front of her house. Gurgle. Gurgle. Gurgle. His mouth was a fountain, red with blood. The same type of makeshift weapon that was used to puncture Leon Trotsky, an ice pick, had been used to stab José in the stomach.

José died at Los Angeles County General Hospital. The press set citywide paranoia into motion by sensationalizing his stabbing. They pinned his murder on the worst nightmare of many white Angelenos: roving packs of bloodthirsty Mexican hoodlums. To get to the bottom of José's murder, police arrested six hundred Mexican youths. A grand jury was convened. Ed Duran Ayres, a member of the Los Angeles County Sheriff's Department, submitted a report, blaming José's death on Mexican psychopathology.

> The Caucasian, especially the Anglo-Saxon, when engaged in fighting, particularly among youths, resort to fisticuffs and may at times kick each other, which is considered unsportive, but this Mexican element considers all that to be a sign of weakness, and all he knows and feels is a desire to use a knife or some lethal weapon. In other words, his desire is to kill, or at least let blood.

Sensation magazine published an article by another member of the sheriff's department, Clem Peoples. He called the accused teenagers "baby gangsters" and likened them to wolves.

Twenty-two kids, including Gus Zamora, Smiles Parra, Chepe Ruiz, and Hank Ynostroza, were indicted on murder charges.

People v. Zamora, more popularly known as the Sleepy Lagoon trial, became the largest mass trial in California history.

The Sleepy Lagoon shit show set the stage for the Zoot Suit Riots, a bloody ten-day event named after an eye-catching fashion trend popular among Mexican teens. Dressed in tailored regalia, zoot-suiters cut flashy silhouettes. Pachucos wore broad-shouldered, fingertip jackets that tightened at the hips to create a V shape. Baggy slacks that tapered at the ankle and a duck's ass haircut brought further flair. Pachucas also wore broad-shouldered jackets and paired these with slacks or knee-length skirts. To assert Mexican pride, some pachucas replaced saddle shoes with down-home huaraches. Crowned by tall pompadours, these early cholas plucked their eyebrows, replacing them with hand-drawn arches. Dark lipstick made their smart mouths pop.

In 1943, white servicemen and off-duty cops armed with sticks, ropes, and other weapons prowled LA by car and by foot, hunting for zoot-suiters. They bashed their victims bloody, stripped them down to their underwear, and cut their hair in front of stunned crowds.

Time magazine reported that some of those assaulted weren't zoot-suiters, just "little Mexican-American youths," and that one mob had attacked a twelve-year-old boy, breaking his jaw. At the hospital, the kid said, "So our guys wear tight bottoms on their pants and those bums wear wide bottoms. Who the hell they fighting? Japs or us?" Meanwhile, the *New York Times* reported that the rioting servicemen and police acted with the spirit "of a college fraternity initiation."

Racists applauded the riots.

Flamboyant Mexicans kids needed to learn humility.

Less than a decade after the Zoot Suit Riots, Bloody Christmas dragged young Mexicans back into the headlines. This was yet another event I didn't learn about in school. I learned about it from *L.A. Confidential*, the neo-noir novel by James Ellroy. On Christmas Eve 1951, cops responded to the call that kids were drinking at the Showboat Bar on Riverside Drive. They arrested seven people, five of whom were Mexican, and jailed them at Central Station. About fifty shit-faced cops took turns beating them with wet towels and wrapped fists. By the time they were done, blood covered the walls.

The victims were then transferred to the Lincoln Heights Jail, a now-defunct Art Deco–style facility that operated a few miles from the kids' house, Eastlake Juvenile Hall.

Chief William H. Parker ruled the LAPD from 1950 to 1966. His involvement in *Dragnet,* the show that created the template for all future copaganda, made Parker the country's most influential policeman. Parker used the show to "publicize his views on law and order" and advisers scrutinized scripts to make sure that *Dragnet* portrayed LAPD officers as "ethical, terse, efficient, and white." In 1960, Parker shared his racial views with the U.S. Commission on Civil Rights, testifying that Mexican-Americans "presented a great problem" and that some of us were "not too far removed from the wild tribes of the inner mountains of Mexico."

Some Mexican kids responded to racism by organizing and creating the Chicano Movement. Its goals ranged from strengthening cultural pride to improving labor conditions. When kids protested the inferior education offered by LA's informally segregated schools, they were met with the usual hostility. Cops brutalized several who participated in the 1968 walkout at Roosevelt High School. A newspaper that grew out of the walkouts, *Chicano Student News,* describes how two teens were "jumped by four full grown armed policemen, beaten to the ground and held with a club to the neck."

DC policy changes also shaped the local persecution of Mexican kids. During a 1971 press conference, President Richard Nixon ranked drug abuse as "public enemy number one." In *The New Jim Crow,* the activist Michelle Alexander notes that while police and prosecutors didn't declare the War on Drugs, they embraced their roles in the conflict. With money to be made, police officers asked themselves, "If we're going to wage this war, *where* should it be fought and *who* should be taken prisoner?" The LAPD answered this question by turning neighborhoods like the one where Desiree was arrested into war zones.

Desiree is one of many Latinas who lost more than a decade of her life to prison thanks to the War on Drugs. Like our male counterparts, Latinas also get stereotyped as lazy drug addicts and deadly hustlers. These tropes are used to justify our high incarceration rate for drug offenses, but our substance abuse rates aren't that much different from the US general population. We use drugs for the same reasons as everyone else. First off, drugs can be a lot of fun. Second, they're medicinal, and as far as medicine goes, let's get real. What other choices do many of us have? Racism and sexism widely limit Latinas' access to decent health care, and statistics related to suicide prove that many of us are in a state of crisis. In 2019, one out of every ten Latinas tried suicide, two out of ten planned a suicide, and half of us reported feeling hopeless.

Desiree used because when she was on drugs, the hurt didn't hurt anymore.

"I started with weed in my early teens. I did coke for a little while. I did PCP for years. Crack too. Anything to keep me numb from the shit that I'd been through. Then I fell in love with meth. That drug was the most addicting ever. I never had to sell my body, but I did a lot of crime to get it. Drugs aren't free, and so I did whatever it took to get that next high. I didn't care what happened to me if I sold drugs. I sold drugs so that I could buy more drugs and guess what.

"I became my number one customer!"

What my cousin needed from the government was health care and housing. Instead, it imprisoned her for self-medicating. Juvenile hall was her training ground, and the homies told her stories about prison. They prepared her for the challenges she would find there.

"I didn't want to live past twenty-five or thirty. And I fell in love with the hustle. The game. The money. I fell in love with the things I had to do to survive. Let's call the things I had to do my 'survival kit.' With my kit came consequences for doing illegal activities. Sybil Brand was the first jail I went to."

Before closing in 1997, Sybil Brand Institute was LA's County main female lockup. I first heard about it when I read *Helter Skelter*, the true-crime book written by Vincent Bugliosi, prosecutor in the 1970 trial of sex cult leader Charles Manson. In 1969, Susan Atkins, a Manson follower, bragged to her Sybil Brand cellmate, Virginia Castro, that she'd participated in the ritual murder of the actress Sharon Tate. Castro tattled, and her revelation led to the arrest of Manson and other cult members. Like many women who die in prison, Atkins was a high school dropout. She had also been sexually abused as a child. She developed brain cancer, and at the time of her death, Atkins had been locked up longer than any woman in California. Her life ended at Central California Women's Facility in Chowchilla, the first prison Desiree was sent to.

Desiree lied when she was taken into Sybil Brand. She told the cops that she was eighteen when she was really seventeen. They didn't bother to check her ID; that's how she made it to the adult house. When she turned eighteen, she fought with the cops and got sent to Sybil Brand again. For her twentieth birthday, she went to Twin Towers, another LA jail. Next was the Lynwood jail and eventually, Chowchilla, home to women on California's death row.

When Desiree was sentenced to her first term at CCWF, the largest women's prison in the country, she got sixteen months.

"How am I supposed to do that?" Desiree asked her public defender.

He answered, "Do what you can and let the state do the rest."

Desiree slid on a very hard mask. She wasn't going to let anybody hurt her, and she wasn't going to prison to make friends.

Desiree traveled from LA to Chowchilla by crowded cattle bus. The women wore ugly floral muumuus and shackles during their four-hour ride. They took the 5, which cut through the San Joaquin Valley, offering hazy views of almond orchards, vineyards, and garlic fields. The bus had one bathroom, and the women begged God that no one would take a shit.

Once at the prison, the women were led to reception, where they stripped naked. Officers ordered them to squat and cough. Cavity searched them. Next, the women got plastic cups and locks for their lockers. When handed their bedrolls, they hoped they'd be assigned a good roommate. Otherwise, there'd be fighting.

They waited.

There was always something to be waiting for.

Waiting for clothes. Waiting for books. Waiting for mail. Waiting for money.

The women sat in cages for twenty-two hours a day.

Waiting.

Waiting.

Getting to take a shower, the feeling of warm water on skin, might be the high point of a woman's week.

Desiree spoke with a counselor. Counselors decided where the women might be shipped next.

Prison food was better than jail food, but the portions were smaller. Way smaller. Like a kid's meal. The women learned to be thankful for it. County jail food was punishing. Slop. You couldn't tell what it was.

Desiree focused on her food and laundry.

Life became food and laundry.

Food.

Laundry.

Food.

Laundry.

Food.

Laundry.

She became a genius at zoning out. She had to. Prison was like jail was like juvenile hall was like the babysitters. Remember the type of playground Eastlake was? Prison was the same type of place. Staff wanted "favors." Like, if you wanted tobacco, you had to give the guards what they wanted. And you couldn't hide. In prison, there's no such thing as privacy and no such thing as private parts.

Desiree recalls an elder whose private parts were turned public.

"There was a woman, probably in her eighties, getting cavity searched. After the first go-around, they told her, 'Cough again! What else do you have in there?'

"They'd found her lipstick. After she exposed herself the second time, they found eyeliner. There's a lot of stuff we can't get in there so some women come prepared from county jail. There was still more inside this lady, so they asked her, 'What else do you have in there?'

"She goes, 'Well, mascara . . .'

"Finally, they went, 'Okay, whatever else you have, just keep it. Now GO!'"

Hypocrites staff prisons. Angela Davis has noted this, writing that "the threat of violence emanating from prison hierarchies is so ubiquitous and unpredictable that some women have pointed out the striking structural similarities between the experiences of imprisonment and battering [relationships]." Desiree has made this same observation, telling me that prison didn't save her from abuse. Instead, it became her new abuser.

"When I got to Chowchilla, I ran into people who'd been living the same as me. It's kind of like a reunion with all the people you've been fucking up with. And some people aren't ever going home.

" 'I'll be back!' we'd say. It kind of felt like home after a while. I didn't want to go back, but I accepted having to. There was a time in my life where I'd think, *I'm never going to be successful. I don't have a driver's license. I don't even have a bank account.* I would cry because I thought I would never have a normal life. I felt that my life was unfixable.

"I went to California Institution for Women in Chino, Valley State Prison for Women in Chowchilla, and California Rehabilitation Center in Norco. I've basically been everywhere in California. The longest I did was my four years at VSPW. You get placed where they can fit you. Your roommate might be a baby killer for all you know. And she might also run the prison's parenting program.

"I worked in the kitchen. I made about eight or nine cents an hour. I didn't get trained. We just got thrown in there. I also worked in the infirmary. You can work yard crew. You can also go to school. It depends. A prison is a little town. The town restaurant is the cafeteria. You have a laundromat. You have your canteen, which is your market. You have your yard where you go for your daily jog. You have a jungle gym. You have a library.

"You focus on doing your time. If you focus on the outside world, it breaks you. You cannot sit and cry over your family. You cannot sit there and cry over your children. That will give you the hardest time. It's sad to say, but you have to build a wall. If I was a long-termer or lifer, maybe I would see things differently, but I was passing through. The holidays were really bad for some of the women. They would always have suicide calls during that time.

"I saw people die in there. I saw people get beaten up. I saw women with other women. You gotta remember, we're a bunch of angry women who've all been thrown in together. I made the best of what I could in there. I had good birthdays in there. You bond with people in there. You're all going through the same thing, but you don't talk about it.

"Unlike juvenile hall, they'll do anything to extend your stay in prison. The state claims to send you there for rehabilitation but I think they send us there for the almighty dollar. It's all about money. It's expensive to keep people in cages. And it costs money to survive in there too. If you don't have money in prison, you're screwed."

Valley State Prison for Women was the last prison where Desiree did time. It was built in 1995, and three years after its completion, a visiting Amnesty International delegation found severe overcrowding. Women reported that it was common for male officers to watch them undress. They also reported that during pat searches, guards touched their breasts and genitals. VSPW was overwhelmingly staffed by men, and women in need of medical attention could only see male doctors who were reported for performing needless pelvic exams. The staff gave the women access to a complaint box, but no one used it. Why bother reporting your abuse to your abuser?

Desiree says, "Prison terms were a revolving door. It was nothing to come back and visit. But that last trip to VSPW was different. It hit me hard. A couple of my lifer friends asked me not to come back. They had a simple request, 'When you get out, eat a hamburger or a steak for me.'" When Desiree was released, she ate that steak, but VSPW wouldn't be her last cage.

California doesn't deserve its reputation as a progressive state. If it were so damn progressive, it wouldn't rely on jails and prisons to take care of its problems. In *Golden Gulag: Prisons, Surplus, Crisis, and Opposition in Globalizing California*, the geographer Ruth Wilson Gilmore asks why California embarked on the biggest prison-building project in the history of the world. In her view, "prisons are partial geographical solutions to political economic crises."

My cousin's understanding of prison is like Gilmore's.

"Let's say you get a scratch on your car," proposes Desiree. "If you paint over it, you know the scratch is still there. When the sun beams down on that area, you're going to see the scratch and be tempted to paint over it again. Instead of getting the body work done, you're taking a shortcut to hide the problem.

"That's how prisons work. They're used for hiding problems."

When Desiree was arrested on her last charge, she faced being hidden away again, this time for fifteen years. While waiting in jail, Desiree heard about the Second Chance Women's Re-entry Court program, a treatment-based alternative to prison for nonviolent female felons struggling with addiction. Judge Michael Tynan, a former public defender, ran the program. Desiree and I had seen Tynan on TV when we were kids. He'd presided over the inescapable trial of the serial killer Richard Ramirez, the Night Stalker. While the chair Ramirez had sat in was still in Tynan's courtroom, the work now happening there was very different. In 2010, Tynan spoke to the *Los Angeles Times* about the women who appeared in his courtroom. "A lot of them have been really, really beleaguered and beaten up, primarily by the men in their lives."

At first Desiree's interest in the program was an addict's ruse. She figured out that she could get out of jail and return to using. She entered the program and, upon release, started sneaking around, doing her grimy stuff. A program counselor confronted her, and she went back to jail.

When Desiree appeared before Tynan, he asked, "Why would you not make use of this program? We could just give you your time."

Desiree glanced at the Ramirez chair. She began calculating the length of her sentence, but Tynan interrupted her thoughts.

"I want to know why you're doing what you're doing. I see something in you that you can't see in yourself."

Tynan asked Desiree to write him a letter recounting her life story. She did.

After reading it, Tynan gave her a second chance.

Desiree says, "By that time, I was tired of doing time. I was getting older. I decided to do like the judge did: I gave myself a chance. I started to face what happened to me when I was a kid. I started peeling back the layers of the onion and arrived at the core. I was doing a lot of therapy and really taking it seriously."

Surrounded by her counselor, mentor, probation officer, lawyer, and fellow Second Chance participants, Desiree graduated from the program in a fourth-floor courtroom in the criminal courts building in downtown LA. In a photo taken that day, my cousin beams with joy. She wears a black dress and a wide grin and displays her graduation certificate. Tynan, a petite, bespectacled man wearing a collared shirt, necktie, black robe, and Ugg boots, stands beside her. He told her, "I'm proud of you. I believed in you when you didn't believe in yourself. You're one of my stars." In his courtroom, Desiree got the things she'd been so starved for, praise and hugs. The program taught her to cry without fear or shame, to release her truth and pain. The felonies that she was originally charged with were dismissed and expunged.

"When I left that day, I said to myself, *You don't ever have to come back to jail ever again as long as you face life one day at a time.*"

However, Desiree did panic when faced with an unfamiliar challenge.

"They told me I needed to get a job. I was like, who's gonna hire a fucking felon with my history?" Her concerns were legit. Though employers often refuse to consider applicants with criminal records, such workers have been found to be more productive and have less turnover. They're also promoted faster.

Fortunately, Desiree was introduced to an employer who, like Tynan, took a chance on her. Desiree has now worked for this employer for close to eight years. "They gave me what I needed," says Desiree. "I needed people to take chances on me."

In the beginning, it was hard for Desiree to get to work and keep appointments. She walked. Rode the bus. Took Ubers. Whatever it took. She stayed at a sober living house. She struggled. Saved money. Paid restitution. A lot of people think that prison is payback, but along with doing time, people like Desiree have to actually pay people back. They have to return the money they stole. Those free lawyers? They have to pay for those too.

When I ask my cousin what might have prevented all of this, she answers that if somebody had listened to her and taken her seriously as a child, she wouldn't have had to carry the burden of so much shame and guilt. "I wouldn't have needed so many masks. I wouldn't have needed to pretend to be somebody I didn't want to be. I took my anger, hurt, and frustration out on society and on other people. I take responsibility for my actions. And I also think that had I been listened to, and honored, things would have turned out very differently."

Desiree and I are still as loyal to each other as the Pope is to sin.

We continue to confide in one another, sometimes loudly.

When people try to shut us up, our inner locas jump out.

We were seated at a restaurant table on a tiled patio at Olvera Street, an LA tourist attraction that mimics a Mexican marketplace. This faux Mexico isn't far from where Desiree graduated from Second Chance. It's also across the street from Union Station, where Grandma first set foot in California. As Desiree spoke to me about family stuff, I chewed on enchiladas. My cousin shot an annoyed look across my left shoulder. Glared.

"Whassup?" I asked.

Quietly, she said, "The white lady sitting behind you has a staring problem."

I turned around. A pasty woman with sandals Velcroed to her feet sneered at me. I looked at my cousin and raised my eyebrows, tilted my head. Desiree said, "If she does it again, she's gonna learn not to."

I knew from the lady's Velcro shoes that she was going to do it again, and when she did, Desiree screamed, "Hey! Karen! You got a fuckin' problem?"

I turned to look at the lady.

She'd gone from white to whiter. She shook her head.

"Good!" my cousin yelled. "Cuz we're not tourists!"

We cackled.

I periodically looked over my shoulder to check on the Velcro lady.

She was hunched over her plate. She would look only at it and the wall.

Good.

Recently, we were visiting our uncle Henry, a Vietnam veteran, at the nursing home where he lives. He was in a deep sleep, and the TV was on but muted. For hours, Desiree and I sat at the foot of his bed, swapping our own war stories, tales of domestic violence and prison. We talked beatings. Stabbings. Escapes. Petty torture. Small forms of revenge, like spitting in your abuser's coffee cup. Suddenly, the curtain separating Henry's side of the room from his roommate's flew back. Startled, Desiree and I turned to look at the man standing there.

With his face beaming, Henry's roommate said, "I have been listening to you two all afternoon and I must say you nieces are better than TV." After chuckling with sincerity, he thanked us and whipped the curtain back into place.

Desiree and I fell over laughing. Henry opened an iguana eye and peered at us. Then he shut it and fell back asleep.

MITOTE

No pude saber mas, porque ha venido
Un Mitote solemne celebrando,
Y cien mil invenciones diferentes,
Con diversos regalos y presentes.
Donde la trompa, el cuerno y atambores,
El caracol, sonaja, y la bocina,
La flauta, los cantares, y dulzores
Suenan con invencion muy peregrina.

—Antonio de Saavedra Guzmán

Before destroying my idols, I lay flowers at their feet.

Siempre les doy flores.

Rosas silvestres y cempasúchil are preferred, but other blooms will do. My tattooed fingers write violets, camelias, red dahlias, florecitas de calabaza, pétalos de hikuri, kieri, calla lilies, and baby's breath into being. Erato, muse of poetry, waters this garden. In tandem, we harvest, gathering an ofrenda that we'll place at the well-worn huaraches of my grandfather Ricardo Serrano Ríos.

The last time I saw Abuelito alive, his machismo smoldered.

It was December, and three generations had descended upon the house where our patriarch would die, a moldering concrete box in the Mezquitan Country neighborhood of Guadalajara. As a girl, my mother stood barefoot in her small front yard, watching black horses pull funeral carriages to el Panteón de Mezquitán, one of the city's oldest graveyards. Murals depicting the afterlife dress the cemetery walls, and today, my grandparents exchange whispers in one of its palm-shaded tombs. My tío Álvaro rests with them. Because my uncle cared for his mother and father until they took their last breaths, the word *spinster* best describes what he became. It's usually daughters, not sons, who sidestep marriage, instead caring for parents who shrivel and shrink, returning to dust.

To honor the love Álvaro gave, I write into being a cup. Next, I fill it with tejuino: la bebida de los dioses. Before I order you to hand this drink to my uncle's thirsty spirit, allow me to add a scoop of crushed ice, a twist of lime, and three shots of the finest tequila.

Now, pass the cup to my spinster tío . . .

Thanks.

But back to December. We were ringing in the New Year, making mitote in my grandparents' living/dining room, a plain, off-white space furnished by a pine hutch and two shelves. Above the plastic-upholstered sofa hung a portrait painted by Abuelita. Its subject: a blond, melancholic mutt, long since dead.

I stood near the table, waiting to grab a torta off the tray brought by my tía. Staring at the canine portrait, I admired how my grandmother had captured the silky bitch's sadness. Abuelita adored stray dogs, birds, and human beings, and before she got sick, her feathered friends had chirped in the living/dining room, filling their cage, and ours, with birdsong.

My turn came.

I lunged at the tortas, snatched one, then thrust it into the nearest bowl of red sauce, drowning it. With my plate resembling a bloodbath, I carried my dinner across the stone floor, in the direction of Abuelita's prized possession.

Hunched over a stool, I ate.

Across from me, Abuelito commiserated with a new best friend. Behind me, Abuelita's piano, a wedding present. (I once overheard an argument concerning the attempted theft of this instrument. My great-aunt had learned that Abuelito was plotting to sell the piano, and for its own protection, she'd tried to kidnap it. She didn't get far, and now here it sat, a dust magnet.)

Abuelita couldn't make mitote with us. Alzheimer's had made off with her memory. Her teeth were gone, and only her face and hands could move. Her bed was her world. Her remaining vocabulary consisted of two words. Depending on the cadence she used, the pair took on different meanings.

Quiero aguita.

Quiero aguita.

Quiero aguita.

A water-stained portrait of la Virgen de Guadalupe kept vigil over her.

My grandmother's absence hung heavily in the living/dining room air. Abuelito seemed not to notice. He was busy holding court. We'd dragged our seats into an oval, and he presided over us all from an armchair with daisies carved into its wood. Despite these flowers, the seat had an imposing quality. It was a throne fit for a cacique, and after daintily crossing his legs, Abuelito lifted his torta to his gray mustache. Nibbled.

Salsa leaked, dribbling onto the plate in his lap.

Abuelito hated the cold, and it was frigid that evening, the temperature dipping below seventy degrees Fahrenheit. To stave off pneumonia, Abuelito had wrapped a wool scarf around his head, knotting it at his chin. To ensure that no heat could escape his ancient fontanel, a gray beanie held his scarf in place.

His ensemble called to mind Dickens's *A Christmas Carol.*

In a film adaptation I'd seen, Jacob Marley's ghostly cadaver wore a bandage wrapped around his head and knotted at his chin. The sight had unsettled me, and I'd turned to my father to ask about the English clerk's dressing.

"It's so that the dead person's mouth won't open," he explained.

"Their mouths can . . . OPEN?!"

My father nodded, lowering his jaw slowly and cadaverishly.

To keep the rest of himself warm, Abuelito had tamaled himself. He wore a white button-down shirt beneath a sweater draped with a serape emblazoned with an eagle. Polyester pants sheathed his chicken legs, and beneath his huaraches, fluffy white socks pulled high.

Instead of asking kin to sit beside him, my grandfather had invited a stranger to take the seat of honor.

"Yo soy el Vaquero," the chosen one announced.

The old man grinned, exposing wide gaps between cheddar teeth.

In contrast to Abuelito, el Vaquero seemed overdressed. Taking in his ecru traje de charro, I mumbled, "Where have his fellow mariachis gone?"

A tasseled silk tie flopped at his neck.

Reptilian boots cradled his feet.

How many rattlesnakes had to die so that el Vaquero could strut in their skin?

Bastantes.

El Vaquero was my cousin Veronica's guest. She was dating el Vaquero's son, a policeman with fewer teeth than his father, and Abuelito was riveted by this duo. When our patriarch turned to speak to the rest of us, he acted like a child doing a chore. He couldn't wait to get back to what really mattered, his güiri-güiri with a couple of cowboys.

Though I craved my grandfather's kindness and respect, I didn't expect any from him. I knew what Abuelito thought of girls because of what he'd told me when I was a tween. It'd been afternoon and I was seated at the living/dining room table, the one currently covered in tortas, tacos, tostadas, salsas bien picantes, y Coca-Cola.

A caged parakeet trilled. I turned the page of a young adult novel.

Shuffle . . .

Shuffle . . .

Shuffle . . .

The sound of Abuelito's dress shoes.

I looked up, expecting to be asked about the book in my hands.

Instead, my grandfather demanded, "When are you going to get married?"

I was twelve.

"Never!" I snapped.

Abuelito looked horrified.

"Why aren't you ever going to get married?"

"Because I'm a feminist!"

Abuelito leaned toward me. His bony hand petted my head.

"Don't think so hard," he moaned into my face.

I wanted to slap the mustache off his lip, but before I could, he'd shuffled away, disappearing down the hall.

The front door opened.

The front door closed.

He was probably on his way to visit a lady I'd heard a lot about but had never seen.

La otra mujer.

I took a bite of torta and watched my grandfather and his new friend ignore us. What was everyone who belonged to Abuelito's other family up to? Who were they celebrating New Year's Eve with? Not their father. He was here, practically playing footsie with el Vaquero, and to fuck with their clique, I blurted, "Hey! HEY! Let's play a game!"

Álvaro perked up. "What game?"

"Two Truths and a Lie!" In Mom's ear, I whispered, "Your dad is gonna be good at this."

She ate a laugh.

Álvaro asked, "What are the rules?"

"They're in the name of the game. We go clockwise. When it's your turn, you say three things total. Two of them should be truthful things about yourself but one has to be bullshit. The people sitting on either side of you each get a turn pointing out which thing you said they think is bullshit. If one of them figures it out, they get a point. If neither of them does, the liar gets the point."

Álvaro glanced at his father.

Abuelito shrugged.

Everyone agreed to play.

The elders never quite got the hang of it.

First they forgot how many lies to tell.

Then they forgot how much truth to share.

They mostly struck to trinities, telling three truths or three lies. At times they told two lies and one truth. Álvaro, for example, said that he'd dated las dos bonitas del show *Friends*, la Yennifer Aniston y la Kurtni Cox. He then added that he'd eaten some bolillo for breakfast.

The math was chaos. It made keeping score impossible.

It turned out that Abuelito wasn't so good at the game, and in passive-aggressive protest, he steered us away from it by igniting a political debate. He and el Vaquero scuttled our attempt at family fun, instead arguing about the origins of Mexican corruption for nearly an hour. At one point, Mom perplexed the men by quoting a passage from Plato's *Republic*. Someone else shouted that Coca-Cola is the sweet but nefarious petroleum of North America, and to the surprise of el Vaquero, Abuelito shot out of his throne and demanded, "Does anyone have a tape recorder?! I think we've developed some solutions to Mexico's gravest political problems! We should record this conversation and send it to . . . Los Pinos!"

"Yes! Excellent idea!" concurred el Vaquero.

I looked at a cousin. Laughter in her eyes.

Our grandfather wanted to send an audio recording of our mitote to the president.

Classic.

After peering at his phone, the policeman stood. He announced that he and his father had another party to hit, and the slow process of farewell began. There was hugging. Kissing. Handshaking. Jokes. Back patting. Jokes. Laughing. Jokes. More kissing and one very dangerous attempt to swallow a torta in three bites.

As el Vaquero and Abuelito made their way down the front hall, my cousins and I followed.

"You mentioned that you're a writer," said el Vaquero. "What have you written?"

Abuelito was reciting titles of unpublished poems when a cousin interrupted him to say, "Myriam writes too!"

"Yes," agreed Abuelito, "but women can't be good writers. Women have too much moral fiber to write well. They lack the sinful inclination required of genius. Women don't practice enough vice. To write well, one must commit oneself to a lifetime of misdeeds." Abuelito paused. Then he jabbed the air with his index finger and announced, "Gabriela Mistral! She is the one good female poet produced by Latin America. And I don't know how she did it!"

I wanted to be mad at my grandfather.

But I couldn't.

He looked foolish puzzling over how a woman could possibly write decent poetry. Mistral's talent scrambled his macho mind, making capirotada of it, and I wanted to laugh. Abuelito had indulged in plenty of vice, but no one could tell by reading his poetry. It simply wasn't that good.

Most of my grandfather's life was spent working as a reporter and publicist. He took extreme pride in the latter profession. The profits it generated purchased his box of a house, and while Abuelito developed PR campaigns for various tapatío figures and enterprises, he most delighted in publicizing himself. Abuelito prattled himself into legend, extolling his gifts and magnetism, insisting that he'd once had to protect himself against the advances of María Félix, Mexican cinema's most celebrated twentieth-century sex symbol. According to his version of events, Abuelito visited the actress's home to deliver documents. Dressed in a barely there caftan, the drunk seductress invited him into her parlor.

It was as if she'd been waiting for . . . Ricardo.

The poor man had to defend himself against her praying-mantis-like advances.

This tall tale would've made an ideal entry into our New Year's Eve competition.

My grandfather foretold that he would outlive the title of a novel written by one of his Colombian acquaintances, *One Hundred Years of Solitude*. But then a stroke ended his life three years short of this dream. At age ninety-seven, Ricardo Serrano Ríos took his last breath in the bed that he shared with his spinster son.

I think of the April morning that his spirit left his body as the day that my grandfather woke up dead.

I didn't go to his funeral. I couldn't. I had to work. I had a mortgage to pay. A wife to support.

I watched video of the wake, my family mumbling a rosary in unison.

My tío Ricardo aimed his camera at his father, shooting a postmortem photograph of his namesake—a photograph that, once again, calls to mind *A Christmas Carol*.

Arms crossed, Abuelito's cadaver rests on a peach blanket.

A gauzy bandage is wrapped around his head to keep his mouth shut.

Mom's half siblings, the children of la otra mujer, attended the funeral too. Offspring who'd been denying the existence of one another for decades were now gathered around the husk of the man who'd made them and hurt them. I stared at these weird family photos, a bunch of mourners with forced smiles clustered around a casket, and it shouldn't have shocked me that these strange faces looked so familiar. I saw Abuelito in their eyes and chins. He especially haunted through their noses.

Some Villa Guerrerenses crashed the funeral. They praised Abuelito, stating that he was a great man, the pride of Villa Guerrero. They took so much pride in him that they wanted to name a street Ricard Serrano Ríos Way. Of course, we would have to pay to have the street registered, and we would have to pay for its sign, and we would have to pay for the sign's installation, and we would have to pay for the street's upkeep, but what a way to honor our patriarch!

We declined their offer.

"In the lands now occupied by the municipality of Villa Guerrero . . . sprawled the houses, shacks, and huts of humble people . . . the closest village was Totatiche, and about every fifteen days or so, the pious longed to kneel at the feet of the Lord."

La vida de Ricardo Serrano Ríos no comenzó en Villa Guerrero.

Before Villa Guerrero was Villa Guerrero, it was El Salitre de Guadalupe, a reference to the region's saltpeter deposits. El Salitre was days away from Guadalajara, and my great-grandparents resided west of this mestizo settlement, making their home where missionaries, anthropologists, and other pests were unlikely to bother them, a Tepecano-style pit house that gripped the edge of a barranca. Abuelito's father, Gumersindo, cobbled its walls using tree branches, stones, and mud. He harvested grass, dried it, and climbed to the exposed roof, thatching its A shape with hay. The house had two rooms, one for sleeping, and one for everything else, and it was up to Abuelito's mother, Magdalena, to care for this handmade world.

Outside, the burro brayed.

Magdalena tossed a stale tortilla at her.

The donkey lowered her head and opened her mouth, long teeth chomping at scraps.

A cigarette hung from Magdalena's lip. Her nostrils exhaled a comforting fog.

Every day, she tended to the fire, to her children, to their clothes, to the corn, to her husband, and to his animal. Her childhood had ended at age thirteen, with marriage. Gumersindo spent most of his time in the milpa. Soon after sunrise, he would reach for his machete or coa, hike to las tres hermanas—corn, beans, and squash—and plead with them, coaxing his cultivars to grow along rocky and inhospitable slopes. When he arrived home, he hunkered down on his stool and ate. Sipped. Smacked his gums.

Toddlers crawled underfoot.

While attempting to stand upright, the little ones sniffed at the earth, inhaling its history. To prevent her kids from kicking up dust, Magdalena watered the ground, smoothing it with a broom made of dried grass. One must diligently care for dirt floors, and Magdalena's were impeccable. Hers signaled to scorpions that they were not welcome.

Life at the barranca's edge smelled of mesquite, mist, pitaya, rue, rosa de castilla, hierba de San Antonio, venison, verbena, roast rabbit, blood, and wild tobacco. It also smelled of saltpeter, an ingredient in gunpowder.

No one has shared with me a memory in which Magdalena wasn't smoking.

Because my great-grandmother was a chimney, my imagination smells her tobacco before seeing it.

As my fantasy comes into focus, my mind's eye traces the contours of a cigarette dangling from her lip.

I follow its orange glow. Its cherry.

Magdalena is walking, as if in a trance, through dark morning.

Arriving at a centuries-old tree, she stops.

Beneath branches, she lifts her skirt.

Squats.

The first light of dawn pierces, illuminating long acorns. Spiky leaves.

This oak will be her midwife.

She pushes and pushes and pushes and pushes and pushes, the puddle beneath her growing and growing and growing and growing and growing . . .

She and Gumersindo wait to see if this one will survive.

The baby lasts, making it to the next day. He drinks from Magdalena and drinks from Magdalena and drinks from Magdalena. He turns a week old. Suck suck suck. Gumersindo strokes his jaw with relief. He has a boy, one that's strong, one that he won't have to unite with the other babies buried nearby.

Twelve days after my grandfather's birth, my great-grandfather descends from his ravine.

Two elders, Cruz and Julian, accompany him.

They walk until arriving at a threshold.

Gumersindo knocks. The three campesinos wait. It's up to Adolfo Llanos Valdes, the man in charge of El Salitre's civil registry, to confirm every newborn's existence. In addition to serving as registrar, Adolfo is also the region's cacique. Bribery, fraud, extortion, and murder are a sampling of the strategies that these civil servants use to swindle, terrorize, and control, and though these real-life strongmen are fearsome, storytellers have been known to rely on caciquismo to advance otherwise inert plots.

The most well-known literary cacique is, perhaps, Juan Rulfo's *Pedro Páramo*.

Named after its villain, the gothic novel takes place in a non-place, an imagined Mexican ghost town. Juan Preciado, one of Pedro's countless sons, introduces the reader to this seemingly abandoned village: "I came to Comala because I had been told that my father, a man named Pedro Páramo, lived there. It was my mother who told me." Juan's mother, the aptly named Dolores, craves vengeance. Pedro treated her and her son horribly, and Juan pledges to find his father and make him pay. As the prodigal narrator struggles to fulfill his promise, the dead become his guides.

They teach Juan that it's impossible to extract a pound of flesh from a skeleton.

Straw hat in hand, Gumersindo fidgets before the cacique.

I imagine my great-grandfather quietly observing Adolfo as he writes about him in the registry. Adolfo records that it is 1915, the twelfth of April. A farmer who lives with his wife on a rancho closer to Azqueltán than Coculitén has presented himself. Eleven days before, this peasant's woman gave birth to a boy. The creature arrived in the morning. Husband and wife have named the infant Ricardo, and he has one living grandparent, Dámasa. The cacique taxonomizes, classifying Gumersindo and Magdalena as "progenitors of the indigenous race." With that phrase, he inscribes the infant Serrano into a fuckable caste.

The Valdés y Llanos clan, a family of hacendados, has been screwing over Tepecanos, Wixáritari, Mexicaneros, and campesinos for generations.

The greed of such clans has spurred an uprising.

The ghosts of this rebellion continue to haunt Comala.

Open *Pedro Páramo* to find them descending upon the home of its spectral cacique.

"We've rebelled against the government and against people like you," a carbine-toting man named Perseverancio tells Pedro. "We're tired of putting up with you. Everyone in the government is a crook, and you and your kind are nothing but a bunch of lowdown bandits and slick thieves."

Ever the strategist, Pedro asks, "How much do you need for your revolution?"

"Tierra y Libertad" was the Mexican Revolution's motto, and one of its goals was the overthrow of Porfirio Díaz, a president who'd managed, with the help of the United States, to stay in power for thirty-five years. My grandfather was born at the heart of this revolution, into its very deadly "middle" (that is, if something amorphous can *have* a middle), and like most Mexicans at the time of this conflict, his father could not read. Sure, Gumersindo could squiggle a signature. He could identify a noun here, a verb there. But not a preposition. And an adverb or a conjunction? No way. Were my great-grandfather to have picked up the Bible and flipped through it, he would've skimmed page after page of holy chicken scratch.

Tyrants revel in the chasm separating the literate from the illiterate.

Hoarding literacy gives them the power to define, defraud, and shatter.

In Comala, the divide between those who can and can't read also separates the guilty from those they ruin. When Pedro's favorite bastard son, Miguel, murders the priest's brother, it is Gerardo, Pedro's lawyer, his trusted document forger, who intervenes.

Gerardo restages the scene so that the murder reads as a suicide.

The lawyer also mops up after Miguel rapes.

The bastard stalks girls.

Spies on them.

Slithers through bedroom windows.

Climbs into beds.

Surprises.

When Miguel's victims protest, when they complain that there are unwanted monsters kicking inside of them, that their tits are swelling with malevolent milk, the lawyer arrives.

"You should be thankful that you'll be having a light-skinned baby!"

He tosses coins at their feet.

Comala fills with madwomen.

None of them can read.

Instead, they mumble to themselves.

For eternity.

"The peasant read the entry and is satisfied with its content. Signed, Adolfo Llanos Valdes."

People with a rigid and unimaginative sense of time say that the revolution ended in 1917, with the creation of a new constitution. Those who prefer to mark time through the rise and fall of great men say that it ended in 1920, when General Álvaro Óbregon, a Sonorense who lost his right arm at battle against Pancho Villa, was sworn in as president. An explosion blew the general's limb off and out of sight. He stumbled around, searching for it, cussing. Finally a fellow soldier produced a coin. He held it up in the air. It caught the light, glinting.

The greedy arm materialized on the horizon.

Flying toward the shiny object, the disembodied hand snatched it.

General Óbregon's injury earned him the nickname el Manco

de Celaya, and his flying limb inspired songs, poems, and jokes, including one cracked by the presidential candidate Manuel de Jesús Clouthier del Rincón. While on the campaign trail, reporters asked Clouthier, "Who's your favorite Mexican president?"

"Óbregon! He only had one arm to rob us with!"

The presidency of Plutarco Elías Calles, another mustached Sonorense, followed on the heels of Óbregon's. A staunch anticleric, Calles worked to loosen the chokehold that Catholicism had on Mexico. In 1926, his administration rolled out secularizing legislation.

Churches began to close.

The devout panicked.

And plotted.

The Vatican mostly looked the other way.

Óbregon was reelected in 1928. Like Calles, he too had an aversion to the eucharist.

(It does lack flavor.)

On July 17, in San Ángel, President-elect Óbregon attended a luncheon at La Bombilla restaurant. So did José de León Toral, a twenty-seven-year-old artist who looked like the love child of James Dean and Sal Mineo.

A popular orchestra entertained, serenading the revolutionaries. Toral approached the bar and ordered a beer. He sipped and prayed, sipped and whispered, "Hail Mary, full of grace, the Lord is with Thee . . ." He signaled a waiter, who showed him into the main room, and Toral told one of the revolutionaries that he was an artist; would it please these great men to have their caricatures drawn? The revolutionary nodded.

At the general's table, Toral drew VIPs enjoying their platos tipicos.

"Limoncito," Óbregon's favorite song, played.

"El limón ha de ser verde, para que tiña morado, y el amor, para que dure, debe ser disimulado: limoncito, limoncito . . ."*

---

* "The lemon should be green, so that it will ripen, and love, so that it will last, must remain hidden . . ."

Toral stood close enough to show the general a sketch of his own profile. With one hand, the artist raised the drawing. With the other, he appeared to reach for a pencil.

Óbregon grinned with approval but his smile soon disappeared.

Toral had drawn a Spanish revolver and fired it into the president-elect's face.

Next, Toral shot him in the back.

When asked why he'd assassinated el Manco de Celaya, Toral explained that he wanted to stop the persecution of Catholics.

The assassin hated that Mexico was losing her religion.

"Our children cannot be baptized, and the last sacred sacraments cannot be administered!"

Ghosts may also lose their religion. When Comala's priest, Father Rentería, runs off to join religious rebels, hordes of men like José de León Toral in open revolt, there is no one left to baptize Comala's newborns. There is no one left to offer peasants their final sacraments.

Comala's infernal heat was always suggestive of hell.

The absence of a village priest confirms it.

Scapular-wearing partisans with Winchester rifles chanted, "Long live Christ, our king!" Nowhere was their zealotry more pronounced than where my grandfather grew up, Jalisco.

Devout peasants pledged their loyalty to Jesus.

Blood spattered and flowed.

The devil grinned.

During his trial, Toral celebrated this violence.

"The Catholic rebels in open hostilities against federal troops in the state of Jalisco are heroes! All of them who perish are martyrs!"

Toral became so popular that during his trial, when the chief defense attorney approached the courthouse, crowds cheered, showering him with roses.

By the time my grandfather was old enough to understand death, El Salitre de Guadalupe had been renamed Villa Guerrero. Education had fallen under secular control, enraging many Catholic parents, and their fury might have had something to do with the disappearance of Manuel Leyva, the local director of schools. On February 12, 1925, Leyva kissed his wife goodbye, mounted his horse, left his ranch, and was never heard from again. The godlessness wrought by Leyva didn't bother Magdalena. She didn't care if her children learned to read from a Bible or a primer, so long as they learned to read. And her skinniest son, Ricardo, would learn to read and write. He wasn't much to look at, but he was destined for greatness.

Amid whizzing bullets, burning fields, cows that had no idea what was going on, and nuns on the run, my grandfather walked to and from school. Well, maybe it wasn't quite this dramatic, at least not every day, but I imagine Abuelito stepping over clerics' corpses on his way to learn his ABCs.

A is for Atheist.

B is for Benito Juárez.

C is for Chamuco.

D is for Damnation.

E is for Execution.

F is for Filial.

G is for Guerrero, Villa Guerrero.

The village schoolhouse had one room and, of course, one teacher. All students, regardless of age or ability, followed the same curriculum. They learned their numbers. They learned to add, subtract, multiply, and divide. They learned to read. They learned about great moments and great men in Mexican history. (There were no great women in Mexican history except for la Virgen de Guadalupe, but she was currently blacklisted.) The boys learned that Mexico is a great country with a glorious government and that they might someday be great men.

They were seated according to their marks.

Those who earned the highest scores sat at the front of the room.

Those who received the lowest sat at the back, near the door.

These fools got called donkeys.

My grandfather encountered his first nemesis in this setting.

We shall call him Juan.

Juan was Ricardo's most precocious classmate.

His talents earned him a seat close to the teacher's desk.

Ricardo envied Juan's position. Like a little cacique, he plotted to take his seat.

The classroom became Ricardo's game board, and he verbally sparred with his classmates, knocking out opponents in academic duels. Seat by seat, he leapfrogged to the front.

On the day that the teacher ordered Juan to sit behind him, Ricardo beamed.

He was a king.

A conqueror with a freshly whittled pencil.

That, at least, is the story that my grandfather tells.

My grandfather told my mother that his parents left Villa Guerrero for his sake, that Magdalena knew how talented he was, that she understood that his gifts would be wasted on a rancho. Mom describes her grandparents' descent from the region as "estilo Joad," à la *Grapes of Wrath*, their burro standing in for a Model T, lumbering under the weight of their belongings.

After schlepping for days, the family arrived in Guadalajara, settling in the city's Aranzazu neighborhood.

Near el Teatro Degollado, Ricardo watched boys play soccer.

His skin burned with envy.

Some of the soccer players looked like him. None of them dressed like him.

A handwoven straw hat covered my grandfather's black hair. A knotted bandana hung around his neck. He smoothed his white cotton shirt and pantaloons, rubbed his huaraches together. The soccer players wore button-down shirts and trousers. A few wore jackets and ties.

An orange pocket square erupted from the coat of one tiny gentleman.

Ricardo swore that he would someday dress like the kid with the pocket square.

He would become a dandy.

With the help of the family donkey, Ricardo set his sartorial plan into motion.

Neighborhood kids admired the animal, and for a small fee, Ricardo let them climb aboard and take the burro for a spin. Magdalena and Gumersindo turned to sugar for an income, operating a roadside stand where they sold soft drinks. They called their puesto "la isla," its customers sipping sweetness from long-necked bottles, enjoying the shade cast by the stand's modest awning.

Swallowing his last gulp, a customer would hand his empty bottle to Gumersindo.

Gumersindo would set it in a crate, trying not to make any noise, not even a clink.

He had a hangover that lasted thirty years, a hangover that would eventually be cured by death.

Magdalena's hand clutched her broom. She swept debris away from her stand. From her lip hung a Faro, an unfiltered cigarette sweetened by rice paper. Being offered a Faro before facing the firing squad had become a death rite back during the revolution.

Those who'd survived the conflict somberly puffed away.

Because he was intent on continuing his education, on fulfilling Magdalena's prophecy that he'd become one of Mexico's great men, Abuelito pretended to love Christ, his king. The attempt to secularize Mexico had failed, and with the church back in business, Ricardo enrolled in el Seminario Conciliar de San José, a colonial institution established in 1699.

In class, Ricardo felt tiny. His scores were among the lowest, and he envied the boys who outperformed him. One of these boys was Juan. This Juan, last name Rulfo, excelled at geography and history but sucked so bad at Latin that he had to take it twice. When Juan was six years old, an assassin murdered his father, Juan Nepomuceno Pérez Rulfo. Maria, Juan's mother, sent him to Instituto Luis Silva, an orphanage in Guadalajara. Later that year, Juan learned that his mother had made the journey to join his father.

Books consoled Juan. So did Ricardo, who might as well have been an orphan. He shared nothing about his parents or Villa Guerrero with his classmates.

During childhood visits to Guadalajara, I heard my grandfather tell story after story about Juan. He'd sit at the living/dining room table and go on and on and on about his frenemy.

His prattle drowned the birdsong. Laced with resentment, his nostalgia prickled, and my eyes rolled as he accused Juan of theft. The first thing my grandfather accused him of stealing was a poetry manuscript that he'd shared with him. Juan had never returned it and Abuelito insinuated that Juan had pillaged it for language, ideas, and style. That seemed weird to me. Juan wrote short stories and novels, not poetry. Poetry was my grandfather's thing. The other way Juan had supposedly ripped off Abuelito was by selling him an incomplete set of encyclopedias for two hundred pesos. He still carried a grudge about those missing volumes.

The moment Abuelito uttered the phrase, "Pues, mi amigo Juan . . ." I knew to hide.

I wanted to hear ghost stories, not Juan stories.

A few days after Abuelito had harassed twelve-year-old me about marriage, he trapped me in the living/dining room, launching into an impromptu lecture about Juan. He'd gone to the room no women were allowed in, the one Abuelita called his lair, to fetch a portrait. I'd seen it before. We all had. In the photo, Abuelito appears alongside Juan.

It's labeled, "Third year preparatory students, Section A, 1933–1934."

Three rows of seminarians, some looking as young as twelve, fill its frame.

Dressed in a suit, my grandfather looks beatific. His gaze is fixed on the bright future Magdalena predicted for him.

Juan looks lost. Depressed. Perhaps his spirit is already wandering the ruins of Comala.

It was, in the end, Juan who achieved the great-man status that Magdalena had prophesied for her son, and this mistake left a foul taste in Ricardo's mouth. Through prose that detailed the sort of lives my great-grandparents had lived, the people my grandfather felt so much shame about, Juan became a literary celebrity, catapulted into orbit with the likes of Carlos Fuentes, Octavio Paz, and Mario Vargas Llosa. His fame was cemented by the genius of *Pedro Páramo,* a book that many Rulfistas say established the genre of magic realism.

In theory my grandfather published a few essays about Juan. In truth, these works primarily focus on the person my grandfather most loved publicizing. Himself.

In one of these pieces, Abuelito describes meeting a woman named Maria Elena, "one of the most beautiful women in Guadalajara, Jalisco, and Mexico." The church be damned: this beauty became his new vocation. He pursued her and read her poetry. He sweet-talked her into loving him, but Ricardo wanted Maria Elena to prove her loyalty.

He expected sacrifice.

Maria Elena's friends had entered her name into a contest, nominating her to serve as the queen of Guadalajara's fourth centennial celebration. The winner would be crowned on Valentine's Day and the festivities included a literary competition. From this contest, a centennial poet would be chosen to address the queen.

Ricardo prayed for anyone but Maria Elena to be crowned.

She was his queen and his queen only.

Only he could worship at her altar.

"Renounce your candidacy and I'll marry you!" he threatened.

"Wait!" Maria Elena urged. "Maybe I won't win! Can you please just wait?"

Ricardo shook his head.

Maria Elena refused to make the sacrifice.

She dumped the poet.

On the evening of the coronation, Don Aurelio Hidalgo stood onstage, reading verse to the queen.

Ni modo.

Like Willy Loman, Ricardo went to work as a traveling salesman, clomping from door to door, perfecting his smooth-talking skills. Mom says she has no idea what her dad was selling so let's imagine that he was peddling mystery. He walked the cobblestones, reached for Hand of Fatima door knockers, pounded them, and charmed whoever answered, convincing them to buy his enigmatic wares.

In his spare time, he wrote poetry that no one wanted to touch.

He considered becoming a journalist but when he learned how much reporters earned, he laughed.

When he learned how much publicists earned, he knew he'd found his calling.

He could advertise himself as a first-rate exaggerator and clients would pay him to use these skills!

He founded a one-man agency and initiated multiple publicity campaigns. The most elaborate of these targeted Maria Elena.

He sent unwanted floral arrangements to her workplace, Fábricas de Francia.

He paid mariachis to perform outside her bedroom window.

Night after night, trumpets blared, ruining her sleep.

Night after night, guitars strummed, ruining her sleep.

Night after night, music harassed the most beautiful woman in Mexico.

The bags under her eyes were the products of Ricardo's obsession.

My grandfather's campaign was desperate, creepy, and expensive. It was also adulterous. After being dumped by the most beautiful woman in Mexico, Ricardo had married a teenager he'd knocked up. That girl was la Señorita Arcelia Garcia de Alba, my grandmother.

Abuelita was not from Villa Guerrero. The "natural" daughter of a seamstress, she was born in Guadalajara and spent part of her childhood in an orphanage. She never complained about her time spent there and said that an orphanage teacher taught her to read and write. She also said that while locked away, she discovered a talent.

She could draw and paint.

Ricardo began incorporating Arcelia's designs into his publicity campaigns. His most successful initiatives featured his wife's artwork.

Ricardo paid Arcelia nothing for her labor.

Some people in my family mention my grandfather's misogyny as if it were a charming yet harmless quirk. Something to giggle about.

Ricardo made Arcelia beg for money to buy new underwear. She had to wear hers until they disintegrated.

He infected her with gonorrhea.

When a man leaves his wife and children to subsist on water for seven days, it's the opposite of charming.

My mother, la Bebé, has two birthdays. This is common in Latin America.

There's the day that she was born, the day that her mother pushed her into the world.

Then there's the day that her father went to the registrar to have her birth recorded.

He was in no rush. My mother was a baby girl. Nothing to get excited about.

A baby boy would've sent him sprinting to the registrar.

We celebrate my mother's first birthday in August and her second in September.

She is Leo and Virgo.

My favorite childhood photograph of my mother is of her wearing her first Communion dress. La Bebé stands in church, a tiny bride. She holds a candle as large as her arm. She looks ready to club a seal with it.

Ricardo issues a household decree. He no longer wants to eat store-bought tortillas, he only wants homemade, and so he orders the female members of his household to devote themselves to tortilla making. Before leaving, he tells Arcelia and his daughters, "When I get home, I expect to see all of you cooking."

Arcelia goes to the kitchen.

She prepares the masa and sits on the apartment floor, making tortillas with her girls.

When Ricardo returns, he finds a pleasing sight, a pregnant wife flanked by obedient daughters.

"Look," says Arcelia. "These are the tortillas that la Bebé made."

Father examines daughter's tortillas.

They're the ugliest he's ever seen.

Funky-ass huaraches.

"You made these?" he asks.

La Bebé nods.

"You're not making tortillas anymore."

When he turns his back, La Bebé grins.

Her plan worked.

It's a muggy afternoon in Guadalajara. Ricardo is daydreaming about his second favorite subject, women. He rounds a corner and walks down a wide sidewalk, along the avenue where his parents have been selling Coca-Cola for more than a decade.

As Magdalena turns her head, he crosses the street.

His eyes avoid her eyes.

Those peasants. They aren't his people.

Who are they?

They're poor.

He isn't.

He wears a suit.

His wife irons it for him.

She starches his collar.

And he has another woman too. And she's pregnant. Again!

He has two families. Two women.

How could he be poor?

He's earned enough money to buy a house and he didn't even have to sell his wife's piano.

Magdalena watches her son.

Smoke billows from her nostrils.

It disappears, just like him.

Ricardo walks toward el Templo de Nuestra Señora de la Merced.

It is surrounded by beggars.

One of these beggars, the one holding out his hand, the one with the worst limp, is Ricardo's brother.

Ricardo crosses the street.

In March 1955, *Pedro Páramo* debuts.

The journalist Edmundo Valadés writes its first review.

> Disconcerting, ready to unsettle critics, Juan Rulfo's first novel, *Pedro Páramo*, is already in shopwindows. It unfolds in a series of dreamlike transpositions, delving beyond the death of its characters. One is unsure of what these voices are sharing—lives, fables, or truths—but they've been heard by an extraordinary writer with ruthless and accurate insight.

• • •

The poet Alí Chumacero also reviews the novel.

He describes it as having a messy structure and lacking a core.

He also reminds readers to be kind. *Pedro Páramo* is the author's first novel.

Arcelia gives birth to a baby in the room where she will one day wake up dead.

The baby is dead.

Arcelia denies that Miguelito was born this way.

He's an archangel.

He can fly.

Ricardo can't stand to hear Arcelia sob.

He leaves the house.

He returns with a small pine box.

"Give him to me."

Arcelia walks in circles, carrying Miguelito.

She walks in circles.

Walks in circles.

Walks in circles.

On the third day, she sinks to her knees.

She dreams of Comala.

Ricardo dislodges the cadaver from her arms.

He places the child in the box.

He secures the lid on the box.

With the coffin tucked under his arm, he marches to the front door.

La Bebé hears it open.

La Bebé hears it close.

La Bebé knows there will be no funeral.

"What happens with these corpses that have been dead a long time is that when the damp reaches them they begin to stir. They wake up . . ."

• • •

La Bebé is supposed to be at school.

Instead, she's adventuring through Guadalajara.

She's trying to enjoy her girlhood.

She sees a man in a tan suit walk past a shoe store. He turns his head slightly.

The starched collar!

The necktie stitched with silk cobwebs!

It's her father!

He's supposed to be at work.

La Bebé follows him.

Ricardo walks to a neighborhood that la Bebé has never visited.

He approaches a door.

Stands at the threshold.

Knocks.

Holding a baby, a strange woman answers.

Ricardo leans forward. He kisses the woman on the lips, just like he kisses Arcelia.

Abuelito,

I heard that when you were an old man, you got yourself a new girlfriend.

Álvaro told me.

He said that though she was eighty-seven, she could easily pass for eighty-three.

Abuelito,

Te busco.

Tengo flores.

Tenemos flores.*

---

* I'm looking for you. I have flowers. We have flowers.

• • •

Abuelito,

The last time I saw you alive, your machismo burned brightly.

The last time I saw you dead, you scared the shit out of me.

"Educating women is a waste of money," Ricardo says to la Bebé. "I'll give you bus fare to go to church. But not to university."

He laughs at the thought of his pretty daughter achieving her dreams.

A girl chemist. Ha.

La Bebé and her big sister visit a medium.

The medium tells the big sister that she will marry a rich man.

The medium tells la Bebé that she will fall in love with a gringo and leave Mexico.

La Bebé finds this funny until she falls in love with a gringo and leaves Mexico.

Abuelito,

I don't hate you.

Not at all.

I'm writing this because I love you.

This is a different kind of love letter.

It's a tribute to who you really were, not who you would have us believe you were.

It's a tribute to the truth.

We can't honor you without knowing you.

And I am you.

Not completely but in part.

How does it feel to be reborn as a girl?

To have a girl carry on your legacy?

You wanted people to speak your name.

Now they will.

Thanks to me.

My grandmother worked as a seamstress so that she could afford art lessons.

The only activity she loved more than feeding stray animals was making art.

She paid a woman who'd been trained by Diego Rivera to teach her to paint the human body.

When my grandfather found out about these weekly lessons, he became incensed.

He told my grandmother that she wasn't allowed to take any more art classes.

"When you stand behind an easel, staring at a nude model, that's infidelity!"

Ricardo ordered her to paint family.

That's how she got stuck painting people like me.

And dogs.

There is a portrait of me painted by my grandmother that hangs at my parents' house.

My aunt claims that its eyes follow visitors, but I guarantee you that while my eyes may move, they see nothing.

"Tell your father it's time to eat," Abuelita tells Mom.

"Yes."

"Can I come with you?" I ask.

"Okay."

My grandfather is in his lair.

His lair is the only room on the rickety second floor.

The only route there is a rusty ladder that dangles from the roof.

I tremble with excitement and climb after Mom.

I've been told that his lair is dominated by a single scent.

Paper.

If we listen carefully, we can hear two Mexicans bickering.

They sit in a house between Pedro Loza and Santa Monica.

Juan holds Ricardo's manuscript, his first poetry collection.

Because he doesn't know how to tell his friend that it stinks, he begins with the title.

"Why not call it *Hidden Sob*?" asks Juan.

Ricardo cringes. He didn't come here for advice.

He came here for praise.

"Why that?" he demands. "It's impossible to hide a sob! Besides, I've got nothing to cry over. When I lose a woman, ten even more beautiful women usually appear in her place."

Juan doesn't hide his sigh.

Psalms.

Intimate Joy.

Through the Grasslands of the Sun.

My Hands on Your Heart.

Before Dying.

Jalisco in Poetry.

Brother President.

These seven poems comprised *Illuminated Absence*, the manuscript that Abuelito claims Juan stole.

"Brother President" was supposed to ensure my grandfather's immortality. Ricardo was certain that because of it, paisanos would line up to lay flowers at his feet.

• • •

"One thing is absolutely true," wrote Ricardo Serrano Ríos. "I am humbler than Juan Rulfo . . ."

After suffering a heart attack, Juan took up residence in the ghost town of Comala.

It was 1986.

Because my grandfather had a knack for commodification, he found a way to monetize having known him. During the twilight of his life, my grandfather traveled the state, giving lectures about his dead friend.

Álvaro chauffeured him to his talks. They came and went in a green Volkswagen Beetle whose engine muffled conversation.

One afternoon, Ricardo and Álvaro were at yet another speaking engagement. Abuelito presented to an audience of Rulfistas, yammering about his years in seminary with Juan, emphasizing that had it not been for his having introduced Juan to the short story writer Juan José Arreola, the novelist wouldn't have had the literary career that he enjoyed. Upon concluding his lecture, he said, "You may now ask questions."

He immediately regretted having said this.

He was tired and needed to sit. A hand shot up.

"Yes."

"What do you make of Rulfo's claims that autobiography is absent from his work? Is this true? You knew him. You were his classmate! What's the truth?"

Ricardo was very familiar with this question. It was one that he'd answered over and over and over. He'd answered it in his sleep, and he'd answered it while awake. It was also a question that Álvaro had listened to his father answer over and over and over.

"Sir," Ricardo replied, "this question is painfully rudimentary. As a point of fact, it is so basic that my chauffeur can answer it. Chauffeur!"

"Yes, at your orders, sir!"

"Come up here. Answer this man's question!"

The chauffeur and the Rulfista exchanged places, my uncle taking his spot at the podium, my grandfather sitting in his son's chair. Mouths agape, the audience listened as the chauffeur lectured, with passion and humor, on epistemology and Mexican autobiography.

The audience gave him a standing ovation.

"Brilliant chauffeur," they murmured.

The last time I saw my grandfather, we had come to help my grandmother die.

My grandfather had died in April.

It was now August.

Our help worked.

Arcelia died.

We buried her in the palm-shaded family tomb.

At her wake, we ate pigs' feet while being serenaded by mariachis.

We sang "El Rey."

My godmother arranged for a rosary to be prayed in Abuelita's honor.

During the golden hour, everyone left for church.

I stayed behind. The pig's foot was acting up.

I felt it kick. It was powerful. Strong enough to ruin the rosary.

I saw my grandfather that night.

At least, I think it was my grandfather.

He looked . . . different.

Amber light filled the boxy house.

I felt my grandmother.

She drew me to her deathbed, still covered in the sheets she'd died with.

I climbed into her bed.

I looked up at the ceiling fan.

I looked at the wall.

The water-stained portrait of la Virgen de Guadalupe continued to keep vigil.

In her bed, she held me.

In her bed, Death held me.

The light changes.

It dims, a warning.

I scramble out of the bed.

Plink. Plink plink plink . . .

Rain.

It's pouring.

Lightning.

THUNDER.

I sit in the living/dining room.

Lamps flicker on and off.

• • •

I sit at the table, trying to read.

I can't.

Shuffle . . .

Shuffle . . .

Shuffle . . .

I look up from my book.

Above the chair beneath the canine portrait hovers a hand, a right hand.

It is old.

It is dead.

It is his.

We write with our hands.

I write with his hand.

My hands hold flowers.

I set them at his seat.

• • •

The hand. It writes, “I leave here a testimony regarding my literary restlessness. Thank you for allowing me this pleasure and liberty. Thank you for tolerating this joke of sorts, my contribution of fact. In the future, I shall be known, people shall know the name Ricardo Serrano Ríos, native of Villa Guerrero, Jalisco, the capital of the world. Unless I publish under a pseudonym, or pseudonyms, I also have a right to mystery.”

The hand remains restless.

THE WHITE ONION

Amado Vazquez, a Mexican horticulturist, named an orchid after Joan Didion. While that was a chic gesture, I don't think of her as an orchid. I think of her as an onion. She was *very* white, *very* crisp, and even in death, she makes people cry.

Didion blew into my consciousness during senior year of high school, when our English teacher herded my classmates and me into the library to take an Advanced Placement literature test. We sat on wooden chairs, reading, grinding our teeth, annotating, flipping exam pages. At the end of the booklet, I scanned an essay whose opening line grabbed me by my anxious balls: "There is something uneasy in the Los Angeles air this afternoon . . ." The essay, "Los Angeles Notebook," described a place I actually cared about: California. When we read for English, we often "traveled" to places I didn't want a passport to. The Roman Senate. Winesburg, Ohio. Boats.

But here was home. And home was the star. And I understood the weather that this white lady was writing about! She described regional winds, the Santa Anas. These had touched my family. The Santa Anas had played with strands of my dad's long hippie hair, but Dad was bald now so instead they shook the windows of the business Grandma ran with her second husband, Bob. Hertneck's Furniture Store sat on Artesia Boulevard. With the help of the world's least friendly dog, a Yorkie named Mitzi, Grandma ran its cold showroom. Cataracts had turned Mitzi's eyes opalescent. She hid under French provincial settees and walnut armoires, growling at customers, cousins, and deliverymen. Mitzi hated everyone but Grandma.

Curled on her lap, she let Grandma pet her silver head and fluff her crocheted sweater.

Our local winds behaved as devilishly as those in "Los Angeles Notebook." As I trudged to Dad's office from the school bus stop, gusts spat grit and bugs into my eyes. Lodged against my sclera, gnats went to heaven. Their corpses burned. Gales seized sycamore leaves, cigarette butts, and candy wrappers and blended them with dirt, hair, and pigeon feathers. The debris whirled in small trash cyclones along cement gutters. Some of these dust devils rose two and a half feet. Half of me since sixth grade.

The weather turned out to be a pervert. During a windstorm, invisible hands grabbed my skirt. They tossed it above my stretch-marked ass. Then they flipped it up in the front. I looked like an inverted umbrella in girl form. The hands grabbed my black hair and wound it around my neck. They choked me.

Getting jumped by the weather is the price we pay to live in California.

I wanted to read more by the author who I'd already begun to think about as the windy bitch, but I'd arrived at the excerpt's final line: "The wind shows us how close to the edge we are." Exhaling through my nostrils, I stroked the writing bump on my middle finger and scribbled an enthusiastic analysis I would've preferred to write in the first person but that I wrote in the third.

I doubt that my abuelito read Joan Didion. His current state, deceased, complicates asking him if he's familiar with her work. My Mexican grandfather was a nationalist, bibliophile, and machista who actively avoided prose written by women. I'm sure that Michiko Kakutani's claim that "California belongs to Joan Didion" would've made him laugh. He'd have whipped a pencil out from under his serape and fixed the line: "California belongs to Joan Didion because her ancestors stole it."

In my imagination, Abuelito's interpretation of history wrestles

Didion's. The Mexican presence haunting her work could really do this if those of us living outside Didion's prose lent a hand to those trapped inside it.

The white literary establishment handed California to Didion.

I propose we pry it away from her. Give her a rest. She's dead. And doesn't the place deserve a living ambassador?

I'm not suggesting mutiny because I hate Didion. On the contrary. Her work guides me as much as it scoffs at me, and I admit it: Her voice has been instructional. It mentored me in irony, detachment, and condescension. It invited me to experiment with gringa coolness, tutoring me in first-person omniscience and word snobbery. Didion's regionalism validated that California, a place I love so much and sometimes get the urge to put in my mouth (and do), is a worthy muse. Didion's prose rhythms are found in music I love to take meandering walks to, music that it would be criminal to dance to. Didion modeled how writing yourself into the story of a place convinces the reader that the place is yours. You, the author, fuse with rhetoric and fact. Your body joins the topography.

What irks is Didion's racial grammar.

A conceptual metaphor developed by the sociologist Eduardo Bonilla-Silva, racial grammar is what gives racism its elemental quality, the sense that its natural, no different from earth, wind, or fire: "Racial domination generates a grammar that helps reproduce the 'racial order' as just the way things are." The sociologist Karen Fields and historian Barbara Fields make similar observations in *Racecraft: The Soul of Inequality in American Life*. The Fieldses liken racecraft to witchcraft, describing it as "a kind of fingerprint evidence that *racism* has been on the scene." They write that racecraft "plants mines in our language," and to illustrate how racism curses communication, the Fieldses examine the word *welfare*. While the term "conjures up lazy Afro-Americans and cheating immigrants," it stops having this effect once white people line up for government cheese.

You can't racialize without racism. My go-to definition of this phenomenon was developed by the abolitionist geographer Ruth

Wilson Gilmore. In *Golden Gulag: Prisons, Surplus, Crisis, and Opposition in Globalizing California,* Gilmore describes it in a way that emphasizes murder: "Racism . . . is the state-sanctioned or extralegal production and exploitation of group-differentiated vulnerability to premature death." When racecrafting, racists tend to reach for "the usual suspects"—skin color, ancestry, and birthplace to name a few—but they have every earthly difference at their disposal. You could make a race out of girls with mustaches if you had the right people helping you.

In a landmark social experiment performed in 1968, Iowa schoolteacher Jane Elliott used visible difference to help her white third graders learn about racism. Elliott further differentiated her blue-eyed students from her brown-eyed students by giving the blue-eyed kids green armbands to wear. She told the brown-eyed kids that they were better, way smarter than the blue-eyed kids. Elliott said that blue-eyed kids "sit around and do nothing. You give them something nice and they just wreck it."

She characterized the blue-eyed kids the same way that I heard Mexicans described when I was a kid.

Elliott watched racism ensue.

Its spell is that easy to cast.

Didion's first book, *Run River,* establishes her California racial grammar. According to Bonilla-Silva, this grammar "shapes how we see or do not see, how we frame, and even what we feel about race-related matters." Set in the Sacramento Valley, the racial grammar that shapes *Run River* is identical to the racial grammar that shaped my upbringing in the Santa Maria Valley.

I was born in what used to be the only hospital in Santa Maria. Marian Hospital is still there. So is the place where every egg I ate as a child came from, Rosemary Farm. The egg farm was once visible from the hospital. Three miles away, past broccoli and cauliflower fields and train tracks, were chickens, chickens, chickens. George Allan Hancock, the millionaire who owned the Santa Maria Valley Railroad, named Rosemary Farm after his only daughter.

Public-school kids got to know the Hancock chickens well. School buses drove us from campus to the farm. We smelled it before we saw it. Teachers escorted us to a white room full of caged chickens. Their lives consisted of laying breakfast, clucking, and dying. At the Santa Barbara County Fair, Rosemary Farm always staged a live exhibit. I waited all year to visit it.

This exhibit wasn't part of the midway. It was inside a windowless gallery where local businesses set up folding tables and gave out free stuff and coupons. Rosemary Farm's exhibit was staffed by baby chickens. Next to a table piled with maps, pamphlets, and keychains advertising nearby vineyards and wineries, a table displayed the poultry's miniature county fair. Bumper cars, refreshment stands, a carousel, and a roller coaster made it look just like the one we were enjoying. Chicken feed was sprinkled across the replica and chicks followed the food, hopping rides. Beaks pecked at grain. A chick fell off the carousel, got up, and jumped back on. I got dizzy from watching birds ride the Ferris wheel. Some sat three to a seat. They seemed oblivious to us.

I hoped the young chickens were having the time of their lives.

I knew what was in store for them.

I call Santa Maria "Fresno by the sea." The town sprawls in the northern part of Santa Barbara County, where tri-tip is queen, and strawberry is king. At the same fairground where the chicks have their mini-fair, the Strawberry Festival queen receives her tiara. Strawberries, which have just enough arsenic not to kill you, thrive along the Central Coast. Even inland, the Santa Maria Valley's dirt might as well be sand. Temperatures stay mild year-round. Tourist brochures compliment the region, calling it "Mediterranean."

Strawberries sweeten Santa Maria's reputation but harvesting them is risky. Wearing layers of protective clothing, those who pick this crop crouch in fog, wind, or sun. They bend at the waist. Hands are their only tools. Bees and wasps hover. Tourists drunk driving through wine country ignore these pickers. They shouldn't. They should marvel at their agility, grace, and precision.

Harvesting berries is a ballet.

An audience of crows watches from a bank of eucalyptus trees.

A hairy tarantula crawls across a soft country road, avoiding tires.

Shy of sunset, rattlesnakes slither out of their dens.

The Bureau of Labor Statistics consistently ranks agricultural laborer as one of the country's most dangerous jobs, more dangerous than policing. Among the occupational hazards are human trafficking, wage theft, and debt bondage. Pesticides seep into farmworkers' clothing, skin, and bloodstreams. Farm machinery maims. My dad recalls a mother and father who couldn't afford a babysitter and so they brought their kids to the fields. One of them got plowed by a tractor. Dad also remembers when there were no porta-potties in the fields and women had to walk in pairs to the eucalyptus groves. As one would squat, the other would do her best to hide her coworker behind an old blanket.

On the streets of Santa Maria, people speak to each other in Mixtec. That's because many Santa Maria Valley farmworkers are Indigenous migrants from Oaxaca. The Department of Homeland Security classifies these employees as H-2A "guestworkers," but our government extends these guests the worst hospitality. DHS makes clear that the H-2A program is a matter of mi casa es su casa until a businessman decides that he doesn't need you anymore: "Employers in the United States have often faced a shortage of available domestic workers who are able, willing, and qualified to fill seasonal agricultural jobs. The H-2A program was instituted to meet this need for seasonal and temporary labor, *without adding permanent residents to the population*." Labor organizers describe this visa guestworker program as the little brother of the Bracero Program, an initiative instituted during World War II to bring temporary manpower to the US. In addition to controlling employee visas, the H-2A program gives employers control over where their employees live and how they are transported to and from the fields. They even control what they eat. Oversight of the H-2A program is minimal.

Santa Barbara County's annual agricultural crop report proves that employers can afford to pay pickers way more than $2.10 a box.

In 2021, the industry generated a gross production value of nearly $2 billion. Still, most farmworkers live in the northern, and poorest, part of the county. The posh neighborhoods in and around the city of Santa Barbara stand in violent contrast to the shacks that house strawberry pickers. One of these neighborhoods is Montecito. After marrying the writer John Gregory Dunne, Didion and her husband stayed at Montecito's San Ysidro Ranch, the same hideaway where the Kennedys honeymooned.

In *The Year of Magical Thinking*, Didion gives the ranch a bad review. She writes that it was so dull that she and Dunne hauled their suitcases south and checked into the Beverly Hills Hotel. What were they expecting from a ranch named after the patron saint of farmworkers? The Catholic Church claims San Ysidro is a miracle worker, but I don't believe it. He let my classmate, son of migrant farmworkers, fill his lungs with dirty water. Fortunato had tried doing like Huckleberry Finn out on the Bradley Basin, floating on a homemade raft. It capsized. Fortunato didn't know how to swim. After we lost him, the Santa Maria Valley YMCA began offering free classes to migrant kids. My dad got the funding for the program. He also got funding to make sure that every kid got a bathing suit.

The title of Didion's first novel, *Run River*, alludes to the waterway where she learned to swim, the Sacramento. Published in 1963, *Run River* begins in the summer of 1959. Its first word is *Lily*, a flower hopelessly associated with Christian purity. Like Didion, the protagonist is a "strikingly frail" white woman. Fresh out of the shower, she daubs a cologne advertised as "The Costliest Perfume in the World" between her "small bare breasts."

A .38, which was once used to kill a rattlesnake, is gone from its drawer. We don't see Lily's husband shoot her lover. We hear it.

The characters implicated in this love triangle are the great-great-grandchildren of Anglo settlers, a people whose celebration always prompts an eye roll from my dad. Whenever Conestoga wagons roll into a story, he grumbles, "If there's someone there to 'greet' you when you arrive, you can't call yourself a pioneer."

Run River reduces Mexicans to "goddamn wetbacks." If you live east of the Mississippi, this slur might be new to you. It's a good example of how racists manipulate geography to make racial difference. When Mexicans get called wetbacks, we're being called invaders. The slur suggests that we had to do the thing that Fortunato couldn't to get here. Our town newspaper, the *Santa Maria Times*, printed the word *wetback* a lot. On June 19, 1957, the newspaper published the headline: "The Wetback Season Has Opened." A reporter describes this season as "when Mexican nationals try to sneak across the Rio Grande toward *American* farm jobs . . ." The reporter uses the word *wetback* eleven times.

In 1970, the *Santa Maria Times* published an article titled "'Sheep Dog Cowboy' Star for National Horse Show." It's accompanied by a photo of a monkey riding a dog that's herding sheep. The monkey's name is Wetback. He's a "sheep dog cowboy" slated to perform at the Earl Warren Showgrounds. Audiences should expect to see him dressed for the part, in "leather vest, chaps, sombrero, boots . . ." Wetback's performance promises to be one of a kind: "When 'Wetback' rides the range inside the 3,000-seat main arena—helping to corral sheep herds—it should prove to be one of the most unique acts ever put on in the [Santa Barbara National Horse Show's] history."

The word *wetback* makes me see red.

A classmate who once referred to my mother as one got kicked in the stomach more than once.

Run River, a book full of wetbacks, is divided into three sections.

After the domestic violence murder, part two winds back to 1938, a period scarred by the Great Depression. As is often the case during economic calamity, white nativism surged. Racists alleged that Mexicans were sneaking into the US for contradictory reasons. We were going to fatten ourselves on white charity while stealing white jobs.

To stop the supposed plunder, cops raided Mexican communities throughout the Southwest. Authorities captured suspected Mexicans and repatriated them. Some of those "returned" to Mexico were US citizens whose families had been living here a lot longer than any

Anglos. Estimates of the repatriated population range from 335,000 to 2,000,000.

At the start of the depression, the eugenicist Roy L. Garis presented a report on Mexican immigration to the US Congress. His beliefs are still in style.

> [Mexicans'] minds run to nothing higher than animal functions—eat, sleep, and sexual debauchery. In every huddle of Mexican shacks one meets the same idleness, hordes of hungry dogs and filthy children with faces plastered with flies, disease, lice, human filth, stench, promiscuous fornication, bastardy, lounging, apathetic peons and lazy squaws, beans and dried chili, liquor, general squalor, and envy and hatred of the Gringo.

Garis paints "high-class Mexican" women with the same filthy brush, calling them "sneaking in their adultery." And yet this phrase describes none of the Mexicans in *Run River*. It does, however, describe Lily McClellan to a T.

Part two of *Run River* opens on the morning of Lily's sixteenth birthday. She and her father, the state senator Walter Knight, are talking in her bedroom. Lily believes her dad is a great man. He's destined to become governor of California. Walter creepily drops a stack of sixteen silver dollars on his daughter's bed. She entertains her most "inadmissable wish." Lily wants to play plantation mistress Scarlett O'Hara on the big screen.

Walter slices an apple and instructs Lily in racial grammar, reminding her that "if a lot of people a long time back hadn't said what they wanted and struck out for it you wouldn't have been born in California." With that statement, Walter summons John Gast's famous painting, *American Progress*. The spirit of Columbia, embodied by a dishwater blonde in a white tunic, floats across a prairie. The star on her forehead guides pioneers west. Buffalo run from her.

Traditions of hypodescent abet Lily's secret wish to play Scarlett O'Hara. The teen is consecrated by white blood, made superior to those of us who can't prove our racial purity. "Historically, those people counted as Black have been those people with any known Black ancestry," writes Yaba Blay, author of *One Drop: Shifting the Lens on Race.* Hypodescent rules were developed and codified in the US to give Black blood an additive quality, endowing it with the power to make any resident with Black ancestry a member of the country's Black population. Held to this standard, Mexican California's last governor, Pío de Jésus Pico IV, becomes Black. Held to this standard, so do I. I'm descended from Afro-Mexicans who were probably enslaved.

Anyone who isn't white becomes a shadow in *Run River*. We blend with its literary landscape, as important to the book's agricultural setting as the artichokes, strawberries, and asparagus that receive passing mention. The Mexican presence that whispers through the novel remains mostly nameless. There are "neighborhoods of heavy Mexican penetration." There is Sacramento's West End, where Lily "could eat tacos with her fingers." While Lily sits in a car waiting, a Mexican stands on a sidewalk and makes a face at her. There are "drunken wetbacks," "bars frequented by Mexicans," and Mexican "whores." A "Greyhound bus [is] crowded with Mexican pickers and sailors." There is "that Mexican place in Jackson" where "Mamacita" works.

The only Mexican who develops more depth of character than a head of lettuce is Gomez. Unlike the other characters in *Run River*, Didion doesn't bother giving him a last name. Still, Gomez is the mostly unseen, and unheard, axis of the book's universe. Without him, Walter Knight would have to work. As the senator literally fucks around, Gomez sweats. "[He] ran the ranch, even bargained with the fruit buyers, while Walter Knight sat in the familiar gloom of the Senator Hotel bar and called at the white frame house on Thirty-eighth Street where Miss Rita Blanchard lived." We can see who Lily inherited her plantation mistress fantasies from.

While mangling Spanglish, the novel's omniscient and contemptuous narrator degrades the ranch manager: "Gomez was the most dolorous of men; one might have thought him intent only upon disproving the notion that our neighbors from south of the border were so *muy simpatico*." Like head lice, racial grammar travels from person to person, tête-à-tête. When Walter ritualistically complains about Gomez, he teaches Lily how to feel about Mexicans.

> Patiently, [Gomez] illustrated Walter Knight's contention that honesty could be expected of only native northern Californians. "I pay that bastard more than any Mexican in the Valley gets paid . . . Yet he cheats me, finds it necessary to steal me blind. Add that one up if you will. Rationalize that one for me."

The racial grammar spouted by Walter Knight reminds me of the racial grammar spouted by a Santa Maria politician, George Hobbs. Throughout my entire childhood and adolescence, Hobbs was our mayor. His obituary described him as "plain-spoken" and "blunt."

I remember him as an asshole.

When I was thirteen, the Santa Maria Valley Economic Development Association held a lunch in Hobbs's honor. Important men gathered at the Far Western Tavern, a frontier-themed steakhouse then located in the small town of Guadalupe. Mexicans probably harvested, prepared, and served every bite that Hobbs and his audience ate. Instead of saying thank you, Hobbes delivered a campaign speech that attacked the people feeding him.

> "At this time in Santa Maria, we have a Mexican problem. We have a difficulty with scads of illegal aliens that have come across the border, and they've made our neighborhoods look not like Santa Maria."

The former mailman proposed a solution: concentration camps for Mexicans.

My parents were plainspoken and blunt in their assessment of Hobbs. They said that our mayor had a racism problem and that we shouldn't be surprised if he began to grow a very small, black mustache.

My dad started his career in the Santa Maria Valley by teaching fifth grade at Robert Bruce Elementary School. Many of his students were the kids of Mexican strawberry sharecroppers. When kids came to school with blackened hands, he knew they'd been picking. One of Dad's students grew up to be the same thing as Walter Knight, a state senator. One of the future senator's classmates, Miguel Angel, grew up to be a custodian. Miguel Angel never stopped loving Dad. When he rang our doorbell, I ran to let him in. He always brought flats overflowing with massive strawberries. Some were the size and shape of a burly man's fist. Others, the size and shape of a pig's heart. I swear I saw one the size and exact shape of a dainty woman's foot. When Miguel Angel visited, we made strawberry shortcake and baked strawberry pies. I ate so many berries I worried the arsenic might kill me.

The kid who became state senator never brought us fruit.

He became a Republican.

My parents rebelled against the California racial grammar that surrounded us. In turn, they enabled change. Through rebellion against Didion's racial grammar, we can unseat her as California's thin-lipped literary grande dame. We can make way for other windy bitches, otras cabronas que quieren soplar.

Joan Didion is best recognized for the kind of stuff I first read, her nonfiction. She published her first essay collection, *Slouching Towards Bethlehem*, in 1968. In its preface, she sets readers straight, bitch-slapping us before we've even gotten to part one: "Almost all of the pieces here were written for magazines during 1965, 1966, and 1967, and most of them, to get the question out of the way at the outset, were 'my idea.'" The theme loosely holding the twenty essays together is "things falling apart" and her preface ends with a warning: ". . . one last thing to remember: *writers are always selling somebody out*."

Didion flaunted her nihilism with nicotine-infused style.

"Guaymas, Sonora" is the eighteenth piece in *Slouching Towards Bethlehem*. It reveals why Didion believes Mexico exists: "It had rained in Los Angeles until the cliff was crumbling into the surf and I did not feel like getting dressed in the morning, so we decided to go to Mexico, to Guaymas, where it was hot." This line, which has the unbridled energy of a run-on sentence, tells us that Mexico is a pastime, something for gringos to do on a rainy day. The point of journeying there can be likened to the purpose of camping. Campers seek recreational suffering. In Didion's case, she wants "to become disoriented, shriven, by the heat . . ."

The author and her undressed family drive through Nogales, the Sonoran Desert, and Hermosillo. The farther south they drive, the more Didion dips her pen in infernal ink.

Lost
Hot
Grotesque
Claustrophobic
Limbo
Moaning

Arriving at her destination, Didion goes into Gothic overdrive, plopping a symbol of death on top of a symbol of everlasting life: a vulture perches atop a crucifix in the town square. To help us see Guaymas in our mind's eye, she offers an Anglophilic reference: "As far as the town goes, Graham Greene might have written it." Greene wrote *The Power and the Glory*, a fine novel about La Cristiada, a Mexican religious war, but I find the reference a little galling. I've been to Mexico many times and never once thought, "*Ah, Mexico . . . just as the British described it!*"

Didion belongs to a well-documented spiritual tradition of pale strangers using Mexico as a transcendental portal. "We went to get away from ourselves," Didion explains. Now, if the author left herself, and most of her wardrobe, in Los Angeles, who, or what, is vacationing in Guaymas? Didion answers this question by comparing her journey south to the one made by the mythical queen Alcestis. Prior to her rebirth, Alcestis descends into the underworld. Didion's parallel transformation requires her to slip below the waistband of the Americas: the US-Mexico border.

Terrible things populate underworlds, and while Didion is in Guaymas, she comes to approximate a terrible thing. Sun, inertia, and liminality conspire. Joan hatches a persona that I call Juana: "For a week we lay in hammocks and fished desultorily and went to bed and got very brown and lazy." Didion's punctuation succumbs to sloth. By giving up on commas, she conjures an enduring controlling image: the shiftless Mexican.

The sociologist Patricia Hill Collins created the concept of the controlling image. It's a device that dictates social scripts. Controlling images erect social borders. They limit who we can and can't be. The literary scholar Lee Bebout explains the boundaries marked by the shiftless Mexican: "Whether taking a siesta or laboring continually, Mexicans are often scripted as lacking entrepreneurial energies and a self-reliant, Waspy work ethic."

Because whiteness is spun in opposition, Didion relies on this controlling image, just like Walter Knight relies on Gomez. Becoming a lazy Mexican purifies her. Hibernation restores her Waspy womanhood. Like Alcestis, she rejects the permanent sleep offered by the Hispanophone underworld. She will never, at her core, become lazy enough to quit caring about the work that beckons to her from Hollywood.

By week's end, Joan is over Juana. Wanting "something to do," she returns north. Sloughing off her brown persona, she leaves Juana to the den of sloth so masterfully rendered by that Englishman.

Didion's most disturbing and off-the-cuff Mexican mention appears in the title essay of her second nonfiction collection, *The White*

Album. The iconic piece is a vertigo-inducing account of the author's life in the late 1960s. It features Didion glamorizing the deadly sequence of events that culminated in the Manson trials.

By the end of "The White Album," Didion has proven two things.

One: that in LA in the sixties, even the rich feared having their guts ripped out.

And two: there was no one she didn't know.

She recalls that the filmmaker Roman Polanski ruined her wedding dress by spilling red wine on it at a Bel-Air dinner party. She follows this ominous anecdote with a thumbnail sketch of how she became personal stylist to a Manson girl.

At Linda Kasabian's request, Didion made a shopping trip to Beverly Hills. Her mission took her to a luxury department store on Wilshire Boulevard, I. Magnin. (The store is gone now, but the Hollywood Regency–style building remains. It became the Saks Fifth Avenue where surveillance cameras caught the actress Winona Ryder shoplifting in 2001.) Didion perused the racks. She chose the dress that Kasabian would wear to testify about an atrocity where she was the lookout: the stabbing of Polanski's pregnant wife, the actress Sharon Tate.

> "Size 9 Petite," her instructions read. "Mini but not extremely mini. In velvet if possible. Emerald green or gold. Or: A Mexican peasant-style dress, smocked and embroidered." She needed a dress that morning because the district attorney, Vincent Bugliosi, had expressed doubts about the dress she had planned to wear, a long white homespun shift. "Long is for evening," he had advised Linda.

What twenty-one-year-old would don a "Mexican peasant-style dress" to go tell a judge about how she, at the urging of a little white pimp, waited in the car while her best friends stabbed an about-to-deliver sex symbol? A hippie chick defecting from a racist and apocalyptic sex cult, that's who. And what *is* a Mexican peasant-style dress? Did Kasabian mean a huipil, the kind my mom used to pair with velour sweatpants and pleather loafers on her days off? Or did she mean the ruffled, ankle-length dresses worn by women who fought in the Mexican Revolution?

My ancestors were Mexican peasants and I have a hard time imagining anyone but a pig-tailed dishwater blonde getting away with wearing their clothes to a high-profile murder trial. *They* didn't even want to wear their clothes. They were trying to get out of them. That's why they revolted.

Kasabian got her way. When she appeared to testify, it was reported that she wore "a demure, long-sleeved, floor-length peasant dress." In a photo taken on August 13, 1970, Kasabian smiles at the camera from behind the window of a white sheriff's truck. She wears a white huipil with geometric patterns embroidered in olive green. Since we can see her only from the waist up, I'm unsure if she paired the cotton tunic with velour sweatpants.

At the trial, Kasabian gave insight into Didion's generosity:

> Mrs. Kasabian, who was offered immunity by the state, disclosed on her sixth day of testimony that she was writing a book about her life with the aid of Joan Didion, a writer for *Life* magazine, and that she was supposed to get 25 percent of the profits.
>
> "It's not about the case," Mrs. Kasabian said. "It's about my life, about me and my travels. I tell about narcotics involvement."
>
> "Do you hope you will become famous?"
>
> "I don't care if I'm famous. I hope maybe young people can relate to me and see the road I took and take another."

During the trial, Didion visited Kasabian at the Sybil Brand Institute for Women. Like I. Magnin, the former jail is no more. Its facilities are now used as a television and film location. (If you've seen the movie *Legally Blonde*, you've seen inside Sybil Brand.)

Didion hypes the terror that the jail struck in her: ". . . I remember mainly my dread at entering . . . at leaving for even an hour the infinite possibilities I suddenly perceived in the summer twilight." Nothing became of her Kasabian book project, and Didion may have scuttled it for fear of the Manson Family paying her a visit. In 1975, when President Gerald Ford visited Didion's hometown, the red-headed Manson girl, Lynette "Squeaky" Fromme, pulled a Colt .45 on him. In 1989, the Sacramento US Attorney's Office donated the failed murder weapon to the Ford Library and Museum.

My cousin Desiree was sent to Sybil Brand twice. Not once did a skeletal magazine writer pull up in a Corvette with dresses from Beverly Hills. The first time she went, cops hauled her there after an incident that they provoked. Desiree was seventeen when police used their fists, feet, and batons on her pregnant friend. She and some other girls intervened and tried to shield her. The cops beat everyone. The girl miscarried.

(Hippies really aren't the threat Didion makes them out to be.

It's people with badges who get away with murder.)

Before Manson became a cult leader, he did time in LA County with Danny Trejo. After getting sober, Trejo got into acting. He starred as Isador Cortez, aka Machete, in the *Machete* film series. Director Robert Rodriguez has said that when he met Trejo, he knew he had a Mexican Charles Bronson on his hands. Machete's fans are everywhere. My optometrist is one. He has an autographed *Machete* film still hanging behind the reception desk.

In his memoir, Trejo puts Manson in his place.

> Prison gang life eluded Charles Manson, and even if he could have fallen into it, he sure as shit wouldn't have been a leader. It was only after he got out that he was able to create the social structure he wanted by finding a bunch of lost hippies in Haight-Ashbury and making them into a "Family." If Manson had tried to pull his game in East LA, he'd never have been at the helm of shit.

Across Trejo's chest there is a massive tattoo of a sexy soldadera crowned with a sombrero. Its brim fills the span between Trejo's nipples. Because Trejo and his tattoo artist were repeatedly transferred to different prisons, it took Harry "Super Jew" Ross two and a half years to finish the masterpiece.

Trejo's soldier girl boasts big tits. Dark hair cascades down her shoulders, rivulets flowing along her rebozo. She proudly refuses to smile. She could kill you if she did.

Linda Kasabian could never.

Joan Didion named her only child, a blond girl she sometimes dressed in clothes to match her own, after one of southern Mexico's coastal states. This semitropical place is also one of the country's most popular tourist destinations.

Quintana Roo.

Ten years ago, I flew to Didion's daughter.

I didn't go to lie in a hammock.

I didn't go to fish desultorily.

I didn't go to be lazy.

I went for a writer's retreat.

I went to force myself to finish a novel.

I figured the retreat's location would do me some good. The novel was set in an unnamed fictional country that behaved a hell of a lot like Mexico.

A nurse in a white dress and cap was stationed at a shiny turnstile when I arrived at the Cancún airport. She held a clipboard and greeted passengers, asking each of us if we had the swine flu.

"Uh," I said. "I don't think so?"

"Welcome!"

English speakers eager to hop planes to Cuba bustled around me. They wore Hawaiian shirts and leis, advertising how shitty Americans are at geography. Outside, trucks laden with armed and uniformed soldiers patrolled the streets. A sleek van was there to collect my fellow writers and me and drive us to Akumal, dropping us off in a neighborhood that catered to summering gringos.

I should've been thrilled. I wasn't. My period had ruined another pair of good underwear and bloat was making me shy about putting on my green bikini, the only swimsuit I'd packed. I was away from my wife, whom I couldn't stand, but the thought of her waiting for me in California made it hard to enjoy the country between us.

I was miserable but embarrassed to admit it.

Embarrassment fortified my misery.

I was assigned to condominium ocho, where I shared a room with Sara and Thomas. Even more intimately, I shared a bed with Sara. I regaled her with stories that made my wife seem cool while Thomas brought me herbal tea to soothe my melancholy and cramps. I wasn't hurl-myself-from-the-balcony depressed (which would've been fine; we were two stories up and I would've landed in plush sand), but I was unable-to-enjoy-the-splendor-of-the-Caribbean blue. Beyond our sliding glass door, the sea twinkled, teasing us with her sequins, and I couldn't bring myself to honor her with a smile or hello. I couldn't even muster a wave. I could only offer sighs. The limpest of breezes.

We wrote, or stared at our computer screens, until noon. Meanwhile, staff toiled outside, raking the beach. I felt weird about this. I also felt weird about being the only writer of Mexican descent at the retreat. I wondered if the playwright, a queer dude whose family was from Colombia, was similarly weirded out. We'd sometimes lock eyes and exchange glances, telepathically acknowledging that we were the elephants in the room, the only Latines in the group.

We went on a few group outings that felt like school field trips, and at a chicozapote forest, our retreat hosts decided that we should tour a cenote. Squishing into a palapa, we put on plastic helmets and then trudged after a tour guide. This man looked like my dad's friend Mr. Gabaldon, a Chicano with a pet donkey that a mountain lion had eaten during the last drought.

We made our descent. Deep enough inside Mexico that it mattered, deep enough inside Mexico to create the illusion that we were on another planet, our tour guide illuminated pink stalagmites, coppery stalactites, and bountiful mounds of guano. He trained his flashlight on an obscene-looking mineral deposit and said, "We call this one Mick Jagger's tongue."

It did look like the Rolling Stones logo. The other deposits resembled breakfast foods. Bacon. Eggs. Pizza.

Back on the earth's surface, sunlight burned my eyes. I squinted and moved like a bat, echolocating myself to a refreshment stand. I bought a can of Didion's favorite soft drink, squatted, and sipped. An envious spider monkey scampered over. Reaching her opera-gloved hands through the wire fence, she hissed and grabbed me by the greñas. Baring her teeth, she tried to yank the Coca-Cola from my grip. My knuckles tensed and I defended my can, expelling simian fingers from my hair.

Despite the subterranean magnificence and monkey attack, my depression continued.

In my lesbian gloom, I reached for my go-to coping mechanism: extreme exercise. At the condo, I threw on shorts and a threadbare T-shirt and jogged into the heat, sweating all over thickets of salt-loving mangrove trees. I knew that it was probably a bad idea to do this, that a long run might dehydrate me, but what else was I supposed to do? Go wrestle a marlin?

I ran and ran and ran but slowed when I noticed movement in my peripheral vision. I thought for a second that a dog was trotting alongside me, but dogs aren't green. I turned and looked. The iguana raised his head slightly, winked, and scurried into the trees. He made me feel less lonely, and for that, I am grateful to the reptiles of Quintana Roo.

Didion pronounced the first part of her daughter's name gringishly, à la Anthony Quinn-tana, and she belonged to an elite club of parents who don't have to worry about what they name their kids. They can call their babies X Æ A-Xii, Pilot Inspektor, or Apple without fear that these expressions of "eccentricity" might mangle their offspring's future. What luxury to be able to unfurl a map, latch onto a foreign place-name, and then claim it as your daughter. That's how

Quintana Roo Dunne was named. The child was the living embodiment of Didion mining Mexico for language, and while Mexico is one of the most linguistically diverse countries on earth, the place's words were a mystery to Didion. For her, Mexico's sounds supplied ignorant amusement, a smorgasbord of "unique" baby names.

Many readers don't know that Mexican wood haunts "Los Angeles Notebook." To discern that wood, you have to know some Mexican history. You also have to know about weather.

My parents usually left the TV tuned to the news. Because of this, I kept abreast of LA's weather. I could recite Malibu's surf forecast, describe dolphin stampedes spotted off the coast of Catalina Island, and announce at what time Santa Monica was expected to become overcast. I knew the Santa Maria weather too, but it wasn't as exciting. All I had to do was stand outside to see it. With rare exception, it was predictable. We woke to whipped-cream fog that the sun quickly burned. Temperatures lingered in the low seventies. After lunch, light winds made the coyote bush shimmy. At sunset, temperatures dipped but stayed warm enough to keep strawberries happy.

The fog tiptoed back.

Every year, TV meteorologists with big hair warned about the Santa Anas. I sat on our rust-colored carpet, pondering their name. Were these winds Mexican? Were they Catholic? Did they sweep into mass to ruffle priests' vestments and upturn the collection box? Had someone baptized them, tossed holy water in their invisible direction? Were they named after Santa Ana, the city in Orange County, or were they named after the eighth president of Mexico, General Antonio López de Santa Anna? Maybe they were named after the Mexican who played guitar on "Black Magic Woman." No one seemed to know.

A 1958 edition of *Western Folklore* proves that Californians have been asking about this weather for decades.

> Soon the summer whirlwinds will come, and with them the annual discussions about their name. Are they Santa Anas, after the city in Orange County? Or Santanas? Or, as we used to call them as youngsters here, Santyanas? Anna de Zborowska contends they were named after Gen. Antonio Lopez de Santa Anna, who trapped Davy Crockett in the Alamo. When his army was on the move it was visible from far away by the clouds of dust it raised. In later years when dry winds created dust clouds in the distance, Mexicans would say, "Por Dios! It looks as if Santa Anna were coming."

I've heard Mexicans say camarón que se duerme se lo lleva el corriente.*

I've heard Mexicans say los niños y los borrachos siempre dicen la verdad.†

I've heard Mexicans say este arróz ya se coció.‡

I've never heard Mexicans say that stuff about the wind.

Because I was educated in California, I'm used to teachers calling President Santa Anna a villain. In the index of my high school history textbook, he's listed as "Santa Anna (Mexican dictator)." He makes his first appearance on page 258, in a section titled "The Lone Star of Texas Flickers."

> The pioneer individualists who came to Texas were not easy to push around. Friction rapidly increased between Mexicans and Texans over such issues as slavery, immigration, and local rights . . . When Stephen Austin went to Mexico City in 1833 to negotiate those differences with the Mexican government, dictator Santa Anna clapped him in jail for eight months. The

---

* The shrimp who falls asleep is swept away by the tide (common saying).

† Children and drunks always tell the truth (common saying).

‡ This rice is now cooked (common saying).

explosion finally came in 1835, when Santa Anna wiped out all local rights and started to raise an army to suppress upstart Texans.

A black-and-white lithograph on page 259 portrays the Battle of the Alamo.

Ever since watching the movie *Pee-wee's Big Adventure,* I can't take anything having to do with the Alamo seriously. This is how *The American Pageant* describes what happened there:

> Early in 1836 the Texans declared their independence and unfurled their Lone Star Flag—with Sam Houston as commander in chief. Santa Anna, at the head of about six thousand men, swept ferociously into Texas. Trapping a band of nearly two hundred pugnacious Texans at the Alamo in San Antonio, he wiped them out to a man after a thirteen-day siege. Their commander, Colonel W. B. Travis, had heroically declared, "I shall never surrender nor retreat . . . Victory or Death." The victims included Jim Bowie, who was shot as he lay sick and crippled on his cot, and Davy Crockett, whose body was found riddled with bullets and surrounded by enemy corpses . . .

My dad and one of his cousins visited the Alamo in the seventies. They followed a docent who led a group tour. When she called Crockett and Bowie "American martyrs," the cousins began to giggle.

"Sir!" said the docent. "Sir! You and your friend are gonna have to leave! The Alamo is a sacred place. There is no laughing at the Alamo."

The cousins left, their bell-bottoms swishing.

(The singer Ozzy Osbourne also got kicked out of the Alamo. That was a little different.

He peed on it.)

Mexicans killed Crockett, but US soldiers stole Santa Anna's wooden leg. The general lost the original limb in 1838 when grapeshot fired by a French cannon shredded it. Believing that he was going to perish, Santa Anna issued a dying request: "May all Mexicans, forgetting my political mistakes, not deny me the only title which I wish to leave my children, that of a good Mexican." Santa Anna survived. His leg did not. A state funeral was staged for the mangled limb. Santa Anna resumed his military career wearing a cork-and-wood prosthesis fitted with a black dress boot. He fought in what Mexican history books call la Guerra de Estados Unidos contra México* but fled the Battle of Cerro Gordo on horseback. While retreating, Santa Anna abandoned his dinner and a sack of cash. He also left his wooden leg. US infantry ate his dinner and captured his limb, taking the trophy to Illinois. A museum holds it captive.

In 2016, a group of students rode a bus from Texas to Springfield. One of the kids, eighteen-year-old Andre Grajeda, told reporters that his mission was to take back the general's leg. When the students asked the curator Bill Lear to surrender the trophy, explaining that it belonged to Mexico, Lear said no. He told them why the leg had to stay in Springfield.

> . . . the leg isn't so much the story. It's the story of Illinois soldiers and the battle. What it is, is a vehicle for a conversation so that we can educate. You guys have probably learned more about Illinois history because of this leg than you would have if we didn't have it.

I have a feeling that had my dad been present during Lear's lecture, he would've been told, "There's no laughing in Springfield!" I also imagine a museum guard taking Dad's glasses as a war trophy, a teaching tool that would enable Illinois docents to illustrate the ongoing threat posed by Mexican nerds.

Didion writes that we know when Santa Anas are coming "because we feel it." I know Mexicans are in "Los Angeles Notebook"

---

* The War of the United States against Mexico.

because I feel us. Somos Los Angeles. Somos el viento. Somos California. Somos playas y palmeras. Somos piernas invisibles.

In a "Los Angeles Notebook" anecdote, Didion nods at Mexican existence. It's a smoggy and scorching afternoon. Yet again, the weather prevents her from getting dressed. She heads to Ralph's Market wearing "an old bikini bathing suit." A "large woman in a cotton muumuu" who disapproves of Didion's outfit chases her. The hunt follows the format and rhythm of a joke: "She follows me all over the store, to the Junior Foods [SET . . .], to the Dairy Products [UP . . .], to the Mexican Delicacies [PUNCHLINE] . . ."

This instance is the only time that the word *Mexican* appears in this iconic essay. Given how primitive Didion finds Mexico, and Mexicans, it seems that the comedic pleasure she takes is oxymoronic.

How can anything Mexican be a delicacy?

Kids raised in California inherit a macabre history.

Some adults take pleasure in recounting this past, in sharing with children the grim lore of the Donner party, those pioneers who wandered westward, ran out of food, froze, and ate each other. Since I developed a taste for the morbid during childhood, the Donner party's demise titillated me. It was an antidote to the triumphant settler narratives fed to me by TV, politicians, and teachers. Textbooks also imposed these tales. One of these was *A Child's History of California.*

I found the thin, orange volume sitting on a metal shelf at the Salvation Army thrift store. A logo combining a pickax, shovel, rope, and sack of gold nuggets was on the cover. Grabbing the coarse hardback, I opened it to see if it was an antique.

It was.

The California Department of Education published the book two years before Dad was born.

Curious about what Enola Flower, the author of *A Child's History of California,* had to say about my home, I handed some nickels to the cashier and carried the book outside with me. I dumped it into my bike basket and pedaled home.

That night, as I lay in my bunk bed reading "Chapter 17: The Americans Come in Covered Wagons," I could almost hear my dad and grandfather yelling, challenging every word.

> Many Americans began to come to California. They came to make their homes here. They had heard about the pleasant and sunny climate, about the many animals, about the miles and miles of land that would be so fine for farming.
>
> Many families traveled westward. They traveled over plains and mountains and deserts. They had to cross many rivers and climb many high mountains. They had to travel through the Indian country and the land of the buffalo.
>
> There were no roads. There were not even trails in most places. The only men who could show them the way were the fur trappers. It was a long and dangerous journey. Many times, they had to go without water. Often, they had little food. Sometimes, they were attacked by the Indians and killed.
>
> These brave people were called emigrants. Emigrants are those people who leave their old homes and make new homes in another land.

It was true that the settlers had left their homes. Flower left out the part that they were barging into someone's else. Anglos weren't the only ones who took people's homes. Spaniards and Mexicans did it too. They all usurped Indigenous lands.

Among the thieves who washed up on American shores were some of my Spanish ancestors, and when I use the word *American,* I don't just mean the United States.

I mean the Americas.

All of it.

I spent a fair amount of my childhood wondering what California's nineteenth-century settlers tasted like. I wondered how the

Donner party had prepared one another to be eaten. I wondered if I had the wherewithal to eat my family. I figured I did. I was a fingernail chewer and an occasional swallower.

Didion makes a big deal about what happened in the Sierra Nevadas, but it's not like California was the first place where white people ate each other. When I studied history at the University of California, Berkeley, the same place Didion studied literature, I read about people eating people in Europe. The Benedictine monk Raoul Glaber documented entrepreneurial cannibalism. In response to a famine, a butcher's stall at a Burgundian fair sold precooked people. In my head, the scene looks like a southland Renaissance fair. Instead of turkey legs, sunburned serfs chew a human femur.

A Child's History of California dedicates an entire chapter to the Donner party. They came from the place that won't let go of Santa Anna's leg.

> In the spring of 1846, a party of people left their homes in Illinois to go to California. They wanted some of the good farming land they had heard about . . . For the first few months all went well . . . Some of the parties decided to take [a shortcut] . . . It was a great mistake for them to take this cutoff. . . Soon, the Donner Party was caught in the snow. . . . The air grew colder. The chill winter winds began to blow . . . They came to a lake where there was one rough cabin . . . They knew they would have to spend the winter here in the cold, deep snow . . . They ate whatever they could find. They chewed on hides. They even boiled the hides and tried to eat the thick glue they made. They ate bark and pine twigs. But this was not real food . . . Only forty-eight of them lived to reach the Sacramento Valley.

"The tale of the Donner party," writes Michiko Kakutani, "haunts Didion."

Didion's great-great-great-grandmother Nancy Hardin Cornwall traveled west with the party, but she and her fellow travelers split before the settlers established what came to be known as the Camp of Death. Didion celebrates Cornwall's courage, glorifying her as a Daughter of the American Revolution "who never seem[ed] afraid of Indians or [shrank] from hardships."

As I have stated repeatedly and will state again, there was nothing pioneering about the pioneers. California was Indigenous land when the Spanish invaded it. They held power from 1781 to 1821. After New Spain became the United Mexican States, California experienced Mexican occupation. That lasted from 1821 to 1848. Settlers had been here for at least sixty-seven years before Didion's ancestors reared their heads into the Sacramento Valley.

Governor Pico loathed their arrival.

> We find ourselves threatened by hordes of Yankee immigrants who have already begun to flock into our country and whose progress we cannot arrest. Already have wagons of that perfidious people scaled the most inaccessible summits of the Sierra Nevada, crossed the entire continent and penetrated the fruitful valley of Sacramento.

In 2003, Didion published *Where I Was From*, a nonfiction book that timidly explores her confusions about California. At its most promising, she teases us with her ignorance, admitting that she might misunderstand "America" as much as she does California. Unfortunately, she retreats into cowardice, writing that these "misapprehensions and misunderstandings [are] so much a part of who I became that I can still to this day confront them only obliquely."

Like Enola Flower, Didion conflates the word *emigrant* with *settler*. She inventories the "recent graves, wrecked wagons," and "human as well as animal bones" at Donner Lake. She hints at the shadow of "moral ambiguity" falling across the pioneer quest but stops short of diving into this abyss, probing what was so very wrong about a venture that sparked genocide. Didion wallows in the "hardships" that her ancestors took it upon themselves to endure. She says little about the hardships they inflicted.

Didion inherited her great-great-great-grandmother's cornbread recipe along with her "wagon-trail morality." She meditates on the latter in the essay "On Morality."

> . . . my own childhood was illuminated by graphic litanies of the grief awaiting those who failed in their loyalties to each other. The Donner-Reed Party, starving in the Sierra snows, all the ephemera of civilization gone save that one vestigial taboo, the provision that no one should eat his own blood kin.

I inherited my great-grandmother's chile relleno recipe, but I can't tell you much about any of my great-great-great-grandmothers. About my great-great-great-grandmother Micaela Carrion, I can recite a handful of things. I know that she wasn't a settler or an emigrant. She was native. She died in Sayula, Mexico, around the time that the revolution ended.

These are the facts of her death as recorded by a civil servant.

> On June 22nd, 1918, at nine o'clock in the morning, there appeared before me, Arturo Galvez, Municipal President in charge of the Civil Registry of Sayula, a thirty-eight-year-old shawl maker, Rosalio Quintero Jicasado. He said that at five o'clock in the morning, in a house at 42 Cuauhtémoc Street, a widow and indigenous woman, Micaela Carrion, died of senility at age 100. This Mexican was the daughter of Julian Carrion and Petra Casillas. Her cadaver will be buried today at the municipal cemetery.

I hope to someday visit the place where my great-great-great-grandmother is buried. I know it only through books. Literary historians say that Sayula inspired the setting of a novel, *Pedro Páramo*.

Its author, Juan Rulfo, turned it into a ghost town, changing its name to Comala.

> Rain is falling on the fields of the valley of Comala. A fine rain, rare in these lands that know only downpours. It is Sunday. The Indians have come down from Apango with their rosaries and chamomile, their rosemary, their bunches of thyme. They have come without ocote pine, because the wood is wet, and without oak mulch, because it, too, is wet from the long rain. They spread their herbs on the ground beneath the arches of the arcade. And wait.

The account written by Donner party survivor Eliza Poor Donner Houghton states that "eighty-one souls" attempted to reach California. After listing every pioneer's first and last name, she concludes with "Antonio (a Mexican) and Lewis and Salvador (the two Indians . . .)."

Lewis and Salvador were Miwoks who knew not to trust the party. They fled, but the settlers found and shot them, making them the only human beings intentionally hunted and cannibalized. After the settlers watched Antonio freeze to death, they ate him too. Didion's meditation on wagon-trail morality never names Lewis, Salvador, or Antonio, but their presence pervades the wagon-trail meditation. The settlers Didion commemorates carried this human trinity in their bodies. White intestines became the three men's graves.

These days, I find what Didion doesn't show more interesting than what she tells. Literary criticism, along with history, hands me a scalpel, enabling me to slice open the stomachs of those subjects made visible by her prose. I can poke at the exposed contents, smell them, learn from them, and give them a proper burial. Can we make etching their tombstones a collective effort?

A few summers ago, I went to a party in Los Feliz. After taking a seat on a backyard chaise lounge, I unsuccessfully tried not to gawk at my hostess's house. A fellow partygoer noticed my struggle.

She leaned toward me and whispered, "It's beautiful. I think it's a Frank Lloyd Wright."

I nodded.

I was also struggling not to gawk at breasts. They jiggled and hung everywhere. The backyard was Lesbos. Topless women lounged poolside. Others congregated in shallow water. A few floated alone, arms outstretched, eyes closed. A muscular lady in a bikini bobbed in an inflatable plastic doughnut covered in icing and sprinkles.

Lynn Harris Ballen, a widow, invited me to this party. I'll let her spouse, Jeanne Córdova, introduce her. Jeanne continues to speak through the books she left us. In *When We Were Outlaws*, her memoir, Jeanne explains that Lynn is the South African daughter of the freedom fighter Frederick John Harris.

"The fact of her paternity," writes Jeanne, "drove me to investigate her further and in the process, I married her."

Jeanne, whose parents named her after the French tomboy saint, was born to an Irish mom, Joan, and a Mexican dad, Federico. Jeanne's role in her big Catholic family helped her land one of her first jobs. She'd noticed an ad pinned to a UCLA bulletin board. A couple was seeking someone to watch their kid. When she applied, Jeanne convinced the couple that she was their best bet. How could she not be? She'd helped raise ten siblings.

Jeanne worked at the couple's house, and at first, the arrangement puzzled her. She babysat their toddler while the couple stayed home. Jeanne soon realized that both the wife and husband worked, each in their own book-lined office outfitted with typewriters. The couple behaved the way writers often do in one another's presence, ignoring each other's existence, passing the other in the hallway without acknowledgment, eyes distant, faces haunted, minds preoccupied with language.

The couple was the Didions. (That's how I think of Joan and her husband. Everybody knows that she's bigger than him.)

The toddler Jeanne babysat was Quintana.

Working for the Didions gave Jeanne a peek at the writers' life and this exposure revved up her ambitions. She became an activist, organizer, editor, publisher, journalist, and memoirist. I'm able to proclaim that I'm a free queer Chicana because of Jeanne's labor. Jeanne's labor also made it so that Didion could create her canonical vision of California.

Cancer had taken Jeanne by the time I dog-paddled in Lesbos.

She left us in 2016.

Didion inherited a wagon-trail morality from her ancestors. From mine, I inherited a different kind of morality, one that drives me to write for Lewis, Salvador, Antonio, and Jeanne. In this moment, California belongs to them. This sentence is their title, their deed.

NAVAJAZO

I welcome the veneration of Lorena Leonor Gallo, a female folk hero perhaps destined to become the most powerful type of intercessor, a folk saint. Her spirit is needed. Battered wives already have a patroness and protector, Rita of Cascia, Saint of the Impossible. When Rita was twelve years old, she married Paolo, an aristocrat. He tortured her for six years.

As Paolo crept home one evening, an assassin with a blade stepped out of the fourteenth-century shadows. He turned Rita into a widow. Now free, she left the secular world, joining a community of Augustinian nuns that practiced self-mortification. It might seem counterintuitive that Rita went from suffering her husband's indignities to smacking herself around, but in the aftermath of a man like Paolo, self-harm can prove medicinal. It reacquaints oneself with oneself. It is ritualized self-ownership.

The symbols associated with Rita sound like accessories I might've paired with a tattered black dress when I was seventeen.

A flagellum.

An oozing forehead wound.

Roses.

A swarm of white bees.

Thorns.

Pope Leo XIII canonized Rita in 1900, and on May 22, her feast day, those seeking Rita's protection may ply her with honey, hair shirts, and chains. Rita shields and comforts battered wives, but I think we need a sword, a patron saint of fighting back, to complement her. For that position, I nominate Lorena.

The numbers associated with her are seven and eleven.

The symbol associated with her is a red-handled knife.

When I contemplate Lorena's famed weapon, I hear a metronome with a razor-sharp pendulum.

It slashes the past and perforates the present.

Señorita del navajazo,

Se vuelve ella misma la navaja . . .*

Like my mother, Lorena was born south of a fiction, the Mexico–United States border. Both immigrants would eventually live as wives on this side of that cut. As Lorena approached fifteen, her parents gave her two choices. She could enjoy a quinceañera or travel to the East Coast to visit her cousins. She picked Virginia and was dazzled by the Washington, DC, suburb she toured. It was "another planet, another place."

Lorena was born in Ecuador in 1969. When she was five, she and her family moved to Venezuela. Her father worked as a dental technician in Caracas. Her mother mothered. The middle-class family, which included two more kids, numbered the same as mine: five. Lorena preferred Virginia to Venezuela, and after a student visa was approved, she enrolled at a community college near a Civil War battlefield. Despite her homesickness, life mostly seemed "pink and beautiful." Lorena dreamt of cavities and Novocain and fantasized about outdoing her dad.

She wanted to become a dentist.

When I saw Lorena on TV, I was struck by her resemblance to my mother. At five foot two, Lorena towered three inches taller than her. Both women had black hair; high, well-shaped cheekbones; and dark, melancholic eyes. Their jaws swooped sharply, thin lips arching with a pronounced cupid's bow. They painted their mouths in statement-making lipstick, and when Lorena's lips moved, another

---

* Young lady of the slash / She herself becomes the knife.

similarity registered. What her voice box, tongue, and teeth did to English, my mother's voice box, tongue, and teeth also did to English. The immigrants polished our lingua franca's coarseness, turning it, at last, melodic.

The public couldn't get enough of Lorena. Neither could I.

I sniffed at the air when broadcasters spoke her name. Lorena was aromatic, the tree at its root evoking camphor and lavender bergamot. Laurel leaves represent victory, the laureate, and because one of the prettiest girls at my bilingual elementary school had been a Lorena, I associated the name with beauty even before I learned about the petite wife with the kitchen knife. My childhood Lorena was Mexican. She wore her black hair in braids blended with brightly colored yarn. These were folded in half and held in place by bows. When Lorena reached for glue-encrusted bottles, construction paper, cotton balls, or left-handed scissors, the bows above her ears danced.

Mexican Lorena's trenzas reminded me of Princess Leia, a lady I enjoyed looking at. My hair lacked nobility. No one braided it. Instead, my father hastily gathered it in pigtails, securing one on each side of my head with a rubber band. He took my leftover hair and gave me a third ponytail on top. At school, teachers and teacher's aides took pity. They undid the mess, grooming me so that I looked less like my father's daughter.

In 1988, Lorena attended a Marine Corps officer's ball held at a club for enlisted men near the Quantico, Virginia, Marine Corps Base. A twenty-one-year-old Marine spotted the Latina wallflower. The interested soldier shared a name with a Hollywood cowboy, an Iowa-born actor who collected not one but three Latina wives. John Wayne Bobbitt was drawn to Lorena's shyness. He approached her, dabbling in small talk. Though he thought she could "barely speak English," John offered her his number anyway. They dated. John was smitten with the South American girl's "cute accent." When he learned that her visa was set to expire, he proposed marriage.

"Blue eyes," Lorena later mused. "A man in uniform, you know? He was almost like a symbol—a Marine, fighting for the country. I believed in this beautiful country. I was swept off my feet. I wanted my American Dream."

In the summer of 1989, a justice of the peace in Stafford County married Lorena and John. The couple moved into a small studio apartment. To celebrate their first month as newlyweds, John took Lorena to dinner. He got drunk. The meal turned sour. During the ride home, John swerved and swerved, terrifying Lorena. He drove like a man with a death wish.

She grabbed the steering wheel.

He punched her chest.

Her punishment continued at home. John rushed after her and grabbed her by the hair. After slapping Lorena, he kicked her into a wall.

John spent money they didn't have on a satellite dish, a computer, and two cars. The couple bought a house but fell behind on the mortgage payments. The bank foreclosed. John and Lorena moved back into an apartment.

After John was kicked out of the Marines, his hands crept into Lorena's purse, stealing the money she earned as a manicurist and nanny. While she worked ten-hour days six days a week, John blew through nineteen jobs and barhopped. He used military techniques to discipline Lorena. She was tired, bruised, and scared. Despite being Catholic, she felt she could confess her private pain to no one.

While Lorena struggled to survive John, my classmates and I endured Orcutt Junior High School. Every night, I prayed that someone would burn the place down. It was in a different district than where I'd gone to school with my first Lorena, and the welcome wagon consisted of kids pestering me about where I was from. I knew that they weren't asking what elementary school. They were asking what body of water I'd had to cross to come to "America."

When I told a boy that my mom came from Mexico, he snapped, "Uh-uh! No, she didn't!"

Another said, "You look like those girls that do this on top of the radio." It pained me to watch him gyrate his stiff hips. I worried he might break them while doing his imitation of a dashboard hula girl.

My classmates' expertise about my ancestry was confounding.

The grown-ups were even more arrogant.

In history class, I sat scanning the pages of my textbook. The chapter on "westward expansion" contradicted what I'd learned at home. The journalist John L. O'Sullivan, Manifest Destiny's foremost propagandist, described the US as an Anglo-Saxon project. He called Mexico an "imbecile and distracted" country.

I flipped the page by slapping it. Hard.

My teacher looked up at me from her desk. She glared.

I frowned. I came from people who O'Sullivan thought couldn't be trusted to govern a pot of beans. The US *had* to occupy California to save us from our own stupidity. Wanting to "overspread the continent allotted by Providence," Anglo settlers invaded the west. It was their descendants who made us pledge allegiance to a polyester rectangle and run a mile every Friday.

In pen, I scribbled an essay critical of O'Sullivan's manifesto. It was returned to me with a question manifesting across the top.

What's wrong with wanting land?!!!

I got a B.

In art class, I watched my teacher, Mr. White, sketch a man chasing a buffalo. He often incorporated Indigenous people and motifs into the drawings he made while he should've been teaching. He could always be found at his desk, putting the finishing touches on another feathered headdress. Lessons about Indigenous people were rare at school, but TV had taught me that many of Mr. White's figures were Plains Indians stereotypes. He seemed uninterested in the Chumash. Our school festered on their land.

I asked, "Why do you draw Native Americans and Native American things so much?"

Mr. White said, "I admire them. This is how I honor them."

"I think the best way that we can honor people we've stolen stuff from is to give it back."

His cheeks flushed.

"What do you mean?"

"I mean return the land."

"What land?"

"America!"

Mr. White looked like he'd been hit in the head. "And leave our homes?"

I half joked, "I'm pretty sure there's a little room left in Europe."

"That's stupid! This is my home! You can't just make people . . . move!" I recalled Andrew Jackson forcibly relocating the people my teacher admired so much. Then he asked me my least favorite question. "What are you?"

"My family is Mexican. Mexico got made like how the US got made. A bunch of Europeans showed up and took what wasn't theirs."

Mr. White smirked. He seemed to take libidinal pleasure in saying, "The Aztecs and Spanish were savages. They got what they deserved. They were made for each other."

Returning to his buffalo, my teacher gave me the silent treatment.

I rode the school bus home with a shy, racially ambiguous girl who sat alone. On their way to the back of the bus, a group of white boys made a habit of lunging at her. Because no one stopped them, the ugliest boy took to coughing the word *cunt* at her. A beady-eyed boy spat in her hair. After that she sat at the front of the bus, directly behind the bus driver.

No one spat on me, but kids did call me a slut. Lots of girls got called sluts. Being called one had nothing to do with sexual wisdom. I, for example, was a slut who had yet to stare down a penis. Sluts were given our title in one of two ways. Girls who rebelled against popular mores or swung from the bottom rungs of the social hierarchy got dumped into the slut bin. It was assumed that boys could touch sluts and that we'd be unbothered by our molestation. We seemed to exist for degradation.

To get from class to class, sluts ran a gauntlet of boys. I darted along dirt paths while they stalked, reaching up my skirt, touching me wherever they wanted. Replacing skirts with shorts didn't help. Boys continued to creep after me, their hands squeezing and smacking, Tater Tot fingers primed to penetrate.

Adults saw. They did nothing. I lost faith in grown-ups. I developed faith in sluts.

In art class, one rapist-in-training watched me doodle a rose. He asked, "Did your mom work in tia wanna?"

I'd been to Tijuana before. My uncle with the big sideburns worked for one of the city's newspapers.

"No. My mom worked in Guadalajara. For an agency that managed water. Recursos Hidráulicos."

"You sure about that?"

"Yeah. Why?"

"Because I hear Mexican women fuck donkeys in tia wanna. I bet you could work the donkey shows. I bet your mom worked the donkey shows."

As I considered the logistics of his suggestion, the boy reached to grope my flat chest. I recoiled.

That night, I stood beside Mom at the sink. She washed. I dried. Curious about my classmate's question, I asked, "Is it true that Mexican women have sex with donkeys onstage in Tijuana?"

Her wet slap stung.

Thirteen-year-olds need folk heroes too, and the heavens blessed the sluts of Orcutt Junior High School with one of our own.

Our Lorena was the most cholafied girl on campus. She ratted her brown hair into a scraggly sunflower that framed her enraged baby face. She dressed in black and wore her pants sausage-casing tight.

Lorena's walk was the best. She moved pussy first, and I imagined her clit as a bloodhound's nose sniffing out trouble. Fairy-tale figures wear capes, and Lorena did too. She swaddled herself in a Raiders Starter jacket regardless of season.

I rode the bus with Lorena's nemesis, Sandra. Gossips shared rumors about the origin of their feud. Lorena had a crush on Sandra's boyfriend, Jeremy. Sandra found the attraction laughable. She told people that Jeremy would never be interested in someone as trash as Lorena.

It's dangerous to call cholas names.

It's especially dangerous to call cholas trash. Try it if you want to wind up in a landfill.

On a foggy morning, I sat in homeroom, waiting for the bell to ring. A fellow slut turned to me and said, "Did you hear about what's gonna happen to Sandra?"

"No! What's gonna happen to Sandra?"

Excitedly, she explained that Lorena was going to redeem herself by doing what Delilah had done to Samson. She would vandalize the seat of Sandra's power. Sandra was known for her big hair, especially the tall claw that towered above her forehead.

Lorena was going to chop it off.

We found Lorena's plan thrilling. Sluts prayed for her all morning. Once the sunshine burned the haze, the spring day took on a yuletide quality. It might as well have been Christmas.

Sluts understood that we figured into Lorena's plan. We were tasked with keeping it top secret, and in so doing, we became co-conspirators. We were fighting back against those who'd laughed at us from the top. Sandra's crowning glory would become a trophy.

We would have to wait until lunch to witness her undoing.

Focusing on classwork was impossible. My imagination was going bonkers with visions of violent mulletings. I wondered if Lorena would "accidentally" stab her enemy, fillet the snob. Time flew. The lunch bell rang. I sprinted out of algebra, rushing toward sluts.

Forming a mob, we hurried to the gym. Jeremy was there, bouncing a basketball across the court. Sandra sat in the bleachers, cheering for him, a non-slut entourage surrounding her. They wore denim vests paired with matching denim shorts, narrow noses up in the air. Their cluelessness was exciting.

Lorena entered the gym. Sluts gasped. She and her entourage walked the periphery of the court and climbed the bleachers, sitting a few yards above Sandra. Sandra looked over her shoulder. She looked at Brooke, her best friend. The two exchanged "I smell dog shit" glances. They returned their attention to the game.

A line creased Lorena's forehead. She knew she'd drawn an audience. To tease us, she smiled. Lorena opened her jacket and reached inside. She pulled out her weapon. It caught the noon sunlight streaming through the window behind her.

Scissors.

Big ones, the kind Mom cut fabric with.

Wow.

Señorita del navajazo,

Se vuelve ella misma la navaja.

Lorena slid the blades back into their hiding place but soon revealed them again. She did this repeatedly, whetting our appetites.

Sandra stood. So did Brooke. The friends walked to the nearby restroom.

Lorena stood.

This was it.

Chop time.

Lorena and her entourage followed Brooke's footsteps.

We held our breath.

I was too anxious to move. I was on the verge of peeing myself. I squeezed my thighs together.

Lorena darted out of the restroom with fugitive energy. Her forehead was creased with more lines. As always, her crotch propelled her, moving her to the gym exit.

Brooke scrambled out of the restroom and sprinted to a teacher wearing a striped referee shirt. She spoke with her mouth and hands and legs, pointing, flailing, fretting. The ref shoved his whistle between his lips and blew and the two of them scrambled to the restroom together. We cackled. A decapitation must've taken place for a male teacher to brave a room where he might encounter tampons.

Lorena's flight from the gym was the last time we saw her.

She disappeared after becoming Delilah. I think she got expelled for aiming scissors at her enemy's frontal lobe, but we didn't forget our hero. Her story continues to be repeated and I hope that the sluts of Orcutt Junior High School keep singing the ballad of Lorena the barber, the bang bandit.

My parents disapproved of my newfound enthusiasm for sluts. To ensure I'd cut ties with the several I'd bonded with in junior high, they sent me to the northernmost Catholic high school in the Archdiocese of Los Angeles, established by the Daughters of Mary and Joseph. Our faculty had one instructor who, like the institute's founders, hailed from Belgium.

Sœur J was a jelly bean of a nun with a gray, frizzy halo. She smelled of tobacco and clove, and she shared a tract home and Chevy Citation with Sister Angela, a nun who had a crush on Robert Redford and taught English. Sœur J and Sister Angela led consecrated yet modern lives. Instead of habits, they wore knee-length dresses, cardigans, pantyhose, and flats. On weekends, they went to the mall and could be seen eating frozen yogurt by the escalator. Offset by Sœur J's lace collar shone a Chai amulet, to acknowledge that she'd been born to Jewish parents.

Following Sœur J's birth, her mother had loaded her children onto a train. Their father had already left Poland and they reunited with him, settling in a working-class Orthodox neighborhood in Antwerp. He and Sœur J's brothers worked cutting and polishing diamonds. Sœur J went to school until anti-Semitism interrupted her education.

In 1940, Germany invaded Belgium, bringing it under the rule of the Wehrmacht, the Nazi military. A letter arrived at Sœur J's home. It gave orders summoning her to Malines. Her parents prepared to comply, and this terrified Sœur J. Malines was a concentration camp halfway between Antwerp and Brussels. Trains departing from it were bound for death camps. Instead of waiting for her parents to obey the orders, Sœur J ran away with four other Jewish kids. They trekked to Switzerland, sometimes sleeping in barns, sometimes sleeping beneath the North Star. At the Swiss border, officials told the runaways to go home. Seeing no other option, they turned around. They boarded a train.

Having heard rumors about what the Germans would do to them, the runaways discussed doing it themselves. One suggested that they stand in front of a train. Sœur J didn't like that option. She said she'd prefer to be gassed to death, to drift into an eternal slumber. A woman overheard their conversation and told the desperate group to follow her off the train. They trailed after the eavesdropper; eventually, she handed them each a slip of paper with a name and address on it.

The note led Sœur J to a Catholic dentist in Jodoigne. He took her to his mother's home, and she hid there, moved by her protector's generosity. On the Feast of the Transfiguration, the holiday honoring the time that Jesus took some friends to a mountaintop to show them that he could glow, Sœur J became a Catholic.

This history astonished me, especially when I watched Sœur J limp across campus, past open lockers, football players with paint smeared under their eyes, and assholes chucking microwaved burritos into the air. Someone would apologize for nearly elbowing or stepping on her, and I'd think, "She survived the Holocaust for . . . this?" When kids talked over her in class and played pranks, I thought the same thing. The divine had spared this woman, and now she oversaw a whitewashed classroom with a crucifix hanging next to a blackboard. She survived genocide to spend her days organizing canned food drives, drilling teenagers in French vocabulary, and demanding that we conjugate verbs.

When she lost her temper with us, she would accuse us of being clowns and threaten to change the seating chart.

She never did.

I wrote and drew in a notebook that I carried from class to class. I committed French verbs and romantic sentiments to its lined paper. I'd fallen for one of my classmates, une fille masculine, and my desire was torture. I was in love and lust with a large-breasted girl and terrified to say so. Less frightening was expressing myself through poetry. I composed ambiguous verse, odes free of gendered pronouns, and I drew lips, eyes, and long, long knives. The classmate that I loved loved knives. She collected them. My vocabulary had recently expanded to include the words *bull dyke* and *bull dagger*, and while I wasn't sure why lesbians got called these things, I thought that my secret crush was probably a bull dagger, that her attraction to sharp things qualified her as such.

Señorita del navajazo,
Se vuelve ella misma la navaja

The public library taught me that there were bull daggers all over the planet. I spent time researching forbidden things there but worried my parents might be tipped off about my interests if I were to receive a library fine. I couldn't be trusted to return books on time, and notices appeared in our mailbox. To keep my queer studies clandestine, I used a weapon that came with my mother's accidental blessing.

Mom and I were in the kitchen, preparing dinner. I stood at the stove, using a wooden spoon to stir rice in a pan. The scent of warm corn oil made me smile. After opening a can of tomato paste, Mom reached for a knife to bend the lid back. Still attached, the metallic circle looked bloody. Wistfully, Mom said, "When I was your age, I carried a knife."

The revelation of Mom as one of these children who come at you with knives was eyebrow-raising.

"Really? What kind?"

"A small one."

"Did your mother know?"

"My mother told me to."

I was intrigued. I could hardly believe that my grandmother had ordered my mother to arm herself.

"For what?! Why did you carry a knife?"

"The same reason most girls carry one. For protection."

"Who did you need protection from?"

"People. A stranger tried taking me once."

"When?"

"When I was a little girl. We lived downtown. I was playing in a courtyard. I felt somebody pick me up and put a hand over my mouth. I kicked him and bit him and he let go and dropped me and my mother came to see what happened. He ran away."

"What happened to him?"

"Who knows. He tasted like kerosene."

"Can I carry a knife?"

"Yes."

I handed the wooden spoon to Mom and jumped to the silverware drawer. I chose a not-very-sharp steak knife as my weapon and kept it in my lunchbox. In the nineties, using lunchboxes as purses was a standard practice.

At the library, I wandered the stacks and pulled books off shelves. In defiance of the sign prohibiting books in the bathroom, I shoved books into my backpack and smuggled them into a stall. Seated on a toilet, I waited until I was alone and then brought out my knife. I plunged it into Henry Miller's *Crazy Cock*, savaging it, excising the hidden tag that would trigger the alarm. Miller's novels were banned in our house, but I kept a stolen stash of them, along with a book of lesbian photography, under my bed.

Crazy Cock, originally titled *Lovely Lesbians*, featured a namesake character, the dyke puppeteer Miriam (butch name Vanya). By bedroom candlelight, I read the thinly veiled account of a real-life love triangle.

A scene was precipitated during which the word *slut* was bandied back and forth. He listened to them in amazement. Hildred calling her dear sick genius, her princess, a slut! Finally, Vanya retreated to her room, slammed the door in Hildred's face, and locked herself in. After a time, they heard her sobbing.

"For God's sake, go in there and quiet her," said Tony Bring. "I can't stand that noise . . . you'd think she was having her throat cut."

But Hildred wouldn't move. There were some things, she let it be known, that were unforgiveable.

Finally, a novelist who recognized the ingenuity of sluts, that we are people who contribute to the culture! We produce drama! We produce poetry! We drive people mad! We make marionettes! I wanted to be like Miller's sluts. I wanted to make art and taste heroin and turpentine and women. Inspired by *Crazy Cock*, I wooed my Catholic bull dagger with verse. We exchanged love letters by the chapel, and she invited me to her house for a sleepover. We sat in her bedroom, talking after midnight. To impress her, I confessed that I was a book thief and that I'd stolen an art book filled with photographs taken by lesbians.

My classmate leaned back, smiled, and reached under her bed. I was excited. What was she going to pull out? A gun? A dildo? A bag of Cheetos?

She brought out a velvet pouch and loosened the drawstring. She unsheathed a dagger. I thought of Rembrandt's *Lucretia*, a baroque portrait of suicide. Following the Roman girl's rape by Tarquin, the youngest son of Rome's final king, Lucretia had penetrated herself into the afterlife.

"Can I touch it?"

She handed me her dagger. I held it to my mouth and exhaled, watching my breath fog the silver.

I was in a rapturous state, tortured by a love whose name I could not speak but that I wanted to shout from the chapel rooftop.

"I love a girl with a knife!" I wanted to yell. "A dagger!"

Having to keep my love secret was cruel. I hunched over my notebook in French, drawing bones, turning a blank page into a necropolis.

Sœur J had asked me a question. So lost was I in the creation of my catacombs that I hadn't heard a thing. Suddenly, she was at my desk, arms folded across her chest. She scowled.

She shouted my name, turning the *r* guttural, French. Her hand reached for my notebook. I pulled it away. There was no way in hell that any of my teachers were getting their hands on my secrets, not even her.

"Give it to me!"

"No!"

"I said, give it to me!"

"NO." I shoved the notebook in my backpack. I knew Sœur J wasn't going to wrestle me for it, but I hadn't counted on her mocking me.

"Boo-hoo!" she cried. "Poor thing! I am so sad! Is that what you write in your diary? My life is so terrible? Well, it's not! You have a good life."

Remembering her life in Europe, I felt ashamed. She was right. Compared with what she'd gone through at fifteen, my life as an undercover teen lesbian was heaven. She limped back to her dais, leaned against it, and said, "I am going to repeat what I was saying before. I am shocked and appalled by the results of the last exam. How many times must I teach the subjunctive?"

She approached the chalkboard and wrote.

Il n'est pas evident que . . .

Il n'est pas certain que . . .

Il n'est pas clair que . . .

I took out a sheet of paper and copied the phrases. Across the top of my paper, I wrote "Je regrette rien" and then crossed it out.

I was scrambling out of the station wagon when my lunchbox slid out of my hands and clattered to the parking lot pavement. It unlatched. The lid swung open, exposing my pens, pencils, notepad, rosary, strawberry gum, coins, safety pins, and string. Dad ignored these treasures. What commanded his gaze was the kitchen knife gleaming in the Saturday sun.

I stared at Dad.

"Why is there a knife in your lunchbox?"

Not wanting to get Mom in trouble, I said, "I don't know. I thought it was a good idea. For protection."

"N-n-n-NO!" he stuttered. "When we get home, wash that knife and put it back in the drawer. No knives. They're dangerous, honey."

I silently sighed.

When we got home, I carried my knife to the kitchen sink, soaped it, rinsed it, dried it, and returned it to its drawer. I was disappointed. Like Mom, I'd felt safer with it nearby. The blade had given me courage, empowering me to walk with my shoulders back and my chest out. Now I was just a bull, no dagger. I went to sulk in my room.

To console myself, I lit two candles and stared at some blanched thistles I'd stuck in a vase. I knelt, crawled across the carpet, and reached under my bed. I felt for the lesbian art book and pulled it onto my lap. Flipping through it, I arrived at a picture shot by Del LaGrace Volcano. A woman wearing a leather harness and cap stood behind a woman wearing a corset and veil. The brides were painfully romantic.

I wanted my knife back. I figured Dad was in the kitchen, counting the silverware.

I knew why the sight of my meager weapon had made him stutter.

It was 1993 and Lorena Bobbitt had become a household name.

Dad feared Lorena's powers.

A lot of men in this country did.

On TV, we watched photographers mob her as she entered the courthouse. Her face appeared in newspapers and on magazine covers. Male comedians mocked her violence. I suppose self-defense is funny to those who believe you've got no self to defend.

I found it blasphemous to laugh at Lorena. I was in awe of her. I'd never thought to cut off a penis until she did, and she gave a compelling reason for doing so. She testified that on the morning of June 23, her husband came home drunk. He stumbled into their bedroom and jumped on top of her. Lorena told him, "I don't want to have sex." He raped her and fell asleep.

In a fugue, Lorena walked to the kitchen. She retrieved a knife and brought it to the bedroom. Clutching its red handle, she swiped the blade across pink skin, cutting through meat and veins, severing urethra. She carried the dick to her Mercury Capri, turned her key in the ignition, and left. When Lorena realized what she was driving around Manassas with, she screamed. She hurled the dick out the window, into a grassy field across from a 7-Eleven. It's a shame that a cop found the penis by stepping on it before racoons could run off with it. The cops walked it to the 7-Eleven, filled a hot dog bag with crushed ice, and slid the dick inside. At the same hospital where Lorena submitted to a rape kit test, doctors reattached John's weapon.

In religion class, boys talked about Lorena as if she were Satan herself. That she was an immigrant from South America made her even more villainous to these xenophobes. Mimicking Speedy Gonzales, they caricatured, "My husband no make me cum so I cut off his pee pee!"

I exchanged glances with other girls, daggers in our eyes.

Other boys described the chop as the worst crime in human history. How dare an immigrant divorce a Marine from his penis?

"What she did to him is worse than death," they lamented. "She should get the death penalty."

Reporters who asked men to comment on the case found confusion. What perplexed them was Lorena's insistence that her husband had raped her.

Repeatedly. At home. In their bedroom.

"How can a man rape his own wife?" one man begged, his incredulity making it clear that he thought *marital rape* was a contradiction in terms. Yes, the police had visited the couple's home six times and arrested John for hitting Lorena. But it was his wife he'd hit. Consider the possessive.

His wife.

His.

Those who laughed at the notion of raping one's own wife were channeling the spirit of the English jurist Sir Matthew Hale. This seventeenth-century creep developed what came to be known as the Hale doctrine, the legal precept that "the husband cannot be guilty of a rape committed by himself upon his lawful wife, for by their mutual matrimonial consent and contract the wife hath given up herself in this kind unto her husband, which she cannot retract."

When I think of the Hale doctrine, *Saturn* comes to mind. The Goya painting represents Cronus, the Titan who fathered one of Greek mythology's most prolific rapists, Zeus. Cronus came to power by castrating his father, Uranus, but refused to rest on his laurels. He feared one of his kids would do the same to him. To prevent his undoing, he did like a hamster. He ate his babies.

Set against a black backdrop, Goya's Cronus resembles a monstrous Muppet. He is naked, his crude face framed by a gray mane and beard. His eyes bulge; his mouth hangs open. A bloody arm is stuffed into it. Cronus clutches his son's remains by their waist. He has devoured the thinking part, the head. Blood pours from the neck, reddening the shoulders. Ass and legs dangle. This is what Hale thought husbands are entitled to. A wife surrenders. Consumed by her husband, she becomes him. The Hale doctrine renders marital sex masturbatory. There is no him or her. There is only his.

In court, John's friend testified that he boasted that he "liked to make girls squirm and yell . . . make 'em bleed and yell for help." Other witnesses said that they'd seen John hit, shove, and belittle Lorena, punishing her for how she dressed and cooked. John denied doing most of these things. He denied having pled guilty to assault and battery on Lorena in 1991. He said that the only thing he was guilty of was teasing Lorena a little about her butt getting big. He said she was a hot-tempered thing. She scratched and clawed. She was so rough, he'd had to tell her, "I don't believe in violence. It's not ladylike."

On our living room bookshelf sat Hayden Herrera's biography of Frida Kahlo. One afternoon, when there was nothing good on TV, I pulled the book down and carried it to my bedroom. I lay in bed, flipping pages, looking for what Herrera describes as Kahlo's goriest work. I paused at the glossy reproduction, reexamining it. My grandmother used color palettes like Kahlo's. She had painted portraits of me when I was a child and told me stories to keep me still. One of her tales implicated a wife in despair. After the wife learned that her sister was having an affair with her husband, she could only think about killing the both of them. She stepped into her kitchen, reached for a knife, wrapped it in her rebozo, and set out to find her husband and sister. As she walked through the forest, an angel appeared. It was summertime, and I was covered in mosquito welts, so I imagined this entity like my attackers, translucent wings fluttering.

The angel said, "You won't succeed. You don't have it in you to kill him. You probably don't have it in you to kill her either. You'll just stab them a little. And then you'll go to jail. And they'll be together, laughing at you from the outside while you wither and die. Go home. Put the knife back. Make peace with your horrible life."

The would-be killer burst into tears.

The painting I was staring at was a different version of this story, the everyday one. The room is pink and blue. Over its only piece of furniture, a wooden bed, hover a white dove and a black sparrow. There is a banner suspended by their beaks. Green letters announce "UNOS CUANTOS PIQUETITOS."* An exclamation mark stabs the space immediately after *piquetitos*.

---

* A few tiny stabs.

A man wearing a fedora stands at the bedside. He seems not to have eyeballs. Does he have a mustache? The darkness above his lip could be a shadow, some soot, or a crease. A white button-down shirt is tucked into his brown pants. There's no way he'll be able to get the stains out. His right hand holds a bloody knife, his left hand a soaked handkerchief. An array of reds stain the blanket, sheets, and pillow. Blood dapples the floor. (Is it wrong that this painting reminds me of a well-worn maxi pad? The subconscious does what it does.)

The violence cannot be contained by the pink-and-blue room. It spills onto and marks the wooden frame, stained red in places. There are finger smears. The wood is gouged. I wonder if Kahlo stabbed the frame with a knife and then stuck her finger up her nose and scratched, letting warm liquid flow. Did it drip from her mustache and onto the wood? Probably not. She likely dipped her brush in paint, faking blood the conservative way.

The woman on the bed has got to be dead. Her face is a delicate and defeated version of her murderer's. A pink stocking and garter bunch around her ankle. The hair on her pillow, the triangle between her legs, and her kitten-heeled shoe are an identical black. She bleeds from wounds on her face, neck, chest, breasts, stomach, hips, legs, arms, wrists, and hands. The deepest gashes reach for her heart and womb.

Unos Cuantos Piquetitos was one of two paintings that Kahlo made in 1935. According to Herrera, Kahlo had read in a newspaper that a man had murdered his girlfriend. When he was taken before a judge, the killer said that he had given her only a few small stabs. Feeling murdered by life, Kahlo felt compelled to appropriate the femicide, to die vicariously through its re-creation.

Unos Cuantos Piquetitos is constantly reproducing itself.

On the evening of February 8, 2020, neighbors of twenty-five-year-old Ingrid Escamilla Vargas heard screaming and shouting coming from her Mexico City home. What sounded like an argument soon turned to silence. The neighbors welcomed this. They often heard arguing, and it could be difficult to ignore. On Sunday, Ingrid's boyfriend, forty-six-year-old Erik Francisco Robledo Rosas, called his ex-wife. He confessed that he'd stabbed his girlfriend in front of their autistic son. The ex-wife called the police. This wasn't her first time contacting them. She'd reported Erik for domestic violence. So had Ingrid.

The police found Erik standing next to what remained of Ingrid. Her eyes and organs were gone. She had been skinned from her head to her knees. Erik sputtered that he had no idea who had done this to his girlfriend. He didn't know who had tried to flush some of her down the toilet or why some of her was in a green plastic bag by the door.

A picture of Ingrid's remains appeared on the cover of Mexican daily *Pásala!* By comparison, Kahlo's *Unos Cuantos Piquetitos* appears tame. The headline blamed love.

"THE FAULT WAS CUPID'S: DAYS BEFORE VALENTINE'S DAY, MAN KILLS AND SKINS GIRLFRIEND."

Erik, whom the press deemed "lovesick," later confessed to killing Ingrid. Why? Because she called him an alcoholic. Because she hurt his feelings.

Some men will shatter the mirror you hold up to them.

Next, they'll take the shards and stick them in you.

I hate that when I look for information about Ingrid, I mostly find what I have given you, a detailed description of how she died. Accounts will emphasize that she was youthful. That she was attractive. That she was educated. That she had reported her boyfriend for domestic violence and not been taken seriously. What Erik did to her takes up so much space. It crowds her out. Eats her up.

Saturn.

We can make room for Ingrid, help her to reinhabit herself by clearing a space for her on our altars. We can offer her refreshments. A glass of water. A bottle of Coke. A shot of tequila. Tobacco, marijuana, hashish. Chocolate. We can sit with her, our rosaries in our hands, and pray a novena. We can talk to her. We should listen very carefully for her answers.

On this same altar we may also venerate Lorena Leonor Gallo, a female folk hero perhaps destined to become the most powerful type of intercessor—a folk saint. Her spirit is sorely needed.

WATERLOO

Though some people remember it differently, 1998 was a tough year to be queer. The year before, the actor Ellen DeGeneres had come out on her sitcom *Ellen*. This was a huge deal. No one had done it before, and it was like she was inviting the rest of us to come out too.

Casually dressed in black, Ellen appeared on the cover of *Time* magazine. The headline was sweet, simple, and corny: "Yep, I'm Gay." I walked to my neighborhood bookstore, Cody's, to buy a copy of this historic magazine. Back at my Berkeley apartment, I tore off the cover and stuck it to my fridge with fruit-shaped magnets. I felt optimistic. I considered coming out to my parents again. (The first time I'd told them I was queer, they'd answered, "No," and we'd left it at that.)

Events that took place in Wyoming put my optimism on ice.

In October, a mountain biker pedaling through the countryside mistook a bloody young man tied to a fence for a scarecrow. The victim was twenty-one-year-old Matthew Shepard. Two men had robbed, beaten, and tortured him, apparently for being gay. Life support kept Matthew here for five more days. On the day of his burial, members of the Westboro Baptist Church picketed his funeral. They traveled from Kansas, the setting of *In Cold Blood*, a true-crime novel written by one of the gayest writers in human history, Truman Capote. Unlike Capote, the Westboro Baptist Church used language sparingly. They carried signs that rejected nuance. "God Hates Fags." "AIDS Kills Fags Dead." Their leader, the Reverend Fred Phelps, carried the cruelest one.

"Matt in Hell."

Famous gays and gay icons, like Elton John, Madonna, and Barbra Streisand, sent flowers and hounded politicians. At a vigil held for Matthew on the Capitol steps, Ellen addressed the crowd. She began her speech by saying, "I am so pissed off. I can't stop crying."

Maybe I should've felt more anger and sadness about what had happened to Matthew. I felt some, but mostly what I felt was terror shot through with sexual frustration.

Is that selfish?

I didn't want to be kidnapped, robbed, beaten, raped, or killed for being queer, but I also wanted to get laid. Badly.

A month before Matthew Shephard was mistaken for a scarecrow, two people kidnapped a lesbian and drove her to the outskirts of Santa Maria. Mona Masters was twenty-three, two years older than I was at the time. Like with Matthew, her killers tied her up. Their pickup truck rambled past cattle, toward the toxic waste dump, stopping at Black Road, where one can occasionally see wild boars silhouetted against the horizon. After pushing Mona out of the car, the killers doused her in gasoline, sparked a cigarette lighter, and lit her. Her last words were "Oh God." After killing Mona, the murderers went to a convenience store. They bought cigarettes.

A farmworker found her blackened body.

During summer break, I'd come home from Berkeley and worked an internship at the Santa Maria Superior Court. I shadowed one of the prosecutors assigned to Mona's case. He was a tall, leathery Southerner. His drawl had earned him a nickname, Louisiana Mushmouth. I was in Mushmouth's office, helping him to file folders. He was talking about Mona's murder. He kept calling it "the lesbian flambé." My face must've given away that his joke bothered me and Mushmouth gave me a stern look.

"In this line of work," he drawled, "one must maintain a sense of humor."

When he pronounced *humor*, it became *you-mer*.

Summer break was over, and I was back at Berkeley. Despite

Mushmouth, I was still thinking about applying to law schools. A former roommate, Delia, had gotten me an internship with the San Francisco District Attorney's Office, and I'd ridden the BART to the city to put in my usual hours. My day had taken a nosedive after I'd exited the subway station. I stood on the curb. Traffic rustled my skirt. I teetered in heels. Behind me, a banner suspended from a steakhouse awning advertised lunch specials. I stuck out my arm, trying to hail a cab. A drunk buzzed around me. He wobbled. Leered. His speech was too slurred to make out words. He sloshed with every step.

I angled my body away from him, to show him my disinterest, and felt a splash. I turned to see what was going on. The drunk's zipper was down, and with one steady hand, he'd managed to aim his penis at my leg. I was his urinal.

A taxi pulled over. As I got in, I heard the drunk's laughter. It was of the wheezing variety.

In the cab, I began to shake.

"What's wrong?" asked the driver.

"A man just peed on me!"

"Why did you let him?!"

I burst into tears.

I rinsed my legs in a Hall of Justice bathroom.

When my hours were done, Delia drove me back to Berkeley. Instead of taking me home, I asked her to drop me off at the White Horse. I was twenty-one and had never been to a gay bar. On TV, when sophisticated adult characters had bad days, they'd talk about needing a drink. I felt like I'd had a very adult day and so I deserved a drink. I also needed to be in a place where random men wouldn't pee on me, and I figured I could find that at a gay bar.

As Delia drove off, I stepped beneath the White Horse's awning, pushed open the bar doors, and faced a bouncer.

"ID?"

I showed my passport. I'd failed my driving test three times and still didn't have a license.

The bouncer smiled and waved me in.

I bought the cheapest beer on the menu and watched dykes monopolize the pool tables.

I had no idea what I was supposed to do. Sit? Stand? Fake boredom? Lean against the jukebox? Dance with myself? What is one supposed to do the first time she sets foot in a gay bar, especially if she's alone? I had no instructions.

I was in a panic about seeming panicked.

"Hey!"

I flinched. Sweat crawled down my neck, tickling a mole.

My secretarial blouse felt moist.

"I'm Shelby," said the drab but athletic woman who'd snuck up on me. "I'm friends with that dapper person over there." She pointed to a pale figure dressed in a black leather jacket and chaps. "She'd be honored if you'd join us for a drink."

Shelby dangled a bottle of beer like bait. "She thinks you're really cute."

Feigning confidence, I accepted the offering. Shelby led me away from the billiards, and I climbed onto a stool. Through wire-rimmed glasses, my admirer watched.

Cher's voice yodeled through a speaker. My seat vibrated. My vulva felt the music.

"HI!" the leather-person shouted over the noise. "I'M SAM! WHAT'S YOUR NAME?"

"MYRIAM!"

"DO YOU LIKE BUDWEISER, MYRIAM?"

"NOT REALLY. IT'S PRETTY GROSS."

Sam's eyebrows inched closer together. "WHY ARE YOU DRINKING IT, THEN?"

"IT WAS THE CHEAPEST THING ON THE MENU AND I SPENT MOST OF MY CASH ON A CAB."

Sam grinned. "IT'S NOT EVERY DAY THAT I SEE SUCH A PRETTY GIRL SIPPING WHITE TRASH CHAMPAGNE. AND SO DRESSED UP!"

"IF I DON'T WEAR BUSINESS CASUAL, I'LL GET SENT HOME."

"WHERE DO YOU WORK?"

"I HAVE AN INTERNSHIP AT THE SAN FRANCISCO DISTRICT ATTORNEY'S OFFICE. I'M THINKING ABOUT GOING TO LAW SCHOOL. I'M AN UNDERGRAD AT CAL."

I pointed in the direction of the university. Up Telegraph Avenue.

"YOU'RE CUTE *AND* SMART?"

I shrugged.

"IT WOULD BE THE SMART THING FOR YOU TO LET ME TAKE YOU FOR A RIDE ON MY MOTORCYCLE."

I made a caca face.

Sam reached down. From beneath the table, she produced two helmets. She slid the smaller one at me.

I shook my head.

"WHAT'S IT GONNA TAKE TO GET YOU ON MY MOTORCYCLE, MYRIAM?"

"COMPLIMENTS."

Sam laughed, then shouted, "YOU'RE EXOTIC! THAT'S WHY I SENT SHELBY OVER WITH A BEER!"

My nostrils betrayed my astrological sign. Taurus.

Sam's eyes twinkled with curiosity. "WHAT ARE YOU?"

"MEXICAN MOSTLY."

Sam looked elated. "OH MY GOD! I *LOVE* SELENA!"

I wanted to leap across the table and beat this punk's ass. Instead, I restrained myself. I let out an exasperated sigh. If being fetishized was the cost of admission for my first sexual experience with a woman, I was willing to pay. Sam was a grown-up dyke, not at all like the girls I'd messed around with in high school.

"SERIOUSLY, WHAT WILL IT TAKE TO GET YOU ON MY MOTORCYLE?"

"A DANCE."

"I'M TOO NERVOUS TO DANCE!"

"C'MON."

I hopped off my stool. Sam followed me to the dance floor.

I staked out a spot between a twink who vogued solo and a bearded fag doing the twist with a grinning guy in a wheelchair. I bobbed to a Pet Shop Boys remix. I forced myself not to laugh when I recognized Sam's dance moves. I hadn't seen those since eighth grade.

About two months after I-love-Selena-ing me, Sam moved most of her possessions into my rented room.

Leading up to our cohabitation, Sam had taken me on a few dinner dates during which she'd worn a suit, I'd worn a dress, and she'd lectured me about fine cheeses. On our fourth date, she professed her love for me. While Sam was my first grown-up girlfriend, making it so that I had no reference point for such declarations, it seemed premature for her to announce that we should spend eternity together. I figured I should get to know her better. I did know that she believed herself to be a cheese expert. I did know that she looked handsome enough in a sharkskin suit. I did know that she was pushing thirty. I did know that she'd been raised in a four-letter state. I did know that she'd fucked a lot more girls than me.

In the interest of seeing if our sex would evolve from interesting to good, I entertained Sam's romantic excesses.

We spent nights huddled together on my futon bed, where Sam informed me that I belonged to a mystical category of beings. I was a soulmate. *Her* soulmate. I doubted this, but Sam insisted, and so sure was she that she infused my doubts with doubt. Maybe Sam was my soulmate, and I needed her to convince me of it. Maybe that was part of our journey as soulmates. I'd never known anyone who'd had to be sweet-talked into soulmating, but I was open to the possibility. At age twenty-one, my heart welcomed foolishness.

I had begun to wonder if our soulmating had something to do with housing when Sam shared that she was being evicted. We were at her apartment, a Spartan but somehow messy place where she slept on a mattress on the floor. While explaining that she had to be out by the end of the week, she gushed, "It's so perfect that we met. Because now I can live with you!"

I shook my head and said, "That's not a good idea."

Sam's arms flailed. Inches from where I stood, her motorcycle boots kicked the wall, sending chunks of it flying. She roared, "THANKS TO YOU, I'LL BE DEAD IN TWO WEEKS! I'LL BE HOMELESS! I'M NOT GONNA BE HOMELESS AGAIN! I'LL *KILL* MYSELF! I'LL FUCKING *KILL* MYSELF! I'LL BE DEAD AND IT WILL BE *YOUR* FAULT!"

She aimed a finger at me.

Not wanting her to do to me what she'd done to the wall (it now had a hole the size of my head), I said, "Okay, okay, okay! You can move in! You can move in! It's okay! It's okay! You won't be homeless! I'm sorry!"

As quickly as it had begun, the tantrum ended.

Sam straightened her shoulders.

"Okay," she said. "You can help me start packing."

She handed me tangled sheets to fold.

I was ironing Sam's clothes for a job interview when she said, "We should take a road trip. You need to meet my family."

Sam claimed to be a child of the Black Hills of South Dakota, bragging that she was born near Deadwood, burial place of the frontierswoman Calamity Jane. Sam's mom, Peggy, and stepdad, Jim, raised her a few miles from an Iowa locale that one might call a village. Fewer than six hundred people called it home. It had a stop sign, a convenience store, a graveyard, and a bar that didn't discriminate against children. The village newsletter, the *Night Owl*, was a single mimeographed page that circulated information such as pet death announcements, the names of the Lutheran ladies responsible for bringing refreshments to the next Sunday service, and recipes whose main ingredient was Velveeta. Most of Sam's family was still in the state. A daring few had fled to Minneapolis.

I'd never been to the Midwest. Beyond trips to Mexico, I'd left California once. To go to Las Vegas. Aside from Nevada, the rest of the United States was an uninteresting mystery.

Our drive to the heartland took days. And a life. Sam's car squashed a prairie dog somewhere in Wyoming. Nebraska's plains startled me. I'd heard of the region's legendary flatness (who hasn't?), but it hadn't occurred to me that it really would be that horizontal. Land stretched and stretched and stretched. The expanses were deserted, haunting, and drab. I thought about that Andrew Wyeth painting, the one with the lanky girl in the pink dress alone in a field of amber.

I was used to having the Pacific Ocean nearby. I longed to see horizons made of water.

I was used to seagulls, tide pools, terns, plovers, and sand dunes that crept according to the wind. I was also used to fixed categories of work, among them white work versus Mexican work. In Iowa, that distinction didn't seem to exist. Most work was white because nearly everyone there was white, farmhands too, and seated at a country McDonald's, I watched people who I guessed were of Scandinavian descent staff the restaurant. In one corner, a blonde mopped a spilled milkshake. In another corner, a blonde in a visor filled a napkin dispenser. A blonde with cystic acne strained behind the cash register, struggling to hear a blond customer's order. Behind the cashier, European-Americans, the kind from the Northern part of their native continent, cooked.

The view was stunning. I'd never seen an all-blond fast-food crew. As I unwrapped my cheeseburger, I reminded myself not to stare.

We stayed with Peggy and Jim. They owned a farmhouse purchased from sheep ranchers. The acreage surrounding their home was part lawn, part cornfield, and part shooting range.

Everyone Sam introduced me to smiled in a way that made me uneasy.

As we walked toward a dry creek bed one afternoon, Sam said, "You know what my brother said about you when it was just him and me driving to town?"

"What?"

"He said, 'So, Myriam's a Mexican?' I said, 'Yup.' Then he goes, 'Huh. But . . . she's . . . smart.'"

"Did he expect me to have an IQ of seven?"

Sam laughed. "I s'pose."

We plodded in silence. Sam's revelation validated that uneasy feeling I got around her family, but she just as easily could've spared me the truth.

Another disclosure happened after Sam took me to meet her great-grandma. We were exiting her brick retirement home when Sam said, "Hey, wanna know what Great-Grandma said when you went to pee?"

"That she loves Selena?"

Parroting the old woman's voice, Sam croaked, "Is that girl an injun?"

"Your great-grandma actually said *injun*?"

"Mm-hmmm. And she was a little worried you might steal somethin'."

I wrinkled my nose. What did the hag think I was going to steal? Her yellowing doilies? A dented teakettle? She had nothing worth taking. I said, "Your great-grandma's racist."

Sam bristled. "No, she isn't! We're part Indian!"

I stared at my "soulmate."

She snapped, "My hair turns dark in the summertime! That only happens to Indians!"

I was glad we weren't going to be seeing Great-Grandma again. I might knock her teeth out. She'd probably like that though. Great-Grandma had worked as a rodeo clown. It thrilled her to be chased by bulls.

The racial panic continued in Waterloo. With Peggy, we rode to the city renowned for its iconic tractor factories. She parked at a supermarket and hurried inside to grab margarine, milk, and lunch meat. Sam and I waited in the truck. I shut my eyes and breathed through my mouth. The back seat stank of mildew.

The door flew open, and Peggy leapt inside. After slamming it shut, she shouted, "Lock your doors. LOCK! YOUR! DOORS!"

I obeyed, looking around for a SWAT team.

"Why are we locking our doors?" I whispered.

Peggy nodded in the direction of a brown guy who could have passed for a grown version of my little brother. He was pushing an empty shopping cart and minding his own business. His shoelaces were untied. His glasses were held together with masking tape. Maple leaves hung from his tattered sweater.

"He's why we're locking our doors?" I asked.

Peggy whispered, "They steal things."

So do homesteaders, I thought.

I clenched my ass cheeks together as hard as I could and gazed out the window, wishing I could hop into the familiar-looking gentleman's shopping cart and sail west.

Sam was aunt to two platinum-blond nephews. The younger one, Brandon, had skin so translucent it exposed his circulatory system.

As Brandon streaked across his grandparents' lawn, I whispered, "He's clear. We can see his pulse."

Brandon noticed Sam and me whispering. He beat his chest. I thought of a city in the San Fernando Valley. Tarzana.

Peggy said, "Brandon, put your shirt on! It's suppertime."

When the nephews' mom, a very young blonde named Jewel, arrived, we sat on lawn chairs and ate pork chops and sweet corn. Peggy poured me a glass of whole milk. I spilled some on my shirt and excused myself to the bedroom to change.

I pulled open a dresser drawer and shrieked. Dead bugs were strewn across my clothes. Once over my shock, I reached for a body. Examined it. The remains had wings.

Someone knocked at the door.

"Come in!"

Sam entered, followed by Brandon.

"What the hell's goin' on?" she barked.

"Yeah! What the hell's goin' on?" echoed her sidekick.

"My clothes are covered in these." I handed her a carcass.

She recoiled. I turned and presented it to Brandon. He cupped his hands, accepted the insect, and grinned.

"Did you put those in my drawer?" I asked.

He nodded.

"Why?"

"I heard you tellin' Grandma that you like lightnin' bugs. That you never seen 'em in California. You were tellin' her that you like how their butts light up so I caught some and put 'em in your drawer."

I contemplated Brandon's scheme. He'd harvested insects in the hopes that I'd open my drawer and be surrounded by blinking angels. Instead, I got winged death. No matter. The translucent child's intention was beautiful. For the first time, I felt welcomed by this family.

"Thanks," I told him. "That's really sweet."

He blushed and returned the bug to its drawer. Spinning around, he threw his arms around my short legs and squeezed before prancing back outdoors.

Brandon's version of kindness gave me an idea.

So far, I knew that Sam's family thought me a clever young woman with kleptomaniacal tendencies. To counteract this impression, I wanted to prove that I could be modest, generous, and trustworthy. These salmon-skinned Midwesterners had assimilated some shitty ideas about Mexicans into their worldview, and I challenged myself to battle their biases. I schemed to win their affections.

Food would be central to my mission.

After supper one night, while Peggy and Jim sat in recliners, absorbing Fox News, I announced, "I'd like to cook dinner for you later this week."

Peggy looked worried. "What will you fix?"

"Mexican food!"

"Like . . . ground beef tacos?" Peggy went hard on the *a*. She appled it.

"Mmmmmm, probably not tacos. I'll probably make something a little bit more . . . involved."

She looked at me as if I'd made a threat.

I spent the evening on the phone with my parents, discussing menu options. They suggested I make chiles rellenos, sopa de arroz, and frijoles de la olla. Un platillo típico, the sort of meal General Álvaro Óbregon was enjoying when he was assassinated, face-planting into deliciousness. My parents dictated my great-grandma's recipes, and I jotted them down in the notebook where I journaled at the end of each day. The only detail I was pretty certain I'd deviate from was the feet. I wasn't sure how they'd go over. Not everybody finds toes appetizing, and my great-grandma enjoyed serving her rice with chicken feet crisscrossed over it. She saved the extremities for last, a savory desert, and she'd sit by herself at the table, sucking their marrow, her dentures smiling from a nearby napkin, plate, or glass.

Mom told me to make agua fresca with whatever berries were in season. She also advised to arrange a platter of garnish so that its colors might evoke the Mexican flag. Tomatoes and radishes for red. Diced onion for white. Cilantro, lettuce, and jalapeños for green. I'm not a nationalist but I felt pressure to represent. That's how it is for diaspora. The spirit of patriotism grabs you by the intimate parts once you've strayed from the motherland.

"I'll do it," I told Mom. "I'll make crudité al estilo de bandera Mexicana."

When I got off the phone, I looked out the window. Lightning bugs were blinking. I watched their constellations appear, disappear, and reappear. I would cook the rice without feet. For now we would keep our claws to ourselves.

The elephant stuck his trunk in a glass pitcher filled with neon-orange beverage, sucking until the container was empty.

"That can't be good for the animal," I whispered to Sam.

"SHHH!"

We were seated in the bleachers at the North Iowa Fair. A showman was demonstrating his elephant's many "talents," one being its ability to eat a loaf of Wonder Bread in a single gulp. After the pachyderm performed a few more feats, the showman called, "Who wants a ride?"

Kids squealed and scurried to form a line. Brandon and Luke joined them. I thought of Hannibal leading elephants through the Alps.

"I'm gonna go look around," I told Sam.

She nodded.

I left the bleachers and strolled into a neighboring white tent. Wire cages, some of them rusty, sat on folding tables. Inside of them, hens, roosters, and chicks pecked and paced. Another row of cages was packed with rabbits. They huddled in the corners, their feet and bottoms stained yellow. Flies buzzed, taunting them. There was no way for the rabbits to jump safely. They would've knocked themselves out, taken out an eye against the wire. Woodchip particulate made breathing treacherous. The sharp stench of animal pee burned my nostrils.

I'd left my albuterol inhaler at home.

I hurried back out, filled my lungs with fresh air, and saw an olive-green tent festooned with old-fashioned midway banners.

FREAK SHOW! WORLD'S SMALLEST HORSE! $2.00!

There was no line. Save for the pipe cleaner of a carny stationed at the entrance, the tent stood alone.

Everything else had drawn crowds. The elephant. The few rides. The concession stands. The tractor demolition derby.

The freak show was likely the only place where I might enjoy some solitude.

I approached the tattooed man guarding the exhibition and handed him two bills.

He pulled aside a tarp and mumbled, "Enjoy."

I shuffled across balding grass and peered at shelves sagging under the weight of dusty, murk-filled jars. Things with faces floated in them. Piglets. Cats. Dogs. Maybe gophers. Very large eyeballs. Bones. Teeth. Hair. Fur. Human hands had stitched together different animal parts to make the cryptids suspended in the foggy solutions. A taxidermic duck with an extra leg offered up a Mona Lisa smile. Taking in the wax sculptures representative of skin diseases, I ran my finger down my jawline, feeling for acne and abscesses. In a domestic diorama, a family of dusty and frozen mice sat at a table, having tea and scones.

Flowing from one to the next, the shelves curved into a maze that seemed to be ushering me toward the main attraction.

I knew I was getting close when I finally saw a living thing.

Their aquarium was brightly lit. Its handwritten sign, smeared by water, read, "Pete and re-Pete."

Two leathery faces gazed up at me.

They resided in the same shell.

The turtles lived alone in their glass house. They had a small pool of water with a short stretch of pebbled sand. A private beach. I stared at the Petes. I'd never seen a two-headed reptile. They seemed content.

I kept walking, imagining just how small the world's smallest horse would be. I pictured a taxidermy of some sort, maybe a mouse or rat or muskrat manipulated to look like a pony. As a kid, I'd lurked in the public library stacks where the books on the occult and esoterica lived, and I recalled having seen black-and-white pictures of P. T. Barnum's Feejee Mermaid in one of them. She wasn't really a mermaid. She was half mummified monkey, half mummified fish, and entirely terrifying.

Continuing my journey, I arrived at the wire pen where the main attraction suffered.

He stood on a nest of dirty hay.

Flies buzzed around his haunches and ears.

I gasped.

The Shetland pony looked up at me with molasses eyes. His mane was in need of detangling, and an inflated ball sack sagged and lurched between his hooves, nearly touching the ground. The shame was too much. I'd paid money for this experience, to be an audience to this horse's misery. The world's smallest horse seemed to be begging for something. Mercy? He wanted out. Of the fairgrounds. Of Cerro Gordo County. Of Iowa. Of the spiritual plane where he was forced to perform the role of world's smallest horse.

I whispered, "I'm so sorry," and fled the tent, hurrying back into the summer night.

I tried to forget about what I'd seen as I wandered the fairgrounds, looking for Sam and her nephews. I found them having snacks. They were gobbling them out of Fritos bags with plastic forks.

"Want some?" asked Brandon.

"What is it?"

"A walkin' taco."

"I don't know what that is."

"Ain't ya Mexican?"

"Yes." Curiosity got the better of me. "What's it made of?"

Brandon drawled, "Fritos. Chili. Sour cream. Lettuce." After a pause, he added, "Cheese."

We were headed to the parking lot, having been put in charge of dropping the nephews off at their grandpa's. After we'd piled into the car and buckled in, I asked, "Can we please roll down some windows?"

"Why?" asked Luke.

"The car smells like foot."

Brandon and Luke giggled.

"That's not a nice thing to say about our food, Myriam," said Sam. I disagreed but kept quiet. Fritos smell like feet. It's a well-known and rarely disputed fact.

Down the road we passed a sign advertising an architectural tourist attraction. "Oooooh!" I breathed. "There are Frank Lloyd Wright buildings in Mason City. Can we go?"

Brandon said, "I wanna go to the museum with the tractors."

"Where is it?" asked Sam.

"Charles City."

"We'll take you to the tractors in Charles City! We'll go tomorrow!" said Sam.

"Yay!" cried the boys.

At their grandpa's house, Sam and I walked the nephews to the front door. We knocked. No answer. We knocked again.

I whispered, "What should we do?"

Sam had told me stories about her grandpa, and if Jewel's father was anything like him, I didn't want to go inside. When babysitting Sam and her brother, the old man would open a bottle of Jim Beam, pour a glass, gulp, and become jolly.

"Who wants to play a game?" he'd ask.

"I do!" brother and sister chorused.

The old man would herd the two into dog cages and lock them inside. The kids would pretend to be poodles. Pant. Bark. Scratch fleas. The old man would swallow whiskey until he passed out, and the poodles would whimper, waiting for him to come to.

The game lasted hours.

Luke opened the door. Brandon followed him inside. Sam and I stepped into a cluttered living room. Illuminated by the glow of a black-and-white TV was an emaciated man asleep on a couch. His beard grew long. Rip Van Winkle. A cigarette was clasped between two fingers. Its paper and tobacco had become ash long ago. His face transcended time, ancient and ageless. His parchment eyelids rose.

"Hello," he said softly.

"Hi," said Sam. "We brought Luke and Brandon."

"Thanks," he said. He waved at the boys. His eyelids fell.

Luke approached the old TV and turned the knob, flipping through channels. I was glad the TV was there. The nephews had a reliable babysitter.

• • •

The absence of ocean really unnerved me.

Until visiting Iowa, I hadn't known how much the Pacific mattered to me. I hadn't known how much it represented. Now that the sea wasn't with me, its meaning was clear. The ocean was a threshold. It represented other worlds. Baptisms and death rites. Ends and beginnings. To stand on the beach and stare at the Pacific was humbling and invigorating. Nothing brought that combination of sentiments in Iowa. North, south, east, and west, the horizon was land, corn, corn, and land. The visual monotony was a lot to bear. It seemed painfully inert. The rhythms of the sea, on the other hand, remind us that we're alive. The sea blankets us and oozes fog. The sea reaches for us at high tide and abandons us at low. It's also a theater of violence. Sharks attacking surfers. Stingrays jabbing waders. Malibu mansions sliding down cliffs and crashing, vanishing into waves.

In an effort to ease my homesickness, I turned to charms.

One of them was a recently acquired rattlesnake tail. Un cascabel.

I'd fallen in love with rattlesnakes when I was around the same age as the nephews. Dad had taken us to the Museum of Natural History in Santa Barbara. We walked past oak trees, to a whale skeleton next to the parking lot. It was rearticulated and the bones seemed to float in the air. Dad encouraged my brother, my sister, and me to step into the large mammal's mouth. We were happy to enter it and Dad narrated as we traveled through its digestive tract and wriggled out its exit. Overjoyed, the three of us pretended to be turds descending full fathom five.

"Now you all have something in common with Pinocchio! And Jonah!" said Dad. Entering the whale made us part of an elite community. A club.

In a museum gallery, we gawked at honeycomb behind glass. Bees working in a hive, exiting through a hole in the ceiling. While workers came and went, we sought their queen. She didn't look like the others—she was bigger, and a bee handler had marked her with a red dot so that spectators could easily identify her. We gasped once we spotted her. We were standing in the presence of royalty.

My favorite attraction wasn't in one of the galleries. It occupied a breezeway. Inside a large box coiled a taxidermic rattler, ready to strike. My lustful hands wanted to stroke his scales. That's why he was behind glass. To protect him from kids like me. To satisfy our craving for contact, there was a button. I pressed it. The tail rattled. The warning gave me shivers. I pressed it over and over and over and over, until Dad said, "Enough!" I didn't want to hear that sound in our backyard, but I relished hearing that maraca under highly curated circumstances.

I liked reptiles a lot. My dad and brother worshipped them. So did Uncle Henry, Dad's big brother. Like a lot of young Chicanos, Henry had been made to fight in Vietnam. He trained at Fort Sill, Oklahoma, and Huntsville, Alabama, learning to direct artillery and fire. Henry returned from his tour of duty with his mind and spirit cracked. Both were now open to and attuned to sights, sounds, and smells that the rest of us couldn't access. He heard a baby's voice. The infant wailed. Henry wanted to save the baby but couldn't find her.

Unable to sustain friendships with humans, Henry befriended reptiles. He chose a Nile monitor, Osama, and a green iguana, Saint Ignatius, as his companions. Saint lived most of his life perched on Henry's shoulder. The Vietnam veteran and iguana wore matching expressions, suspicious smirks. For recreation, they browsed swap meets together on the weekends.

Sam's uncle Don gave me my reptile charm. On our way to Iowa, we'd stopped at his cattle ranch. We were pulling up to the farmhouse when Don approached in his Jeep, hopped out, and waved.

"Howdy!" he said. "Just finished killin' a snake!" He held out his palm, displaying a fresh rattle.

Inside the farmhouse, by the hall tree, Don showed me a cigar box bursting with tails.

"I collect them," he explained.

"How many do you think are in there?" I asked.

He gently shook the box. "A lot!"

Don sensed my envy. "Would you like to keep this one?"

I was thrilled. Finally, my own rattle!

"Yes! Thank you. Thank you!"

Don handed me the tail, and I slid the charm into the breast pocket of my western shirt. It made dangerous music over my heart, reminding me of my family's intimacy with scaley things.

While on our way to the Floyd County Museum, I told the nephews about the gift.

"Look what Uncle Don gave me." I stretched my arm into the back seat. I opened my hand to reveal the tail. The kids' eyes bulged. Brandon reached for it. I snatched it back.

"Can I touch it?" Brandon asked. "Please!"

"I don't know," I answered. "It depends on how you act at the museum. If you're good, I'll let you."

He smiled. "I will. I'll be good! I promise!"

"We like to hear that," I said, and tucked the tail into my pocket.

The boys followed every instruction at the museum. They did not whine, and they did not touch. Their behavior was impeccable.

"You guys did a really good job today," said Sam. "Maybe later, you'll get to touch the rattle."

We strolled a path near the Cedar River. I pointed to a café. "I'm gonna get a coffee."

"Can I go with you?" asked Brandon.

"Sure."

I opened the door for Brandon, and we approached the counter. We read the wall menu. I asked for a cappuccino.

I looked at Brandon. "Want anything?"

"A caffaccino!"

I smiled nervously, leaned toward the barista, and whispered, "Whatever you do, do not give this child a cappuccino. Please make him a hot chocolate and call it a cappuccino."

The barista winked, made our drinks, and topped Brandon's with whipped cream and sprinkles.

Brandon swiped his treat off the counter and gulped, giving himself a cream mustache. Smacking his gums, he announced, "Ah! Caffaccino!" and chugged the whole thing.

We left and returned to Sam.

"I'm hungry," grumbled Luke. "Can we have pizza?" He pointed at a restaurant a few doors down.

Sam nodded.

We were the only clientele at the Pizza Ranch. The menu listed pizza, chicken wings, and pork tenderloins. I needed fiber. Badly. Peggy and Jim had been feeding us a diet of protein and starch. Meat and potatoes were clogging my personal plumbing.

A blond waitress with feathered hair came to take our order. Sam asked for pizza, chicken wings, and breadsticks.

"Is it possible to make me a big garden salad?" I asked. "Like, just put a regular old garden salad in a bigger bowl and double the ingredients?"

"Yes, honey. We can do that!"

"Do ya eat a lot of salad in California?" asked Brandon.

"I have to," I answered. "I gotta keep things moving."

The server said, "We're gonna fix you a great big salad. You'll see!"

The woman marched past the empty tables and into the Pizza Ranch kitchen. "Get out the big bowl!" she announced to the cook. "There's a girl from California out there and she wants a salad with plenty of vegetables. Put everything we've got in it! EVERYTHING! EVERY VEGETABLE YOU CAN FIND!"

"Everything?" asked the cook.

"EVERYTHING."

I was mortified and delighted. I didn't need a special salad, but the Pizza Ranch people were making me one anyway. When the server brought our food, she saved my salad for last. Arms outstretched and with an air of ceremony, she carried a shiny metal bowl through the dining room. It overflowed with color. I felt queenly.

"Would you like western or ranch dressing?"

"Ranch!"

She brought a small bowl of ranch, and Sam, Brandon, and Luke watched me dig in.

"What's in it?" asked Sam.

Poking at it with a fork, I said, "Iceberg. Romaine. Tomatoes. Purple onion. White onion. Black olives. Mushrooms. Kidney beans. Garbanzo beans. And pepperoncini."

Luke made a grossed-out face. Brandon grabbed a fork and stabbed my meal.

That night, Peggy and Jim treated us to Bonanza Steakhouse. The nephews' parents met us there.

When I saw the salad bar, I lit up. More fiber!

"I'm gonna go help myself." I stood. Brandon said, "I'm doin' the same!"

The adults laughed. Brandon grinned.

My pale shadow followed me. He barely reached the sneeze guard. "Do you like salad bars?" I asked him.

"Yup. I like 'em. And buffets. There's one we go to on a riverboat. Up in Wisconsin."

"What's your favorite thing to get at the riverboat buffet?"

"Frog legs."

"Really?"

"Mmm-hmmm. Tasty."

"I wouldn't know. I've never had frog. I don't think I've ever eaten an amphibian. I once licked a snail. On a dare. In third grade."

"Disgusting," said Brandon.

We loaded our plates and returned to the table.

Jewel watched Brandon shovel beets into his mouth. "I've never seen him eat so many vegetables."

I said, "Maybe you've got a vegetarian on your hands."

Jim laughed. "Not out here!" He gestured at the pile of meat on his plate. We chuckled.

After Brandon finished his second serving of salad bar, I slid the charm from my pocket and held it out to the nephews. “Who wants to touch the rattle?”

Both boys squealed, “ME!”

Luke snatched the tail from my hand and rattled it. I worried about him crushing it, but I had to keep my promise. I prayed it would remain intact.

“HEY!” Jim screamed. Everyone went silent. “What is that?”

“A rattlesnake tail!” said Brandon. “Uncle Don gave it to Mary-um.”

“PUT IT AWAY!” Jim barked. “WE DON’T PLAY WITH PIECES OF SNAKE AT THE TABLE.”

I snatched the tail back. My cheeks burned.

Sam looked amused.

We rode back to the farmhouse with Peggy and Jim. Once in our room, Sam whispered, “HEY! WE DON’T PLAY WITH PIECES OF SNAKE AT THE TABLE!”

I grabbed a pillow and bit it, hoping that the polyester filling would eat my laughter.

Sam and Peggy were following me around a market in Waterloo.

I was hunting for ingredients for the Mexican meal. My parents had warned me against using canned peppers, half joking that the offense could result in my damnation. After picking through the produce section, I feared hell. The other missing ingredient was queso panela. The closest substitute I found was Monterey Jack. At least the store had grenadine, pinto beans, chicken bouillon, and the rest of my ingredients.

At the house, I borrowed one of Peggy’s aprons and got to work preparing. Making the rice and beans was boring, but fixing the chiles rellenos was fun. My favorite part was dragging my knife up the length of each pepper, making a slit that allowed me to dig my fingers in and clear the chile guts. I fed a slice of cheese to each disemboweled pepper and, once stuffed, stabbed the flesh with a toothpick, stitching the flaps back together. I dusted each pepper in flour and then dredged it in frothy egg batter whipped fluffy as a merengue. One by one, I nestled them in an oil-filled pan and fried them, flipping them with tongs once they turned golden. After plucking them from the heat, I placed the peppers on a paper towel, letting them sweat.

I remembered Dad telling me about his grandma preparing chiles rellenos, cooking for a dozen people. Her pestle clacked and scraped, clacked and scraped, clacked and scraped. At the table, his grandma and mom readied themselves, handkerchiefs nearby. The peppers, along with spices, made their eyes water and their noses run. By the end of the meal, the women's faces were wet, like the statues of weeping saints. The best food makes us cry.

I plated my peppers, drizzling each with salsita, serving rice and beans alongside them. I set the table and placed the pitcher of agua fresca de fresa at the center, beside the crudité al estilo de bandera Mexicana. I prayed to matriarchal spirits, including la Virgen de Guadalupe:

I couldn't find fresh chiles poblanos.
I did my best.
Please, bless this meal.
Please, don't send me to hell.
Amen.

The four of us sat at the table. The dining room was apples in every direction. Apple wallpaper. Wooden apples adorning an antique pantry cabinet. Wooden blocks spelling A-P-P-L-E-S.

Jim stared at the food with anticipation. Peggy looked concerned.

I said, "There's something really important you need to know. I don't want anyone getting hurt. There are toothpicks inside these peppers holding the whole operation together. When you cut into them, be sure to remove the toothpick. Don't get stabbed."

Jim laughed and disarmed his pepper. Knives and forks clinked against plates, and the Midwesterners ate everything. The only remnants were some radishes, which I nibbled during cleanup.

"That was a really good supper," said Jim.

"Yes, it was," said Peggy. "And healthy too!"

I smiled. I read their compliments as a good sign. The spirits had forgiven me for using canned chiles. I'd given two Iowans a gentle taste of Mexican hospitality. Maybe next time they saw someone who looked like my brother they wouldn't be so quick to lock their doors; maybe they'd remember a really good supper.

It was a few days after I'd cooked, and Jim and I were alone in the house. Peggy and Sam had gone to run errands. I appreciated having time to myself. Sam was always on top of me. Now I could breathe.

I took a break from reading and left the bedroom to get a glass of water. On my way back to the bedroom, I paused in the living room. Jim was sitting on his recliner. Instead of Fox News, he was watching *The Greatest Story Ever Told*, a 1965 epic about the life and times of Jesus. Even better than half-naked Charlton Heston playing John the Baptist is Telly Savalas, aka Kojak, as Pontius Pilate.

On-screen, white Christ was bathed in ridiculous light. He looked radioactive. His blue eyes twinkled while he yammered Bible verses.

"Would you look at that," said Jim. "Authentic Jesus. That's probably what he looked like."

"Max von Sydow?" I laughed. "No way! Jesus was *not* born in Sweden. He was from Nazareth! Jesus probably looked way more like Cheech Marin than Max von Sydow."

Jim stared at me. I added, "You know, Cheech Marin. The Mexican stoner from Cheech and Chong. You ever seen *Up in Smoke*?"

Jim's thin lips disappeared. His neck and ears turned fuchsia.

"Jesus. Wasn't. Pri. Muh. Tive," he said.

I raised my eyebrows, turned, and hurried back to the bedroom.

I sat on the plaid love seat and stared out the window, at the gravel road. I wished it was nighttime so that fireflies could distract me. Instead, I picked up the book I'd been reading, *Women Who Kill* by

Ann Jones. I dove back into the chapter about the daughter of a mean and frugal banker.

Lizzie Borden took an axe,
And gave her mother forty whacks;
When she saw what she had done,
She gave her father forty-one.

I turned the page, looked up, and felt regret. I wished I'd embellished the sopa de arroz with chicken feet. I should've never hidden our claws.

SLIMED

I wasted countless nights at one of the saddest places on earth, the comedy club.

It was my wifely duty to go; I was married to an aspiring stand-up comic.

On school nights, I sat in club shadows, nursing a warm ginger ale and watching desperate people, most of them men, scramble to the mic. The men could be counted on to scream, stutter, do impressions, pace, look uncomfortable, and complain about women. They talked about dicks, usually their own, wrung their hands, punned, shadowboxed, sighed, flirted, and complained about women. They improvised silly stories, told a few jokes, sipped bottled water, argued with hecklers, took off their shirts, tucked them into their back pockets, and complained about women. (It seemed that in comedy, the worst people in the world were women.)

Sometimes I laughed.

Most stand-up comics aren't that funny. To be fair, neither are essays about comedy. Analytical essays are autopsies and we're not supposed to laugh at dead bodies, not even when the body is a clown.

For my well-being, I laughed at everything my comic did and said. I didn't want her to cry. Comics are notorious crybabies. Mine was. When life didn't go as planned, she wept, gambled, ran up my credit card bill, and cheated.

After getting fired, she'd say, "Myriam, you're so patient. That's your best quality."

I told myself I could handle this. This was life with an artist.

They're supposed to be difficult to live with. The harder they are to live with, the more of a genius they are. The more of a genius they are, the more we must yield to them. The more that we yield to them, the greater their genius shines. I told myself so many lies to make my marriage work.

When I was married, I had a hobby: writing. If I wanted to be funny, I had to put it there. I wasn't allowed to be funny in front of my comic. She let me know this after I complimented myself on having come up with a joke I thought was funny.

"No!" she said. "You're not funny. I'm the funny one! You're the smart one. And the pretty one. You don't get to have everything." Pointing at her chest, and then tugging at the collar of her Sesame Street T-shirt, she snarled, "Funny is mine."

I tried to keep my humor to myself, but it spilled onto the page. My spouse ignored my writing, so it was safe there.

Unlike comedy, my hobby was unserious. Doing stand-up required my spouse to share the stage with men. Her chosen art form was nocturnal and sweaty, a verbal *Fight Club*. Meanwhile, my hobby had a silent audience of two. Making sure not to wake my comic, I'd crawl out of bed at five a.m. and slink to our kitchen to fix breakfast. With half a Snickers bar and a cup of coffee in me, I'd carry my second cup across our cold wood floor, to the jack-and-jill room where I wrote. I didn't have a formal desk. Instead, I typed at a laptop perched on a wall-mounted shelf. Pinned to the wall at eye level was a ravaged photograph of my great-great-grandmother and great-grandmother, a pair of Afro-mestizas seated and standing in a Mexican portrait studio. My great-great-grandmother looks like she's ready to wrestle her photographer.

As I wrote, the sun rose. Once the world was lit, it was time to leave the page and ride my bike to the high school where I taught. My comic rolled out of bed around noon. A few times a week, she drove her lightly dented muscle car to colleges and universities to teach communication. "My students tell me I'm the funniest teacher they've ever had," she'd tell me. Sometimes, I'd come home to find these students in my living room, drinking whiskey with their teacher.

When my comic told me about these compliments, I'd remember two students I'd overheard. The girls had sat in my classroom. One complained to the other about how she was failing a class everyone said was an easy A. Behind her back, kids called the math teacher who taught this class "the lady who looks like Benjamin Franklin."

Looking squarely at her failing friend, the girl said, "You need to walk up to Miss Campbell's desk and tell her she's pretty. Kiss that ass. It works. I did it and I went from an F to a C."

"Okay," said the failing girl. "I'll kiss it."

During my predawn writing sessions, I worked on an unpublishable novel. I also played with experimental fragments. The fragments were attempts at narrating my innumerable sexual assaults. Approaching them even aesthetically provoked distress. This stifled my hobby, depriving it of air. To keep it moving, I reached for absurdity, slapstick, gallows humor, and insult comedy; anything that could protect my psychic wounds.

Here are some prompts I gave myself during those predawn writing sessions:

What if I write about the time that a stranger raped me, but I narrate it from the point of view of an animal witness? Like, a snail?

What if I write about the time I got molested when I was twelve, but I make the molester a mole?

What if rape is actually a practical joke that half the world is in on and the other half is victim of?

At the time of these writing experiments, I was tearing through high- and low-brow books about gender-based violence. I devoured Alice Sebold's *Lucky* and *The Lovely Bones*. I devoured Maggie Nelson's *The Red Parts* and *Jane*. These four books are, for the most part, humorless, a pretty standard characteristic of narratives that feature women and girls being beaten, shot, kidnapped, raped, and dismembered. I wanted to read about these horrors because some of them had happened to me, but Sebold's and Nelson's books didn't sit right. For one thing, they were so white you could hear the *h*. The books also took themselves very, very seriously.

To survive gender-based violence, sexual violence in particular, one of the things I've had to do is *strategically* not take it seriously. By this, I don't mean that I keep a big book of rape jokes by the bed. What I mean is that I've had to teach myself when, where, and how to laugh at rapists, rape, and my own suffering. Humor anesthetizes and has a spatial effect, stretching the distance between rape and me. Paradoxically, humor also lets me approach rape. Those of us who think about it a lot need to get near it.

How close do I want to creep?

Close enough to wet it with my squirting flower.

The experimental fragments I toyed with eventually slid together to form *Mean*, a slim memoir about growing up queer and Mexican in California during the 1980s and '90s. *Mean*'s "plot" is anchored by the kinds of experiences that fuel the obscene comedy in Chantal V. Johnson's *Post-traumatic*. Johnson's novel introduces readers to Vivian, an Afro-Latina lawyer and child sexual-abuse survivor. While exchanging "unrepeatable" jokes, Vivian and her friend Jane smoke a spliff in Jane's Crown Heights apartment.

> The worst thing about child abuse is being the only girl in your kindergarten class with HPV.
>
> I haven't had a virginity since I was five.
>
> I must have been a really cute kid, because I was molested by two *different* people. Wish I could "me too" them, but they're both dead.

". . . child abuse comedy," muses Vivian. "Are we ready yet as a society?"

"I'm ready to bring this voice to the people," answers Jane.

The first experience anchoring *Mean* is a sustained period of sexual abuse that a thirteen-year-old classmate inflicted on me. This boy molested me in the high-ceilinged classroom where he and I were supposed to study world history. As I filled out a worksheet, his hand crept up my thigh and into a place that no one had ever touched but me. I experienced a common and commonly misunderstood response. I froze. Adults had warned me about weirdos in vans kidnapping children from parking lots. They failed to explain that it would be everyday people most likely to trespass between my legs.

As Jane and Vivian pass their spliff back and forth, getting higher and higher, the friends list these everyday people.

> Sometimes little girls were abducted by strangers and then strangled, raped, and dumped. Sometimes they were abducted, raped, and forced to breed like purebred dogs, and Elizabeth Smart and Jaycee Dugard were heroes. But mostly? Mostly they were raped by supposed protectors: by their fathers, their grandfathers, their brothers and cousins, babysitters, coaches, teachers and preachers.

As the weeks wore on, my history classroom shrank, its walls pressing in on me, a vise. The morning that my teacher glimpsed what my classmate was doing to me, I anticipated an intervention. Instead, he blushed and looked away. Because it deviates from standard narratives, those where the molester is an adult, I titled this episode my "avant-garde molestation." I did, ultimately, write about my molester as a mole.

The second experience anchoring *Mean* is what I titled my "classic rape." A classic rape is the type of attack most men will condemn, the type where a stranger ambushes a pedestrian in a public setting, raiding the unwitting victim's body. The classic rape is cartoonishly obscene, a sexual practice joke.

Scholars of humor aren't that into practical jokes. The folklorist and librarian Moira Marsh suggests that their lack of sophistication might be why practical jokes fail to attract serious scholarly interest. Marsh writes that the "objection to practical jokes in general is that they are aggressive and cruel." I agree. Practical jokes are undeniably aggressive and cruel. However, I would also argue that any scholarly attention paid to rape is scholarly attention paid to the most popular practical joke of all.

In *Practically Joking*, Marsh proposes a taxonomy consisting of five practical joke categories:

The put-on. *An example*: A candy dish filled with animal vertebrae and other small bones sits on my classroom desk. A high school student asks, "Miss Gurba, what's that?" I answer, "Melissa." The student narrows her eyes and then glances at the supposed bowl of Melissa with suspicion and concern.

The fool's errand. *An example*: It's our last night at summer camp, and at campfire, the counselors tell us we're going snipe hunting. When we ask what snipes are, the counselors give conflicting answers. One counselor describes them as delicate, birdlike creatures. Another makes them sound almost like elves. A third paints them as prickly things with no arms, no legs, and an abundance of teeth. The counselors tell us to grab our pillowcases and two sticks. With flashlights pointing the way, they lead us into an oak forest. The sound of twenty girls banging sticks together, chanting, "Here, snipe, snipe, snipe . . ." echoes through the trees.

The kick-me prank. Self-explanatory. (As a high school teacher, I've unpeeled many "kick me" notes from the backs of nerds and foreign exchange students.)

The booby trap. *An example*: A group of students pours a bucket of baby oil down a flight of school stairs. They hide next to the janitor's closet and wait for the dean to slip.

The stunt. *An example*: Hot off the sale rack, I wear a formfitting crop top to my history professor's office hours. I sit across from him, asking questions about German history. He leans forward to read the minuscule print stenciled to the stretchy fabric between my breasts: "My penis is bigger than yours." As he prattles on about the Weimar Republic, he turns a violent shade of red.

My fondness for riddles, trivia, puns, knock-knock jokes, and pranks blossomed during my tomboy years. I slid fake ice cubes with fake flies trapped in them into drinks. I bought some rubber dog shit and left it in the kitchen. I was excited to get my hands on a strip of fake vomit until I realized I couldn't really use it. The sight of it made me gag. I kept it in my dresser, beneath some threadbare pajamas.

April Fools' Day is Christmas for practical jokers, and in the fourth grade, I enlisted the help of three classmates, Guadalupe, Guadalupe, and Guadalupe, in the commission of what was to be a highly choreographed practical joke, category: booby trap.

I snuck into my parents' bedroom and darted past my father's weight bench. At my mother's sewing table, I sat at her chair, pulling a wicker sewing basket onto my lap. I thrust my hand into it and groped for a box of pins. Pulling one out, I held it to my ear. Shook it. Metal rattled. A grin took over my chubby face.

On the morning of April 1, the Guadalupes and I passed notes. We strategized. When the lunch bell rang, we walked to the cafeteria with the rest of our classmates. After wolfing some food and guzzling some milk, we went back the way we came, evading hall monitors and returning to our classroom.

It was empty.

I jiggled the door handle.

Unlocked.

Guadalupe crept in with me. The others stood guard outside.

I knelt beside our teacher's cushioned office chair. The rest of us sat on hard plastic. He enjoyed armrests and wheels. He could spin. His chair was practically a throne.

I slid the box of pins from my sweatpants pocket and got to work inserting them into the upholstery. At home, I'd watched my mother use pins to attach fabric to sewing patterns, dotted paper imprinted with the outlines of pants, dresses, jackets, and shirts. On TV, I'd watched cartoon animals use pins for gags that doubled as acts of self-defense. Mice spilled them on the ground to stop cats in pursuit. In a way, our teacher was a cat. He was bigger than us, he was in charge, and he flaunted his status. When his job frustrated him, he attacked us with sarcasm. It stung. Why not sting him back?

I stood and did as our teacher had taught us; I double-checked my work. Tilting my head back and forth, I noticed that depending on how the light struck my pins, they became visible or invisible. When lit from the right angle, our teacher's chair reminded me of a photograph I'd seen in a library book, of a bearded fakir asleep on a bed of nails.

I asked Guadalupe, "What do you think?"

She nodded and gave me a thumbs-up.

We exited. The Guadalupes and I scampered to the playground.

Once recess was over, we formed a single-file line outside our classroom. Our teacher opened the door and we marched inside. I hadn't experienced this sort of anticipation before. I felt ready to explode. The tension came from knowing a secret that I shared with co-conspirators. They looked ready to explode too.

After lunch every day, our teacher read aloud to us from a book. The current selection was Roald Dahl's *James and the Giant Peach*. The novel rested on the chalk ledge, and on this special day, our teacher seemed to approach the book in slow motion. He picked it up, spun around, and headed to his chair. Yawning, he stretched his arms wide, and then opened *James and the Giant Peach* to a dog-eared page. Our teacher's big feet kicked into the air, and he dropped ass first onto our bed of tiny nails.

What I saw that April Fools' Day I haven't seen since. As pins penetrated our teacher, his face was replaced by a dragon's, nostrils flaring, exhaling steam. The man in charge of us flew, dick first, several yards through the air before landing on his feet. Post-prank, he looked shorter.

"WHO DID THIS?" he screamed.

Most of the class looked confused.

No one laughed.

I realized that what we'd done wasn't funny.

A Guadalupe sniffled. She cracked under the weight of guilt. Her hand went up in the air.

"You did this?" our teacher asked with shock.

She nodded, then ratted the rest of us out.

That four Mexican girls had pranked the teacher stunned him. We were not the expected culprits.

After realizing I'd hurt my teacher, I got scared. Then I felt sorry. Regret humbled me. So did the spanking I got from my mother. Putting needles in my teacher's chair taught me that the pranks we daydream about can translate to horror in real life. This new awareness didn't kill my love of practical jokes. It made me more discerning about which ones I went along with. I gave up sharp pranks, jokes that might cut. I said no to gags that had to be followed by tetanus shots.

The next time I went along with a practical joke was high school. I excelled at typing and had finished my classwork. I sat at my keyboard, bored. Bernice, the blond lady who taught both typing and psychology, walked past our row. A girl sitting near me clapped her hand over her mouth and pointed at Bernice's backside. The rear hem of our teacher's calf-length skirt was tucked into the elastic waistband of her control-top pantyhose. As she paced, I stared. Aside from the time I accidentally walked in on Mrs. Brooks pumping her breast milk, this was the most intimate view I'd ever had of a teacher.

When you're a child—and teenagers are children—it's a thrill to witness adult demotion. To see a member of the class that reigns over you chopped down to your level, or even lower, is a treat, a spoonful of sugar to get you through your day. We let Bernice's pantyhose chew on her skirt for an hour. We let her figure out that she was exposing herself to us on her own. Once I became a teacher, I got a taste of this prank. My students let me teach half a Tuesday with my zipper down. I was relieved I'd worn underwear. I was also relieved that I'd worn the pair with "Tuesday" printed on them instead of the ones with "Monday."

Since comedy isn't a mainstay of school curricula, most of us develop our understanding of comic logic through observation or accident. In his memoir *Born Standing Up*, the comedian Steve Martin recalls this process.

> . . . I opened my textbook—the last place I was expecting to find comic inspiration—and was startled to find that Lewis Carroll, the supremely witty author of *Alice's Adventures in Wonderland*, was also a logician. He wrote logic textbooks and included argument forms based on the syllogism, normally presented in logic books this way:
>
> *All men are mortal.*
> *Socrates is a man.*
> ___
> *Therefore, Socrates is mortal.*
>
> But Carroll's were more convoluted, and they struck me as funny in a new way:
>
> *Babies are illogical.*
> *Nobody is despised who can manage a crocodile.*
> *Illogical persons are despised.*
> ___
> *Therefore, babies cannot manage crocodiles . . .*
>
> These word games bothered and intrigued me. Appearing to be silly nonsense, on examination they were *absolutely logical*—yet they were still funny. The comedy doors opened

wide, and Lewis Carroll's clever fancies from the nineteenth century expanded my notion of what comedy could be. I began closing my show by announcing, "I'm not going home tonight; I'm going to Bananaland, a place where only two things are true, only two things: One, all chairs are green; and two, no chairs are green."

Two years my father's senior, Steve Martin studied philosophy at the same school where my father studied history, California State University, Long Beach. Early in his career, Martin became a well-known prop comic. When I think of him and my father walking the same university hallways, I imagine Martin wearing a headband that makes it look as if an arrow is piercing one side of his skull and exiting the other. Buoyed by gigantic bell-bottoms, my father floats past Martin's prosthetic head injury.

While I admired the flesh-and-blood comedians I saw on TV—John Candy, Rodney Dangerfield, and Carol Burnett to name a few—I learned just as much about comedy from local puppets. It was Saturday, and after taking us to lunch at a steakhouse, my father walked us to a small, square fountain at the bottom of the steps of Mission San Luis Obispo. My fingers were greasy from onion rings. They glistened as I held my hand out. My father gave my brother, my sister, and me each a penny.

"Make a wish," he said. "But keep it a secret if you want it to come true."

I made the safe wish. I wished for more wishes.

After we tossed our coins into the fountain, my father led us to a sunny spot in the bustling plaza. We knelt in front of a red-and-gold puppet stage. I recognized the characters. I'd seen them in a book my father read to me at bedtime, one where a hamster escapes from his cage, explores the seaside, and happens upon a Punch-and-Judy show by the pier.

In a Cockney accent, Mr. Punch screamed at his wife. His bright pink papier-mâché face had a large, hook nose and a mouth frozen in an alarmingly wide smile. His tall, pointy red hat and costume evoked a court jester. His wife, Judy, matched his ugliness. Her cheeks, chin, and nose glowed red. Her eyes nearly touched. Her nose was a toucan's, and tufts of silver hair peeked out from under her torn bonnet. She was missing teeth.

The show was a domestic violence comedy. Mr. Punch's rage moved each scene forward. When Judy forgot to have his dinner ready for him, he pulled a cudgel out from his coat and womped her in the head. Most of the dads in the audience found this funny, and so the rest of us laughed too. Judy clasped their baby to her chest. We could hear it crying. Waaaaaaah! Waaaaaaah! Waaaaaaah! Mr. Punch didn't care. He kept beating Judy and beating Judy until she screamed, "You've gone and killed the baby again!"

Mr. Punch twirled its limp body in the air. The baby's blanket flew into the audience, landing on a boy in the front row.

Everyone laughed.

The puppets at home were just as violent. One winter night, my cousin Desiree and I sat on the carpet in Grandma's dark bedroom. Our only light came from the TV. A puppet show came on. We watched, not understanding that *D.C. Follies* was political satire meant for an adult audience. I remember one skit well. A Margaret Thatcher puppet strolls into a barbershop. She tells an Irish barber to give her a cut everyone will like. He grabs a razor and slashes the British prime minister's throat, and her decapitated head flies, landing in a chair.

The most important puppet in my world was Miss Piggy. I appreciated Miss Piggy for her strength of character. Her integrity, grit, loyalty, and muscular belief in her right to happiness inspired me. Yeah, she was a pig. So what? She was beautiful, smart, and chic. She was also ambitious.

In *The Muppets Take Manhattan*, Miss Piggy shares a scene with the stand-up comic Joan Rivers. The two blondes play department-store sales associates offering customers free samples of French perfume Quelle Difference. After returning from her lunch break with a broken heart, Miss Piggy shouts, "Get your Quelle Difference! It's French! It's feminine! It'll help you grab one of those rotten, stinking men!" Rivers asks her what's wrong. Miss Piggy answers, "My frog turned on me." Miss Piggy begins to doubt herself. Rivers reassures her that she's more than gorgeous; she's unique but she could "use a little rouge." Rivers gives her an aggressive makeover. Makeup flies. A powder-puff dust cloud forms. Maniacal laughter from the perfume counter gets louder and louder. The blondes toss makeup into the air. Customers stare with disapproval. The store manager huffs to the perfume counter and declares, "You are fired!"

Miss Piggy and Rivers look at each other and burst into crazed laughter.

That's how I'd like to get fired, I thought. *By having too much fun.*

When I finally got around to getting fired, it wasn't for having too much fun. The summer after I finished high school, I got a job making smoothies and hot dogs at the mall Orange Julius. Our boss was a retired engineer who only hired teenage girls. He massaged our shoulders and stared down our shirts. In retaliation, we stole. One coworker, a chola and teen mom, would have her boyfriend meet her after her shift. He wheeled their empty baby carriage into the back room so that the chola could fill it with hamburgers, French fries, sandwiches, pickles, and condiments. Tossing a fuzzy blanket over the bags, the boyfriend wheeled his lumpy, chili-dog-scented baby home.

What my coworkers and I didn't steal were several boxes of secret powder that nonetheless went missing. The secret powder was the Coffee Mate–like ingredient that gave the Orange Julius its signature creamy flavor. Our boss used the breakroom whiteboard to threaten us, scrawling, "Whoever stole my secret powder will be prosecuted to the FULL extent of the law."

I regretted not having stolen his powder the afternoon that I showed up and found unfamiliar boys staffing the kitchen. They were young, like twelve, thirteen, and fourteen. I stood at the counter, staring. A tired woman who looked related to the kids came face-to-face with me. In spite of my wrinkled green uniform, which clearly indicated that I was an employee, she asked, "Can I help you?"

"I work here."

"Well, my husband and I bought this store from Mr. Douglas. Our children will be staffing it. I'll need you to hand over your uniform." She stuck out her hand.

"I don't have anything on under this thing but a purple bra."

The new owner grimaced. Her sons looked intrigued.

"Keep the uniform," she said.

A year after I got fired from Orange Julius, I got raped not far from the mall. The attack happened one block from a haunted hotel, the Santa Maria Inn. I'd just crossed East Park Avenue and was making my way up South McClelland when I felt him. Some elements of this rape are still unknown. One of these is my attacker's reason for choosing me. I used to fantasize about sitting across from him at San Quentin State Prison and asking, "Why me?"

I don't anymore. He probably chose me because I was easy. A female pedestrian who daydreamed while walking.

No joke, I had friendship on my mind when he grabbed me.

Another thing I don't know about my rape is how long I was followed. That question makes me shiver. It's one thing to be casually observed. It's another to not know how long a stranger has been walking behind you, enjoying your ignorance as they mentally rehearse a blitz attack. Did my rapist think about killing me? Maybe. He beat another victim to death in a park and took her green card. The police arrested him after he tried to abduct another woman at knifepoint.

My best friend TT says that my voice saved me. I screamed and the guy let go. He ran away. The assault had interrupted my walk to my mother's workplace. She was teaching second grade at the elementary school I'd gone to. In the immediate aftermath, I disassociated, my mind and spirit exiting my ears like two plumes of steam. These hovered above my body, commanding it to complete the journey to my mother's classroom. With the understanding that my attacker had an appetite for fear and terror, I played stoic. I did not cry. That would be giving him what he wanted.

It did not occur to me to call the police.

The only thing I wanted was my mom.

Arriving at Miller School, I took the same route to my mother's classroom as I had on the April Fools' Day that I made my teacher bleed. I walked from the cafeteria down a breezeway, and turned left. My mother now taught in my teacher's former classroom. I'd learned a lot about practical jokes in there. I was about to learn more.

When I threw the door open, I saw my mother standing at the chalkboard. She was inches from the chalk ledge where our teacher had kept *James and the Giant Peach*. Now that it was safe to show emotion, I sobbed.

It wasn't until I began writing my experimental fragments that I started to think of what had happened to me as a practical joke. If my rapist had pulled a misogynist prank, then telling the story of it should be scaffolded by humor. Using humor to fashion my prose would be tasteless but not more tasteless than rape itself.

Shouldn't style match content?

In *Practically Joking*, Moira Marsh defines the practical joke as "a scripted, unilateral play performance involving two opposed parties—trickster and target—with the goal of incorporating the target into play without his or her knowledge, permission, or both." Marsh further emphasizes that the "distinctive part of the practical joke as performance is that the unwitting or unwilling participation of one of the protagonists is a central element." There is no part of this definition that doesn't sound like rape. Rape happens according to social scripts so familiar that movie audiences can anticipate on-screen rapes. Rapists set unilateral play into motion with the goal of transgression. They seek to sexually violate victims without our knowledge or consent. Most important, the victim's unwitting or unwilling participation is rape's central element. Absence of consent is what makes rape rape.

A rapist doesn't have to be a stranger for their attack to conform to the practical joke format. In *Coercive Control*, the forensic sociologist Evan Stark inventories the tactics used by male misogynists to subjugate their wives and girlfriends. He likens their tactics to the violence used by kidnappers and hostage takers. Stark describes one husband who would hide in a closet and then jump out of it to "surprise" his wife when she arrived home. Starks writes that "although he claimed this was only a joke," the husband knew that his actions incited terror. His wife had confided in him that during childhood, "an uncle had lain in wait in a closet, then raped her." Seen through the lens of his wife's personal history, the husband is guilty of a meta practical joke, a rape reenactment likely to trigger incest memories.

The husband justifies his behavior by minimizing it. His claim that his surprise was "only a joke" obscures that his prank puts him in overwhelming control. Practical jokers occupy a position of dominance. Pranksters seek to humiliate, shame, and degrade their targets—humiliation, shame, and degradation also being tactics regularly employed by men who use coercive control to dominate women.

Stark writes that when interviewed, victims of coercive control "reveal the prevalence of rituals of degradation like those to which POWs, prisoners, hostages, kidnap victims, or residents of total institutions' are subjected." He adds that the husband of one of his clients repeatedly told her children, "If your mother isn't here when you come home from school, look under the ground in the back yard, right where the dog is buried." Whether we like it or not, this terrifying statement *is* a misogynist joke. That it's a joke doesn't mean it shouldn't be taken with all due seriousness.

Jokes can be death threats. And jokes can come true.

It is widely but wrongly believed that jokes are supposed to make us laugh. While jokes sometimes have this effect, laughter is beside the point. What jokes do is reorganize social space for varying degrees of time. Practical jokes do this in unsubtle ways. When I was in high school, a student reorganized our Spanish classroom's social space by playing a practical joke on our Spanish teacher.

No one liked this teacher. She taught by the book, treating it like a bible. If we used a Spanish word that wasn't printed in our textbook, she penalized us. She maintained that if a noun, verb, or adjective was missing from the book's glossary, then it didn't exist. This was infuriating to those of us who actually knew Spanish. She did not. She spoke German and German-inflected English. The little Spanish she knew came directly from her teacher's copy of the textbook. One day, when her back was turned, a boy nabbed one of her beloved knickknacks, a feathery parrot perched on a small sign that read "No fumar." After swiping the bird from her desk, the prankster tossed it behind a wooden cabinet against the back wall. Because I sat at the back of the classroom, I had a clear view of the parrot wedged among dust bunnies, spitballs, hardened wads of gum, and trash.

"Where is Polly?" the teacher screamed.

While this practical joke made the class laugh, it also temporarily reorganized social space. We knew where Polly was, but we weren't telling. For the rest of that period, Spanish students, not the teacher, commanded the classroom. Our prankster had inverted the academic hierarchy. Teacher torturing kids had become kids torturing teacher. She never did find Polly.

Practical jokes are also used to strengthen, deepen, and multiply existing hierarchies. That's how rape is usually used. Rape is an act of dominance. It degrades and demotes. The rapist shrinks their victim. They turn them from person to toy. But rape is different from other practical jokes. What sets it apart is its ubiquity and duration. Its scope and scale of impact are also unique.

Once a person has been victimized through rape, they remain raped. For this reason, some survivors grimly quip that sexual assault is the "gift that keeps on giving." In *King Kong Theory*, the filmmaker, writer, and rape survivor Virginie Despentes recalls how she arrived at the understanding that rape is always with us.

> For the first few years, we avoided talking about it. Then, three years later, a friend of mine got raped on the kitchen table of her own home . . . by a guy who had followed her in from the street. The day I found out, I was working in an indie record shop in the old town center . . . Rape doesn't disturb the peace, it's already part and parcel of the city. I lock up the shop and take a walk. I was more outraged than I had been when it happened to us. Through her, I realized rape is something you catch, and can never get rid of.

In my imagination, rape as something you catch and can never get rid of looks like this: When I was in elementary school, I watched a Canadian variety show called *You Can't Do That on Television*. The show was attractive to me because instead of adults, it featured kids doing comedy. In one sketch, Ross, a man, asks Christine, a girl, "What is the big holiday in April that we celebrate what used to be the Roman New Year?"

Christine begins to say something but catches herself, chiding, "Ah, you almost caught me! Forget it, Ross."

Ross says, "Oh, no, no, no, no, no! Seeing as this show is about holidays, you get a holiday from being slimed."

On *You Can't Do That on Television*, kids lived in constant fear of slime. Buckets of it were suspended above the stage, and the crew waited for cues to pour it over kids' heads. It took three words to trigger a sliming. *I, don't,* and *know.*

"No slime?" asks Christine.

"No slime," promises Ross.

"Okay, Ross, what was that question again?"

He repeats, "What is the big holiday in April that we celebrate what used to be the Roman New Year?"

Christine confidently answers, "I don't know!"

A trickling sound, and then slime coats Christine's head. Her jaw drops as the muck runs down her shoulders. A glob turns her nose the color of guacamole.

"What is it?" she asks with exasperation.

Ross says, "April Fools' Day!" and taps her nose.

Rape is sort of like being slimed. It's gross and embarrassing and hard to hide. Some people laugh at you for it. Others feel sorry. A fair number think you deserved it. The slime never fully goes away. You can wash it, scrub it, and bleach it, but it persists. Something will eventually happen to remind you of the sliming, and you'll smell it, see it, taste it, touch it, and hear it all over again. The slime burrows into your pores and seeps into your bloodstream. It eats away at you. At age seventy, you might be found wandering the streets in your nightgown, unable to remember your name, thanks to two boys who raped you at a house party when you were fifteen. Women who've been sexually assaulted are at higher risk of developing a type of brain damage linked to cognitive decline, dementia, and stroke.

Both of my grandmothers developed severe dementia.

The neverendingness of rape is expressed by Shiori Ito's memoir *Black Box*. After the journalist is drugged and raped by her mentor, the journalist Noriyuki Yamaguchi, she tries to get rid of his slime.

> When I got home to the apartment I was renting in Tokyo, the first thing I did was to take off all my clothes and hurl Mr. Yamaguchi's T-shirt into the garbage can. I put everything else into the washing machine and turned it on. I wanted to wash away every trace of what had happened that night.

Five days after the attack, Ito goes to a Harajuku police station. For two hours, she recounts what happened to a female traffic officer. The woman says, "I'm going to get someone from Criminal Affairs." Ito spends another two hours recounting the same story to a male investigator. She writes, "This may have been the first and second time I would describe the details of the attack to the police, but it was only the beginning."

Every indignity and injury precipitated by the acute phase of rape is an extension of its initiatory violence; Ito will be experiencing what Yamaguchi set into motion for the rest of her life. A blatant example of rape's neverendingness arrives when police inform Ito that to confirm certain details about her rape, she must participate in its "reenactment."

The reenactment takes place on the top floor of the Takanawa Police Department. In a room reeking of sweat, a police officer orders Ito to lie down on a blue mat. He places a life-size doll on top of her and asks her to help him arrange it. As they reenact her rape, a photographer takes pictures. When Ito tells a colleague at Reuters about the reenactment, the colleague says, "That was a second rape."

After I began to sob in my mother's classroom, my mother called the school principal. The principal came and escorted me to the nurse's office. A detective arrived. I told him what had happened to me, and then he drove me to the intersection where I was attacked. We reenacted parts of the rape. I can recall standing on the sidewalk with the detective, but post-reenactment, my memory goes blank. There's nothing there. It's like the rest of that July day never happened. Rape slimes past, present, and future.

When I worked on *Mean*, I wrote against books written by Alice Sebold and Maggie Nelson. Taking its cue from certain true-crime conventions, Sebold's memoir *Lucky* opens with her attack at Syracuse University.

> In the tunnel where I was raped, a tunnel that was once the underground entry to an amphitheater, a place where actors burst forth from underneath the seats of a crowd, a girl had been murdered and dismembered. I was told this story by the police. In comparison, they said, I was lucky.

Lucky describes the night of May 7, 1981, in detail. Sebold fights. Bites. Pushes. Tries to run. He has a knife. He strangles her into unconsciousness. When Sebold comes to, the attacker orders her to stand. She recounts looking into his eyes "as if he was a human being." He orders her to take her clothes off. She pleads, "I'm a virgin."

Lucky's lexicon immediately maps borders. It delineates, perpetrator versus victim. The former is subhuman. Monstrous. The latter is human. Innocent. On command, Sebold removes her oxford-cloth shirt. She likens this to "shedding feathers. Or wings."

"Nice white titties," says the rapist. Another contrast is drawn.

Sebold repeats that she's a virgin. It becomes mantra.

When the rapist is finished, he says, "I'm so sorry . . . You're such a good girl."

The police take Sebold's rape seriously. Her parents are loving and supportive. She continues going to Syracuse. She studies writing. Six months post-rape, Sebold makes a quick trip to get something to eat. She spots a Black man who has the same height and build as her rapist. She crosses the street, enters a store, and emerges with a peach yogurt and soda. The Black man has vanished. She mentions that ever since the rape, she's felt fear around Black men.

Suddenly, Sebold sees a Black man crossing the street.

He says, "Hey, girl. Don't I know you from somewhere?"

That somewhere must be the tunnel.

On campus, Sebold calls her parents and tells them that she saw her rapist. Her next stop is the office of her teacher Tobias Wolff. To him, she announces, "I can't come to class. I just saw the man who raped me. I have to call the police."

Sebold has faith in her country's criminal justice system.

She really seems to believe that it exists to serve her needs.

Sebold tells the police that there was an officer on Marshall Street when her rapist appeared. They speak with him. He identifies the man who greeted her as Gregory Madison.

The police arrest Madison. When they assemble a lineup, Sebold chooses a different Black man, failing to pick the man she saw on Marshall Street as her attacker. No matter, Madison goes to trial.

A letter written by Assistant District Attorney Gail Uebelhoer begins, "There is no question this was a rape. Victim was a virgin and hymen was torn in two places." It ends, "Good luck. Victim is excellent witness."

Sebold understands the advantages she holds as a special kind of rape victim. Sebold describes a series of contrasts that seem to distinguish her from her rapist but that also distinguish her from rape victims like me. I imagine her gazing down from the top of this implied hierarchy, at the rest of us.

> . . . I was a virgin. He was a stranger. It had happened outside. It was night. I wore loose clothes and could not be proven to have behaved provocatively. There were no drugs or alcohol in my system. I had no former involvement with the police of any kind, not even a traffic ticket. He was black and I was white. There was an obvious physical struggle. I had been injured internally—stitches had to be taken. I was young and a student at a private university that brought revenue to the city. He had a record and had done time.

A judge finds Madison guilty of rape, sodomy, and other charges.

When I finish *Lucky*, I feel slimed by it.

Sebold was a very good rape victim.

Apparently, I wasn't. I was wearing leopard-print platform shoes, a black velvet miniskirt, and a gauzy black blouse when I got grabbed. I had no (angel) wings to lose. I'd been molested by a classmate and, soon after turning fourteen, had "lost my virginity" at a house party where I guzzled vodka, drinking so much that I couldn't walk. I became a puddle on a living room floor. As I bobbed in and out of consciousness, an older boy scooped me up, slung me over his shoulder, and carried me to a bathroom. He locked me inside, knocked me around, and did what he wanted. He took my underwear. I wore turtlenecks and jeans to hide my bruises. I arranged my hair to hide the bump on my head.

Sebold emphasizes that she's repeatedly congratulated for her cooperation with the criminal justice system, for being an "excellent witness." A bailiff tells her, "I've been in this business for thirty years. You are the best rape witness I've ever seen on the stand." I refused to testify at the trial of my attacker, Tommy Jesse Martinez. I didn't want to see his face again, and I didn't share Sebold's dogged faith in the police or our criminal justice system. The police have given me many reasons not to trust them. At a time in my life when my politics were more unrefined, I'd thought I might join the criminal justice system as a lawyer. I was an undergraduate at the University of California, Berkeley, and had applied for an internship at the District Attorney's Office in San Francisco. I was accepted, and two police officers, a working female detective and a retired male detective, supervised a fellow intern and me.

I was upstairs in a large room with the male detective and needed to walk past him to get to a door. As I did, he grabbed me. As usual, I froze. His jowly face flew at mine, kissing me on the mouth, smearing me with saliva. I was slimed.

When he pulled away, I was shaking.

Who was I supposed to tell?

The police?

"Why did you do that?" I asked.

He answered, "Because you remind me of my wife when she was young."

Back to *Lucky*.

No joke, after finishing Sebold's memoir, I asked myself, what if she picked the wrong guy? *Lucky* gave the impression that Sebold didn't spend much time with Black people. Meanwhile, she ached to send the Black person who'd hurt her to prison.

I decided to give Sebold's novel *The Lovely Bones* a try. On December 6, 1973, Mr. Harvey, neighbor of fourteen-year-old Susie Salmon, rapes and murders her. Susie's spirit goes to heaven and gazes down on her family. Again, another white female victim perched high as an angel. Susie narrates, "The police in those first weeks were almost reverent. Missing dead girls were not a common occurrence in the suburbs." I finished reading *The Lovely Bones* but passed on seeing the movie. The trailers were enough. The film's protagonist looked like one of Botticelli's angels.

I swiped Maggie Nelson's *The Red Parts: Autobiography of a Trial* off a bookshelf in Mexico and read it on a plane that flew me to the United States. *The Red Parts* explores Nelson's relationship with her family, in particular her relationship to an aunt she never met, Jane Mixer. Nelson's prior book, the poetry collection *Jane: A Murder*, folds into *The Red Parts*, as does the murder trial of Jane's killer, Gary Leiterman. As Nelson narrates, questions are answered. Jane's murder moves from unsolved to solved.

The Red Parts acknowledges humor but doesn't adopt it as a stylistic or structural element. Nelson quotes James Ellroy, a crime fiction writer whose mother's murder was never solved, to this effect: "All men hate women for tried-and-true reasons they share in jokes and banter every day." Nelson shares that for as long as she can remember, her grandfather has mistakenly called her Jane instead of Maggie, his confusion feeling like "a hoax." Nelson nods at comedy when she writes, "I tried to find a sense of humor about the cinematic, self-aggrandizing images I had of discovering some crucial piece of evidence that the 'professionals' had overlooked, or of someday reading from *Jane* at a bookstore with her killer clandestinely seated in the audience."

Nelson goes to dinner with the producer of *48 Hours Mystery*, a true-crime television show. The producer asks her if, while she was writing *Jane*, she felt herself channeling her aunt. Nelson answers no, that in the book she doesn't try to speak for Jane. Instead, she lets her aunt speak for herself, through her journal entries. In conversation with the producer, Nelson articulates a highly individualistic understanding of death.

> . . . I have tried to imagine her death, there's really no way of knowing what she went through—not only because I don't know what happened to her on the night of her murder, but because no one ever really knows what it's like to be in anyone else's skin. That no living person can tell another what it's like to die. That we do that part alone.

I come from cultures that don't treat death this way. Death is our confidante. Death answers our prayers, intervening in our lives. Like rape, death is always with us. Because of that, we know death well. Death gives us gifts. One of these gifts is intimacy with the dead.

We never die apart. We always find a way to die together, to die into one another. Nelson herself socializes Jane's death, expanding it, making it shared by strangers. In death, some of us make friends. I have a relationship with the spirit of Sophia Castro Torres, the Mexican migrant woman murdered by my rapist. I play music for her. I cook food for her. I pour water, coffee, soda, and tequila for her. I light candles for her. I burn copal for her. I talk to her. When I see a special kind of sunlight, I wave hello to her.

The man who killed Sophia rehearsed for her death by assaulting several women, myself included. I don't know exactly what it felt like for her spirit to be forced out of her body, but I do know what it's like to turn around and find that man standing there, grinning. I know what it's like for that man to put himself where he's unwelcomed. Sophia and I share that knowledge. It is an obscene point of connection.

Nelson writes about what's left behind after a sudden death, the birth of an archive.

> While writing *Jane* I became amazed by the way that one act of violence had transformed an array of everyday items—a raincoat, a pair of pantyhose, a paperback book, a wool jumper—into numbered pieces of evidence, into talismans that threatened at every turn to take on allegorical proportions. I wanted *Jane* to name these items.

I aspired to create such an archive for Sophia but had little to work with. The most detailed record I was able to locate was her autopsy report. In terms of archival creation, Jane was a better murder victim. She wasn't poor. She owned a lot of things and had places to keep them. In terms of archival creation, Sophia left little. She had no home, no place to keep herself or her things. She was shy and depressed. Her boyfriend had been murdered. She spent her days at the Salvation Army, sipping coffee and staring into space. At night, she walked. When her life ended, television producers mostly ignored it. They couldn't be bothered to say one of the few things that remained, her name. Reporters called her a "transient." As she ran for her life, her toothbrush fell out of her purse.

I didn't think that writing about Sophia would be therapeutic and it wasn't. Not at all.

I kind of gave myself a second rape writing about what happened to us.

I retraumatized myself.

I pored over legal documents and learned that the young man who had hurt us wrote poetry. I learned that he had a girlfriend. I learned that he had a child. I thought about this child a lot. A judge condemned this child's father to death row.

I learned that before standing trial for rape and murder, the young man who attacked me had robbed people. On February 23, 1994, when my future rapist was sixteen years old, he and a friend walked to Pepe's Liquors. They pulled a knife on the cashier and demanded money. He triggered the silent alarm. My future rapist and his friend ran. Cops arrested them. My future rapist told the cops that yeah, he'd been to Pepe's and pulled a knife on the cashier, but the guy had overreacted. It was just a joke.

I wasn't the only reader who felt funny about *Lucky*. Other readers also questioned the conviction of Gregory Madison, real name Anthony Broadwater. Timothy Mucciante, a producer who worked on a planned film adaptation of Sebold's memoir, was one of these skeptics. Mucciante told the *New York Times* that while reading the script and the book, "he was struck by how little evidence was presented at trial." He hired Dan Myers, a private investigator, to further explore his suspicions. Meyers validated the producer's hunch. He also thought the wrong guy had been convicted.

Broadwater had always insisted on his innocence, never confessing to Sebold's attack. Still, he served sixteen years in prison. After his release, he lived as a registered sex offender for twenty-three years. Myers contacted Broadwater and connected him with a criminal defense lawyer. A legal team found flaws in his case. Their legal efforts culminated on November 22, 2021. Broadwater was exonerated. Eight days later, Sebold issued a statement.

Writing for *Bitch* magazine, Melanie Dione credits Sebold with expressing "sorrow and sympathy" for what happened to Anthony Broadwater. However, she also draws attention to the statement's detached quality, writing that Sebold's words read as if penned by "a casual observer caught by the circumstance of proximity and little else." Sebold made a mealy and passive attempt at apology: "I will forever be sorry for what was done to him."

With that phrase, I envision Sebold hovering above the horrific mess, watching Broadwater's ordeal, unwilling to acknowledge her hand in his fate. Her hand authored *Lucky*, a work of copaganda that turned Broadwater into her literary victim. Dion characterizes Broadwater as a "young man without so much as a mugshot on file . . . who had the misfortune of speaking to a scared white woman." A stranger upended Sebold's life. In turn, she upended the life of another.

When I consider how *Lucky*'s lexicon maps contrasts, juxtaposing victim against perpetrator, perpetrator against victim, I'm unsurprised by Sebold's unwillingness to name what she did. She clings to an imagined innocence that won't save her. Angel wings aren't Sebold's, yours, or mine. We're human.

Humor can go only so far. It can protect me from a lot, but it can't protect me from myself. With or without my sense of humor, I'll always be raped. When walking alone, I look over my shoulder. When touched without warning, I leap. Maybe I'll develop dementia like my grandmothers. Of all the things they forgot, I hope they forgot that.

Because rape is so horrific, it can feel as if using everyday language to write about it falls short. This prompts some writers to raid the vocabulary of religion in order to confer solemnity. They write about us having wings. They write about us with reverence. They take refuge in the laughable construct of virginity.

My Catholic parents sent me to catechism and mass, and during worship, I came to relish neither scripture nor sermon. Instead, my mind and spirit soared during moments that validated our fallibility, our common and grotesque humanity. These moments arrived in the form of mistakes, trespasses, and accidents, clashes with rules. I felt connected to my fellow parishioners when one fell asleep and his ogre-like snore punctuated the gospel, waking up everyone, even our priest. Unable to help himself, the priest laughed. That snore seemed to rattle the stained-glass windows, mutating the experience. It tickled divinity. It made church finally feel alive.

When I find moments of humor in survivor narratives, I smile. Toward the end of Chantal V. Johnson's *Post-traumatic*, Vivian decides to go to therapy. As she and her friend Jane discuss this choice, they joke.

> Jane was full of opinions about this and said she could only ever have a Black therapist. "I'm not telling white people my secrets," she said.
>
> Vivian thought having a white therapist might actually be easier. "Less pressure? To be some kind of Black, you know," she said. "I'd be so busy thinking they were going to judge me for listening to the Carpenters or whatever that I wouldn't be able to *get well*."

"Or maybe," Jane said, peering down over her in a pair of oversized glasses worn for show, "you just grew up around a bunch of white people and are more comfortable with them."

"You're not wrong. But seriously, it's really comforting being around white people! If they ever challenge you, you can just always accuse them of being racist."

Jane laughed. "You know what, Vivian? Don't overthink it, just do you."

When asked how he knows that a trauma patient has recovered, Dr. Jack Saul, director of the International Trauma Studies Program, answers that a survivor's ability to exercise spontaneity is his sign. Spontaneity happens when avoiding death or injury stops being a survivor's primary concern. Spontaneity happens when one is able to dwell in a moment for its own sake.

The philosopher Mikhail Bakhtin wrote that "laughter has the remarkable power of making an object come up close, of drawing it into a zone of crude contact where one can finger it familiarly on all sides, turn it upside down, inside out, peer at it from above and below, break open its external shell, look into its center, doubt it, take it apart, dismember it, lay it bare and expose it, examine it freely and experiment with it." When I was a tomboy, these were things I wanted to do with a broken antique clock. The old clock sat by the fireplace, always stuck at the same hour. The only way to fix it was to further break it; the key that wound it was trapped inside. This key was visible through the small panes of glass framing the clock on either side and these panes could be moved just enough to insert bobby pins and paper clips that I twisted straight. Shoving these into the clock's innards, I tried to free the key. With each attempt at rescue, the key moved deeper and deeper into the clock. The clock devoured the thing it needed in order to function.

I don't play with that clock anymore. Instead, I play with words and ideas. I think about horrible things, like rape, because I don't want them to happen to anyone and I don't know how to make them stop. Rape has supplanted my childhood fascination with the broken clock. It is the thing that I want to finger familiarly on all sides, turn upside down and inside out, peer at from above and below, break open, look into, doubt, take apart, dismember, lay bare and expose, examine freely, and intellectually experiment with. To do that, I need to be protected by laughter. I want for laughter to protect everybody who has ever been slimed.

ITCHY

The problems started when my father found me using the wrong math book. I was doing my homework at our kitchen table and had asked him for help with a word problem. The instructions said to multiply some loaves by some fish. I didn't get it. My father picked up the book. He turned the page and knitted his brow. The strange math book belonged to Mrs. Woodcock, my sixth-grade teacher. She was an octogenarian whose neck hung like the most American bird of all, the turkey. She was proud to be from Kansas and even prouder to be a Christian. That's why Mrs. Woodcock used Christian math books.

My father stared at an illustration of the twelve apostles. One of the book's previous users had given them giant penises. My father turned the page. After seeing what they'd done to Jesus, he slammed it shut.

"Myriam, you don't have to finish this homework." He paused. Then, with terrifying calm, he added, "I'm speaking to Mrs. Woodcock tomorrow."

My dad had taught fifth grade for years. Now that I was twelve, he worked as an administrator for the school district's Migrant Education Program. When I asked my dad to explain his job, he said, "I make sure that teachers do their jobs properly. I make sure teachers don't discriminate against kids whose parents work in the fields. Some teachers don't like what I do."

My parents gossiped over dinner and told my brother and sister and me not to repeat what we heard. We listened and learned that our father had done as he'd said he would. He'd dropped in on Mrs.

Woodcock to ask, "Why are you using Christian math books at a public school?"

Leaning against her cane, she answered, "Mr. Gurba, I've been using those books for over twenty years. They're not going anywhere."

"We'll see."

It was a short walk to the principal's office. My father brought my math book with him. He showed the principal the apostles and told the principal that he didn't pay taxes so that Mrs. Woodcock could do the Lord's work. She had to get rid of those books.

After my father left, the principal summoned Mrs. Woodcock to his office. My father had left my book and the principal showed my teacher the picture of the apostles. He reminded her that she worked at a public school and told her to get rid of those math books. Mrs. Woodcock argued that no one, except for that Mexican, had ever complained. The principal told her that tomorrow morning, Mario, the janitor, would be coming to our classroom with the handcart. The math books needed to be stacked and ready to go.

In the morning, we collected the math books and set them on the concrete outside our classroom door. Mario carried three boxes of new books into our room. I rubbed my hands together. I couldn't wait to smell them.

Days later, I joined my classmates at the back of the room for our advanced reading lesson. Before I could sit down, Mrs. Woodcock shook her head at me. Her neck skin swung.

"Go back to your desk, Myriam. You're in the yellow group now."

Yellow was remedial.

When I told my father that I'd been demoted as a reader, he looked ready to grab his guns.

My mother used a different weapon. She went to St. Mary's Catholic church, lit a candle, and prayed.

Two weeks later, my best friend TT and I walked into class to find a substitute teacher half Mrs. Woodcock's age standing at the board. Mrs. Lambert introduced herself. She had bad news. Mrs.

Woodcock had slipped, fallen, and shattered her hip. She'd be gone for the rest of the year. She might have to retire.

I turned to TT, stuck out my palm, and said, "Gimme five!" She slapped my hand hard. I pictured Dorothy's house crushing the Wicked Witch. I knew my Kansas history.

I also knew why some teachers hated being told what to do by my father. These were teachers who acted like Mexicans should be seen and never heard. The place they wanted to see us was stooped in a field, harvesting strawberries. They wanted us in a constant state of humble servitude. When our light shone, these teachers tried dimming it.

My father had told me a story about a six-year-old Mexican girl who had come to school wearing a new jacket she was proud of. Kids gathered around her on the playground to admire it. She showed off its ribbon-trimmed hood and matching belt. She kept the jacket on all morning, even after the sun came out and the classroom warmed. The teacher had walked over to take a look at it, and before lunch, she motioned for the girl to come to the chalkboard. The woman smiled. Without saying a word, she bent down and pinned a note to the jacket.

The girl was ecstatic. She couldn't read the note—it was in English—but she knew that it had something nice to say about what she was wearing. At lunch, the girl held her head high as she carried her cafeteria tray. On the playground, she pumped higher than anyone else on the swings. She couldn't wait to show the note to her mom. Her mom had made the jacket.

The bell rang, and the girl walked home from school.

She felt like a star. People were staring and pointing.

At home, the girl's mom puzzled over the note. Unable to read English, she unpinned it from the jacket and brought it to the neighbor. When she returned, she slapped her daughter's face.

"How long were you wearing this?" She threw the note in the girl's face.

"All afternoon."

She slapped her again and said, "Bring me the scissors. Do you know what this paper says?"

The little girl shook her head.

"It says, 'Stay away from this dirty Mexican girl. She has head lice.'"

The next day, the girl came to school wearing an old sweater. She was bald.

Some people might argue that what happened to that little girl wasn't racism. That Mexicans are a nationality and not a race.

I think that's pedantic.

Why split hairs? Racists don't.

Whether it was racism, xenophobia, or some combination that inspired that white teacher to write that note doesn't matter. What matters is that that lady used her power to crush a child's pride.

Though I was born in the United States, my fellow "Americans" have called me a Mexican for most of my life. I like to think that they mean I'm Mexican in the tradition of the beloved ranchera singer Chavela Vargas. Her voice is a tender wound. Like my grandfather, she wrapped herself in jorongos. My grandfather kept a typewritten sonnet beneath his. On occasion, he would whip it out, hold it to his face, and read its verse. The first time he shared his sonnet with me, I was giddy. He had composed something for me! Then I saw him read the sonnet to a cousin. And then to a woman my uncle was planning on hiring as his "secretary." And then I saw him recite it to another uncle's friend, a blond newscaster named Yudi.

I fumed.

It was an all-purpose sonnet. One line was always blank.

The space for the name of the girl he was reading it to.

Chavela kept tequila under her jorongo. Alcohol helped her perfect a genre of singing indistinguishable from weeping, and while Chavela respected Mictlantecuhtli, the lord of death did not frighten her. Seducing the wives of businessmen, politicians, and muralists also didn't scare her. The only thing that terrified Chavela was the place she needed to be. The stage. She needed to drink to conquer it. That came naturally. Chavela bragged that she was born an old drunk.

From hole-in-the-wall cantinas to Parisian halls, Chavela's audiences cried into glasses of beer, champagne, and mezcal. Beautifully handsome and handsomely beautiful, she dressed like a man while stubbornly thanking the Virgin for having made her a woman.

Born Isabel Vargas Lizano, the tomboy singer left home at fourteen. According to legend, Mexico called to her. It promised to be her teacher. It promised to teach her how to be herself. To arrive in Mexico City, the girl traveled across Guatemala, Honduras, El Salvador, and Nicaragua. Her Mexican metamorphosis began at fifteen. Psychic and physical pain twisted her, misfortune turning her into Chavela, a dyke vessel for exquisite sound, music that remains at once morbid, seductive, ecstatic, perfect, and unambiguously Mexican.

At ninety-three, Chavela released her final record, *La Luna Grande*. While promoting it, she told the press, "Life doesn't owe me anything, and I don't owe anything to life. We're good."

On August 5, 2012, the ranchera singer and my grandmother accepted the invitation we must all eventually say yes to. La flaca* called. The day was overcast. I'd eaten a sweet tamal for breakfast. I stood at Abuelita's bedside and stared at her dresser mirror. It reflected her, the crooked print of la Virgen de Guadalupe hanging over the bed, a rosary, a rag, and me. The men from the mortuary hadn't come yet so Abuelita continued to cool on the mattress where she'd lived for more than a decade. Her mouth hung open. Even slack-jawed, she radiated elegance. Every bone in her face was regal.

In the days leading to her death, my grandmother's face had worn pain. She wailed and groaned. We took turns sitting with her. We told her that everything was going to be okay. We told her that dying is hard work and that she was doing a good job. It seemed as if the

* The skinny girl (Mexican nickname for death).

sum of her life's anguish—being locked in an orphanage, the babies she'd buried, the suffering my grandfather had inflicted—was suffocating her. But when la flaca took her by the hand, something beautiful happened. Abuelita's ninety-year-old face relaxed. The lines and wrinkles disappeared. Death was Botox.

"I can't believe it," said my uncle Álvaro. He pointed at the newspaper on Abuelita's dresser. The front page announced Chavela's death. "Both! On the same day!" Álvaro mustered a wobbly grin. Then he sobbed.

In the days to come, we would bury my grandmother in the family tomb and offer prayers for her spirit's journey. Álvaro unhooked a black-and-white portrait of her from the wall and set it on the couch. Newspapers published pictures of Chavela's jorongo-draped coffin. I took silent pride in the coincidental deaths. Who better to escort my grandmother to heaven than Chavela? What more beautiful woman to accompany Chavela to Saint Peter than my grandmother? I imagined the two of them, ascending arm in arm, my grandfather watching from behind a curtain of flame.

Throughout her life, insecure men worked to keep Chavela out of places she belonged. They wrestled her to the outskirts of masculinity. They confined her to tiny stages. They barred her from Mexico's recording industry.

One man took it as provocation when she proclaimed, "I am a Mexican!"

"But, Chavela, you were born in Costa Rica."

She snarled, "Mexicans are born wherever the fuck we get the desire to do it."

Chavela smoked cigars, aimed pistols at arachnids, and made love to women with silky mustaches. I consider these activities to be Mexicanizing, and I participate in them when given the opportunity. Like Chavela, I believe that Mexicans are born wherever the fuck we want. Still, on certain documents, I become a hyphenated Mexican, a Mexican-American.

"Mexican-Americans," writes the essayist E. Michael Madrid,

"tend to be identified not by what they are, but what they are not." In this way, Mexican-Americans are like lesbians, another group of people who tend to be identified not by what they are, but what they are not. I belong to a diaspora defined by deficiency, and I keep a running list of things I'm supposedly missing. Some leaders, like the California school superintendent who made the following statement, think I lack the same thing as the scarecrow from the *Wizard of Oz*: "Some Mexicans are very bright, but you can't compare their brightest with the average white children. They are an inferior race."

The *Saturday Evening Post,* a magazine whose Norman Rockwell covers made whiteness look wholesome, promoted the idea that Mexicans lack restraint. Why else would we reproduce with the "reckless prodigality of rabbits"? The *Post* also called Mexicans "half-breeds," implying that we're impure. This obsession with hygiene, both moral and material, points to the myth of Mexican filth and contagion, a trope embodied by an enduring bit of propaganda so small you've got to lean in to see it.

Come close.

This page is a scalp, and each instance of punctuation, a louse.

.

,

:

;

...

This essay's words are here to be washed, detangled, combed, brushed, twirled, braided, petted, and curled.

They are hair. Lots and lots of Mexican hair.

I have to take a break from lice. Thinking about them makes me itch. Let's spend a little time with another bug. Let's play with roaches.

Roaches lived in my grandparents' house. The sound of them

moving in the walls, drawers, and cabinets made me want to levitate. Roaches can crawl up your legs. They can also drop from the ceiling. To prevent them from wandering into my ears at night, I slept with my pillow over my head. I didn't want them touching my brain.

Some of the roaches at my grandparents' house soared. They were the size of small pigeons. When Álvaro brought home a box of chocolate doughnuts, a family of these very large bugs swarmed him. My mother chased them with her shoe, but they flattened themselves and disappeared into crevices. To kill them, we would've had to borrow Chavela Vargas's gun or read them one of my grandfather's poems.

While I hate cucarachas in my face, I seek them out in art. In high school, I developed feelings for the roach in a library book I stole, a hardcover collection of Franz Kafka's most popular stories. It introduced me to *The Metamorphosis.*

I rationalized stealing this book after I pulled it off the shelf and examined the card tucked into the cardboard pouch glued to the last page. It was stamped with checkout and return dates from a decade ago. That the book had gone unloved for so long made me sad. To give the book a better life, I slipped it into my bag, smuggled it home, and pulled it free once I had some privacy. I stroked its hard cover and sniffed its pages. They had a mildewy stink.

Some stories take a while to suck their reader in. Not *The Metamorphosis.* Its first line hooked me. "As Gregor Samsa awoke one morning from uneasy dreams he found himself transformed in his bed into a gigantic insect." Since I was a teenage girl, Gregor's narrative of alienation held developmental appeal. I read his story while lazing on my bedroom carpet. I thought of my bedroom floor as my fainting couch and reclined against it while bleeding, my period drenching the bulky pads I wore before I figured out how to insert tampons painlessly. (Nobody explained that you don't shove these directly up. Though trial and error, I eventually figured out how to insert them at a slant.)

If I metamorphosed into a roach, I'd have to figure out how to prevent my family from throwing food at me. That's how Gregor's dad killed him. He tossed apples at his son. One sank into his back. It injured and disabled him. The thought of a person reborn as an insect suffering from a pocked exoskeleton, its crater festering with decomposing fruit, made me cry. I cried again at the end of the story, when the housekeeper found Gregor's remains and threw him in the trash.

The Metamorphosis seemed a reinterpretation of the popular corrido lowriders play when you honk their horn.

La cucaracha, la cucaracha,
Ya no puede caminar
Porque no tiene, porque le falta
*Marihuana que fumar**

Gregor was a bug. He was also a person whose indefatigable humanity appealed to my compassion.

Through literature, bugs can become people too.

Head lice are ectoparasites the same size as sesame seeds. Their tastes are unique. They exclusively colonize human heads. Home is usually the hair around our ears and neck, but intrepid lice will explore eyebrows and eyelashes.

Our scalps are everything to them. Bedroom. Pantry. Toilet. Lice can live for up to thirty days, but if they fall off a head, they've got forty-eight hours until la flaca arrives. Grown lice can go only a day or two without blood.

Tiny Draculas, lice are most active at night. That's when we can really feel them thriving, reminding us that we aren't alone, that each

* The cockroach, the cockroach / can't walk anymore / Because he doesn't have, because he lacks / Marijuana to smoke.

of us is a habitat for countless unseen things that will never know our name and don't have to.

Lice do to our heads what settlers are still doing to the Americas. Lice, however, don't expect us to assimilate to their culture. They eat us but let us keep our ways. If lice ever make a home in my pompadour, I'll write about them in English, Spanglish, or Spanish. They can't make me tell their stories in their silent parasitic language.

I used to teach at a California high school where I experienced déjà vu a lot. Ladies like Mrs. Woodcock taught there. I avoided them. Teaching is stressful enough. I didn't need to befriend assholes.

I opened my classroom to kids at lunch; they came and shared school news, tales of what went on inside other classrooms. One of my visitors, Miguel, was sitting on the orange futon near my desk. He was expressing concerns about his teacher, a short wiry runner type rumored to have the ability to put kids to sleep with her lectures. The rumors checked out. Whenever I walked past Mrs. Hume's classroom, I saw rows of unconscious kids, their faces smashed against their desks, mouths agape, drool gleaming under the fluorescent lights. Those who hadn't drifted off to sleep stared at her with bored contempt.

"Mrs. Hume doesn't like us," said Miguel.

"Who?"

"Mrs. Hume."

"Yeah, but who doesn't she like?"

"Us!" For clarification, he hissed, "*Mexicans*."

I sat up straight. "Oh really? What did she do this time?"

Miguel relaxed into shit-talking mode. Rubbing his hands together, he explained that while in Mrs. Hume's classroom, he'd slid off his hat and set it on his desk. Mrs. Hume yelled, "Put it back on!"

Miguel was perplexed. Teachers usually punish kids for wearing hats indoors, not for following the rules. Miguel asked Mrs. Hume why she wanted him to put it back on. She asked, "How do I know you don't have head lice?"

My eyebrows rose involuntarily.

"Do you think she was joking?" I asked. I already knew the answer, but sometimes I succumb to the pressure to give "nice" white people the benefit of the doubt.

Miguel shook his head. "She told us this story about how when she took her daughter to the pool, she wouldn't let her play with the Mexican kids there. She said she didn't want her daughter getting lice. She said they live in our hair 'cause we're dirtier." Miguel looked at his hands. "Mrs. Hume laughed when she said that."

I wanted to rip out Mrs. Hume's tongue. I hated going to department meetings with her. She asked long-winded questions that could've been two-sentence emails, and she acted confused by people's concise answers, passive-aggressively asking us to explain simple things again and again. One afternoon, she had the nerve to waste our time by talking about paper clips for ten minutes.

"That's fucked-up," I told Miguel. "Truly fucked-up."

He nodded.

The high school where Miguel and I gossiped sat fifteen miles away from Westminster, the Orange County city where a Mexican tenant farmer made US legal history. By 1940, Orange County had become the core of Southern California's citrus belt. Its fortunes were built by the Mexicans who worked the region's groves and packing houses. The historian Gilbert G. González estimates that as many as one hundred thousand Mexican citrus workers and their families lived in barrios scattered throughout the area. I have friends from Orange County whose families picked citrus for generations. That job became synonymous with Mexicans, and it seemed that our reason for being was making sure that white people had enough to eat. "It is up to the white population to keep the Mexican on his knees in an onion patch," said one Texas school superintendent opposed to educating Mexicans. Administrators claimed that once educated, Mexicans became "difficult."

During the 1940s, the Westminster School District operated two schools. Hoover was the Mexican-only campus. In a decrepit frame building plopped next to a cow pasture, Hoover teachers punished kids who spoke Spanish. They offered a barely there curriculum. Everyone learned vocational skills and English. Most students already knew English, but whatever; they were going to learn it again. Flies buzzed along the gray piece of meat heated and reheated and re-reheated to make lunch. As they sipped broth outdoors, students stared at the electric fence surrounding their campus. They recalled the terror of classmates who'd gotten tangled in it. When that would happen, teachers had to run to the neighboring dairy farm and beg the farmer to shut it off.

Buses chauffeured white students to 17th Street School. Created by J. E. Allison, an architect who codesigned the Beverly Hills Post Office, its buildings had stylized Spanish facades. As students learned reading, writing, science, math, and history, they gazed out classroom windows, daydreaming, their eyes glazed over. Lost in fantasy, they couldn't see the manicured lawns, fluffy palm trees, and topiaries tended by gardeners. During recess, smiling kids poured into the playground. They climbed monkey bars, soared on swings, and teeter-tottered. They ate sandwiches and drank milk in the cafeteria. At the end of the day, they clambered back onto the buses, returning home to cottages and bungalows.

In September 1944, Sylvia, Jerome, and Gonzalo Jr. went with their aunt Sally to enroll at the nearest school. The group, which also included Sally's two kids, Alice and Virginia, walked from the Mendez family's asparagus farm to the office of 17th Street School. After peering at the three Mendez kids, the clerk at the front desk said, "They'll have to go to Hoover." Smiling at their pale cousins, she leaned close to Sally. The clerk said, "Those two can go here, but no one can know they're Mexican. They'll have to tell everyone that they're Belgian."

Refusing to pledge allegiance to Brussels, Sally walked everyone back to the farm. She told her niece and nephews' parents, Felicitas and Gonzalo Sr., what had happened. Gonzalo met with other Orange County dads whose kids had gone through the same thing, and the men decided to sue. The attorney David Marcus represented the dads at trial. He used social science to argue their case.

When the school superintendent James Kent took the stand, he defended the Mexican-only schools. He explained that they were designed for kids with "language handicaps." When asked to clarify what that meant, Kent said that this problem was unique to students of Mexican ancestry, and that he assessed the language abilities of incoming Mexican students "by orally talking to them." When prompted to describe the results of these assessments, Kent answered, "We usually find them retarded."

Kent was emphatic that Mexican kids lacked the social habits of white kids. Because of this deficiency, it would be "silly" to transport Mexican kids to white schools. Before integrating, Mexican kids needed to be taught "cleanliness of mind." They needed to be trained "how to get along with others." Kent added that mixing white and Mexican students would "retard" the "English-speaking pupils," that that was why administrators sent the "Mexican-speaking" students away. He bemoaned Mexican hygiene, arguing that Mexican kids couldn't even take care of their own heads. He alleged that this failure fostered "lice, impetigo, and tuberculosis." Classifying Mexicans as a race, Kent believed uncleanliness to be one of our essential traits.

Mrs. Hume was probably unfamiliar with *Mendez, et al. v. Westminster School District of Orange County, et al.* But she was extremely well versed in the ideas expressed by Superintendent Kent. She preached the gospel of supreme Anglo-Saxon hygiene.

What a hypocrite.

The custodian told me that her classroom had roaches, all our classrooms did, and I hoped that a bunch of them were laying eggs in her paper-clip drawer.

• • •

In 1946, Judge Paul McCormick decided *Mendez v. Westminster* in favor of the dads. He wrote that "a paramount requisite in the American system of public education is social equality. It must be open to all children . . . regardless of lineage." On paper, California became the first state to desegregate its schools. In real life, they're still segregated.

It was after school when Mrs. Hume barged in. I'd left my door propped open and was sitting at my desk, lesson planning.

What now? I thought.

Earlier that day, President Donald Trump had done something awful, I can't remember what, and Mrs. Hume had chosen me as her audience to complain about it. "Mrs. Hume hates Donald Trump," the kids would complain. "It's her whole personality!"

I watched her shake her head, wave her arms, huff, and purse her mouth. She squealed, shouting, "He's Hitler! He's just like . . . Hitler!"

I went limp, hoping she would go away.

The anti-Trump rants by people like her were tedious. They could go on for an hour about how diabolical Trump was, which was true but lopsided. On days that I felt like stirring the shit, I'd wait for the complainer to quiet. Then I'd say something like, "You know, Obama earned the nickname Deporter in Chief because he deported more people than any US president before him. Were you as concerned about the enforcement of immigration law when he was in office? I don't remember you caring this much about immigrants a few years ago. What changed? What are you doing to support migrant kids in your classroom?"

I waited for an answer. Liberals looked at me in disgust. I look at them with disgust when they yell at me to vote. Yeah, yeah, yeah, voting matters, but it's just one political tool out of many. It's also one that can be used to corrupt democracy. Germans voted for Hitler just like more than 70 million Americans voted for Trump. This country isn't the opposite of the Third Reich. One of the histories that inspired the Nazis was ours.

In *Mein Kampf*, the manifesto he wrote while in jail, Hitler defined race as something "in the blood." To "Germanize" a non-German population would require a commingling of bloods, a transformation Hitler believed "impossible." As proof, he pointed in our direction, at the Americas.

> North America, whose population consists in by far the largest part of Germanic elements who mixed but little with the lower colored peoples, shows a different humanity and culture from Central and South America, where the predominantly Latin immigrants often mixed with the aborigines on a large scale. By this one example, we can clearly and distinctly recognize the effect of racial mixture. The Germanic inhabitant of the American continent, who has remained racially pure and unmixed, rose to be master of the continent; he will remain the master as long as he does not fall a victim to defilement of the blood.

Hitler drew more inspiration from Manifest Destiny. This doctrine argued that Anglo-Saxon settlers had a "right to independence—to self-government—to the possession of the homes conquered from the wilderness by their own labors and dangers . . ." Hitler fused Manifest Destiny with Lebensraum, a concept developed by German geographer Friedrich Ratzel. It was first defined "as the geographical surface area required to support a living species at its current population size and mode of existence," and in Hitler's geopolitical imagination, unconquered Lebensraum beckoned. The Wild East, made up of Poland, Lithuania, Ukraine, and other territories, became the Nazi answer to the Wild West. Hitler dreamt of Germanizing this "wilderness." Nazi scientists and engineers pioneered new forms of mass murder to achieve this goal.

During the Trump presidency, intellectuals and pundits constantly name-dropped the German Jewish political philosopher Hannah Arendt. I read as much of her work as I could. I wanted to study her ideas in context. Some of Arendt's writing helped me to understand what was happening in the United States. Some of it helped me to understand myself. Some of it, like the essay "Reflections on Little Rock," is awful and bigoted.

Arendt studied with the philosophers Martin Heidegger, Edmund Husserl, and Karl Jaspers. In 1933, as she was leaving the Prussian State Library, the Gestapo arrested her. A librarian had reported her for being too studious, and police discovered that she was breaking the law; it was illegal to research anti-Semitism. After a week in jail, Arendt talked a detective into freeing her. She left Berlin and fled to Paris. In 1940, she was arrested again. French officials sent her to Gurs, a concentration camp at the foot of the Pyrenees. Arendt ran away again. In 1941, she sailed from Lisbon to New York, one of the last Jews to escape Nazi-occupied France.

In *The Origins of Totalitarianism,* Arendt distinguishes homicide from genocide, writing that when a "murderer leaves a corpse behind" he "does not pretend that his victim has never existed . . . he destroys a life, but he does not destroy the fact of existence itself." In the death factories of Auschwitz-Birkenau, Belzec, Chelmno, Majdanek, Sobibor, and Treblinka, Nazis developed radical measures that treated people "as if they had never existed."

"The insane mass manufacture of corpses," writes Arendt, "is preceded by the historically and politically intelligible preparation of living corpses." These walking dead are created through processes of dehumanization, and one medicalized model was developed in a place rarely associated with the Nazis, El Paso, Texas. In 1917, the surgeon Claude C. Pierce announced that everyone entering the US from Mexico needed to be quarantined. Typhus was spreading, and US officials wanted to ensure that "vermin-infested" Mexicans weren't bringing the disease with them. Pierce took a small redbrick building underneath the Santa Fe Street Bridge and expanded it, converting it into a disinfection plant. It was staffed by three physicians who inspected 2,830 bodies a day.

Alexandra Minna Stern, founder of the Sterilization and Social

Justice Lab, has documented the day-to-day operations of El Paso's disinfection plant. She writes that those inspected were sorted by sex and forced to strip naked. All clothing was chemically scoured; every scalp examined for lice. Clippers attacked boys and men, their hair falling to newspapers that were spread at their feet. The hair was burned. Kerosene and vinegar doused girls' and women's tresses. Covered by a towel, they inhaled fumes for half an hour. Once everyone was deloused, they were herded to the showers and sprayed with soap, kerosene, and water. At the end of the ordeal, each person's clothing was returned, and everyone got a certificate from the "United States Public Health Service, Mexican Border Quarantine." It guaranteed that they were lice free.

Stern notes that "in El Paso, and along the border in general, forced nudity and totalizing disinfections continued into the late 1920s, long after the typhus panic had subsided." One pesticide introduced at the border was hydrogen cyanide, also known as Zyklon-B, a German invention.

When I taught US history, my students studied the Holocaust. While I lectured, I projected images of Jewish captives. I explained that at the camps, people were sorted. Women were separated from men. Children from adults. Guards shaved everyone bald and everyone stripped naked and showered in front of everyone else. Everyone's belongings and clothes were taken. Some captives were chosen for immediate death, others for indefinite slavery, and others for interminable waiting. Numbers replaced names. These were tattooed onto the prisoners' arms.

At the sight of a starving nude Jew, a boy let out a high-pitched giggle.

A Jewish boy turned to him. He said, "Shut the fuck up or I'll beat the shit out of you."

Nobody was beaten, but I did have an uncomfortable conversation with the boy who laughed.

"Why'd you laugh?" I asked him after the bell had rung and everyone was gone.

He looked away. He stared at the wall, his desk, the ceiling, the flag. His eyes were willing to look at anything but mine. He said, "I don't know."

"Did you see something that made you uncomfortable?"

After sucking his bottom lip for a few seconds, he answered, "I don't know. Okay. Yes. Yes!"

"It's normal to laugh when we're uncomfortable. I do it too. All the time. I do it even when I'm not supposed to. But that laughter sometimes hurts people. David wanted to kick your ass because some of his family went through that."

My student looked embarrassed. He said, "Well, how was I supposed to know?"

"Exactly. It's impossible to know what people have suffered unless they tell us. Now you know. I think we're done here."

My student nodded and left in a hurry. I never saw him do anything like that again.

"Antisemitism is exactly the same as delousing," said Heinrich Himmler. "Getting rid of lice is not a question of ideology. It is a matter of cleanliness. In just the same way, antisemitism, for us, has not been a question of ideology, but a matter of cleanliness, which now will soon have been dealt with. We shall soon be deloused. We have only 20,000 lice left, and then the matter is finished within the whole of Germany."

Dr. Gerhard Peters isn't one of the more famous Nazis.

He was a chemist and an authority on the production of insecticide.

When Peters learned that US officials were disinfecting Mexicans at the US-Mexico border with Zyklon-B, he studied their use of the pesticide carefully. In 1938, he wrote an essay about his findings. Published in the German pest science journal *Anzeiger für*

Schädlingskunde, Peters's essay was accompanied by two photos of El Paso's delousing chambers. During World War II, the chemist became the general manager of Degesch, the German Corporation for Pest Control, the agency that held the patent for mass production of Zyklon-B. In 1941, Zyklon-B was put to new use in Poland. Karl Fritzsch, deputy commandant of Auschwitz, began to asphyxiate prisoners of war with it. By 1942, Zyklon-B had become the primary murder weapon used in the death camps. The majority of those murdered were Jews.

When the war ended, a German court charged Peters "as an accessory to murder in 300,000 cases."

In 1955, he was acquitted.

The fumigation of Mexicans continued until the late 1950s.

In 1994, seventy-three Castlemont High School students, most of them Black and Latine, took a field trip to Grand Lake Theatre to see *Schindler's List*. After a scene where a Nazi officer shoots a Jewish woman in the head, a student blurted, "Ooooh! That was cold."

His classmates laughed.

The other theatergoers were already mad at the kids. They'd been talking throughout the whole movie, but the laughter was different. Outraged patrons complained to the management. The theater owner relocated the kids to the lobby, scolded them for making fun of genocide, and ordered them to leave. As they exited, the remaining theatergoers clapped.

When local and national media got hold of the story, reporters and commentators stoked speculation that the Oakland, California, teens were Nazi sympathizers. School administrators issued a public apology. They instituted a Holocaust curriculum to, presumably, cultivate what the kids must've been lacking. Empathy.

I don't think those kids were Nazis. I also don't think they lacked empathy. I think that they laughed at the horror on-screen for the same reasons that I laughed when confiding to a friend that a stranger had raped me. She laughed too. We kept going until we cried. I also laughed at my first funeral. My cousin Desiree and I were sitting on a wooden pew in a Catholic church. Our cousin Franky rested in the coffin on display at the altar. My father had told my brother, my sister, and me that Franky had been murdered on his way home from school. He didn't look like it. He looked strangely asleep.

To distract from the sight of our cousin's remains, Desiree whispered jokes in my ear.

I was thirteen. She was fourteen. Franky was fifteen.

Soon after we buried Franky, his mother joined him. Then his father joined them.

The murder of children takes a wretched toll.

"We see death and violence in our community all the time," one of the Castlemont kids told the *New York Times*. "People cannot understand how numb we are toward violence."

Sometimes, laughter anchors us.

It's the best way of reminding ourselves that we're alive.

A few weeks after Miguel had come to vent about Mrs. Hume, I found myself standing in the same room as her.

We were in the classroom of a teacher who ran an illicit bodega, the kind to which administrators turn a blind eye, occasionally dropping in themselves to buy chips and soda. While Mrs. Hume and the bodega teacher chatted, I opened his fridge. We three were the only ones in the room and the two of them were discussing students, emphasizing the races of the students they perceived to be shitty. Sensing that someone was about to say something that would make me feel murderous, I spun around and blurted, "I'm Mexican!"

Mrs. Hume got the wildest look on her face.

"I thought you were from India!" she said indignantly.

Oh wow. She thought I was a "model minority"?

"I'm Mexican."

Louder, and with more agitation, Mrs. Hume repeated, "I thought you were from INDIA!"

I wanted to laugh. She was acting like I'd tricked her. I knew that now, she feared me.

Something might leap from my body and invade hers. I took a few steps toward Mrs. Hume, shook my head vigorously, and proclaimed, "I'm a Mexican!"

I left her to ponder whether or not I had given her lice and skipped back to my room.

I hoped Miguel would be dropping by.

PENDEJA, YOU AIN'T STEINBECK

My Bronca with Fake-Ass Social Justice Literature

When I tell gringos that my Mexican grandfather worked as a publicist, the news silences them.

Shock follows.

They look ready to explode, and I can tell they're thinking, *In Mexico, there are PUBLICISTS?! What could they possibly have to publicize?*

I grin wryly at these fulanos and let my smile speak on my behalf. It answers, "Yes, bitch, in Mexico, there are things to publicize such as our *own* fucking opinions about *YOU*."

I follow in the cocky footsteps of my grandfather, Ricardo Serrano Ríos, "decano de los publicistas de Jalisco,"[1] and not only do I have opinions, I bark them como itzcuintli. También soy chismosa, and if you don't have the gift of Spanglish, allow me to translate. *Chisme* means gossip. It's my preferred art form, one I began practicing soon after my period first stained my calzones, and what's literature, and literary criticism, if not painstakingly aestheticized chisme?

Tengo chisme. Are you ready?

A self-professed gabacha, Jeanine Cummins, wrote a book that sucks. Big-time.

---

1 His fucking tombstone.

Her obra de caca belongs to the great American tradition of doing the following:

A. Appropriating genius works by people of color,

B. Slapping a coat of mayonesa on them to make palatable to taste buds estadounidenses, and

C. Repackaging them for mass racially "color-blind" consumption.

Rather than look us in the eye, many gabachos prefer to look down their noses at us. Rather than face that we are their moral and intellectual equals, they happily pity us. Pity is what inspires their sweet tooth for Mexican pain, a craving many of them hide. This denial motivates their spending habits, resulting in a preference for trauma porn that wears a social justice fig leaf. To satisfy this demand, Cummins tossed together *American Dirt,* a "road thriller" that wears an I'm-giving-a-voice-to-the-voiceless-masses merkin.

I learned about *Dirt* when an editor at a feminist magazine invited me to review it.

I accepted her offer, *Dirt* arrived in my mailbox, and I tossed it in my suitcase. At my tía's house in Guadalajara, I opened the book.

Before giving me a chance to turn to chapter one, a publisher's letter made me wince.

"The first time Jeanine and I ever talked on the phone," the publisher gushed, "she said migrants at the Mexican border were being portrayed as a 'faceless brown mass.' She said she wanted to give these people a face."

The phrase *these people* pissed me off so bad my blood became carbonated.

I looked up, at a mirror hanging on my tía's wall.

It reflected my face.

In order to choke down *Dirt,* I developed a survival strategy. It required that I give myself over to the project of zealously hate-reading the book, filling its margins with phrases like "Pendeja, please." That's a Spanglish analogue for "Bitch, please."

Back in Alta California, I sat at my kitchen table and penned my review. I submitted it. Waited.

After a few days, an editor responded. She wrote that though my takedown of *Dirt* was "spectacular," I wasn't famous enough to write something so "negative." She offered to reconsider if I changed my wording, if I wrote "something redeeming."

Because the nicest thing I can say about *Dirt* is that its pages ought to be upcycled as toilet paper, the editors hauled out the guillotine. I was notified that I'd be paid a kill fee: 30 percent of the $650 I was initially offered for my services.

Behold my unpublishable cruelty as it rises from the dead!

In México, busy people drink licuados. Making these beverages requires baseline skills. Drop fruit, milk, and ice into a blender and voilà: a meal on the go.

Unfortunately, Jeanine Cummins's narco-novel, American Dirt, *is a literary licuado that tastes like its title. Cummins plops overly ripe Mexican stereotypes, among them the Latin lover, the suffering mother, and the stoic man-child, into her wannabe realist prose. Toxic heteroromanticism gives the sludge an arc, and because the white gaze taints her prose, Cummins positions the United States of America as a magnetic sanctuary, a beacon toward which the story's chronology chugs.*

Mexico: bad.

USA: good.

I pinched my metaphorical nose and read.

Cummins bombards with clichés from the get-go. Chapter One starts with assassins opening fire on a quinceañera, a fifteenth-birthday party, a scene one can easily imagine President Donald Trump breathlessly conjuring at a Midwestern rally, and while Cummins's executioners are certainly animated, their humanity remains shallow. By categorizing these characters as "the modern bogeymen of urban Mexico," she flattens them. By invoking monsters with English names and European lineages, Cummins reveals the color of her intended audience: white. Mexicans don't fear the bogeyman. We fear his very distant cousin, el cucuy.

Cummins employs this "landscape of carnage," a turn of phrase that hearkens to Trump's inaugural speech, to introduce her protagonist, the newly widowed Lydia Quixano Pérez. Police descend upon Lydia's home, now a schlocky crime scene, to pantomime investigation. Lydia doesn't stick around. She understands what all Mexicans do, that cops and criminals play for the same team, and so she and her son, Luca, the massacre's other survivor, flee.

With their family annihilated by narcotraffickers, mother and son embark on a refugees' journey. They head north, or, as Cummins often writes, to "el norte," and italicized Spanish words like carajo, mijo, *and* amigo *litter the prose, yielding the same effect as store-bought taco seasoning.*

Through flashbacks, Cummins reveals that Lydia, "a moderately attractive but not beautiful woman," age thirty-two, operated a bookstore. Her character soon takes absurd shape. As a protagonist, Lydia is incoherent, laughable in her contradictions. In one flashback, Sebastián, Lydia's husband, a journalist, describes her as one of the "smartest" women he's ever known. Nonetheless, she behaves in gallingly naive and stupid ways. Despite being an intellectually engaged woman, and the wife of a reporter whose beat is narcotrafficking, Lydia experiences shock after shock when confronted with the realities of Mexico, realities that would not shock a Mexican.

It shocks Lydia to learn that the mysterious and wealthy patron who frequents her bookstore flanked by "[thuggish]" bodyguards is the capo of the local drug cartel! It shocks Lydia to learn that some Central Americans migrate to the United States by foot! It shocks Lydia to learn that men rape female migrants en route to the United States! It shocks Lydia to learn that Mexico City has an ice-skating rink! (This "surprise" gave me a good chuckle: I learned to ice-skate in Mexico.) That Lydia is so shocked by her own country's day-to-day realities, realities that I'm intimate with as a Chicana living en el norte, gives the impression that Lydia might not be . . . a credible Mexican. In fact, she perceives her own country through the eyes of a pearl-clutching American tourist.

Susan Sontag wrote that "[a] sensibility (as distinct from an idea) is one of the hardest things to talk about" and with this challenge in mind, I assert that American Dirt *fails to convey any Mexican sensibility. It aspires to be Día de los Muertos, but it, instead, embodies Halloween. The proof rests in the novel's painful humorlessness. Mexicans have over a hundred nicknames for death, most of them are playful because death is our favorite playmate, and Octavio Paz explained our unique relationship with la muerte when he wrote, "The Mexican . . . is familiar with death. [He] jokes about it, caresses it, sleeps with it, celebrates it; it is one of his favorite toys and his most steadfast love." Cummins's failure to approach death with appropriate curiosity, and humility, is what makes* American Dirt *a perfect read for your local self-righteous gringa book club.*

The writer Alexander Chee has said that writers interested in exploring the realities of those unlike themselves should answer three questions before proceeding. These are:

"Why do you want to write from this character's point of view?"

"Do you read writers from this community currently?"

"Why do you want to tell this story?"

The introductory letter from Cummins's editor answers the final question. Cummins believes she's important, and expert, enough to represent "faceless" brown people.

Step aside, Jesucristo. There's a new savior in town. Her name is Jeanine.

Saviors terrify me: they always fuck things up, often by getting people killed, and if you don't believe me, look closely at the first four letters of the word *messiah*.

To fit the messyanic bill, Cummins rebranded herself as a person of color. A glance at recent interviews shows Cummins now identifying as "Latinx," her claim to this identity hinging on the existence of a Puerto Rican grandmother. Cummins, however, is still breaking in her Latinx-ness, because four years ago, she wasn't.

I repeat: four years ago, Cummins was white.

"I don't want to write about race," Cummins wrote in a 2015 *New York Times* op-ed. "What I mean is, I really don't want to write about race . . . I am white . . . I'll never know the impotent rage of being profiled or encounter institutionalized hurdles to success because of my skin or hair or name."

Unlike the narcos she vilifies, Cummins exudes neither grace nor flair. Instead, she bumbles with Trumpian tackiness, and a careful look at chronology reveals how she operates: opportunistically, selfishly, and parasitically. Cummins identified the gringo appetite for Mexican pain and found a way to exploit it. With her ambition in place, she shoved the "faceless" out of her way, ran for the microphone, and ripped it out of our hands, deciding that her incompetent voice merited amplification.

By her own admission, Cummins lacked the qualifications to write *Dirt*.

And she did it anyways.

For a seven-figure sum.

A seven-figure sum.

As Bart Simpson used to say, "Ay caramba!"

Dirt isn't Cummins's first book. In addition to several other novels, she wrote a highly racialized true-crime memoir, *A Rip in Heaven*. I also wrote a memoir in this genre: *Mean*. *Mean* features a budding serial killer, Tommy Jesse Martinez. In 1996, Martinez sexually assaulted several women, me included, and his final victim helped police capture him.

In the months between my sexual assault and his capture, Martinez raped, disfigured, and bludgeoned to death Sophia Castro Torres, a soft-spoken Mexican migrant who sold Mary Kay cosmetics and performed farmwork. Martinez stole her green card, kept it as a trophy, and threw it in a trash can once it bored him.

Sophia's ghost haunts me. She's always with me, I supposed you could say she talks to me, and she has words for Cummins: *Mexicanas die en el otro lado too. Mexicanas get raped in the USA too. You know better, you know how dangerous the United States of America is, and you still chose to frame this place as a sanctuary. It's not. The United States of America became my grave.*

Perhaps Cummins's fascination with borders explains *Dirt*'s similarity to other works about Mexico and migration: her novel is so similar to the works she used for research that some might say it borders on the *P* word. In *Dirt*'s acknowledgments, Cummins announces her ignorance by thanking people for "patiently teaching me things about Mexico." She lists writers "you should read if you want to learn more about Mexico" and a slew of authors—Luis Alberto Urrea, Óscar Martínez, Sonia Nazario, Jennifer Clement, Aída Silva Hernández, Rafael Alarcón, Valeria Luiselli, and Reyna Grande—contradicting her characterization of us as an illiterate horde. We not only have faces and names; some of us have extensive bibliographies.

If Cummins had really wanted to draw attention to the assorted crises faced by Mexicans—Mexican migrants in particular—she could've referred readers to the primary and secondary sources she plundered.

Let's take, as an example, *Across a Hundred Mountains*, a novel written by Reyna Grande. At age nine, Grande entered the United States as an undocumented immigrant. She "became the first person in her family to set foot in a university," and obtained both a BA and an MFA. Her lived experience as a Mexican migrant inspires both her fiction and nonfiction and Grande writes intimately about a phenomenon Cummins has emphasized she knows nothing about: racism.

While attending a literary gala at the Library of Congress, a fellow writer misidentified Grande. Instead of assuming she was his peer, he treated her as a member of the waitstaff. Grande wrote about this experience, stating that "feelings of inadequacy" have persisted in spite of her success. These feelings begin early. When I was in high school, I scored better on the Advanced Placement English Language and Composition exam than all of my white classmates. Instead of celebrating my success, teachers openly insinuated that my score was suspect. I must have cheated.

While we're forced to contend with impostor syndrome, dilettantes who grab material, style, and even *voice* are lauded and rewarded.

Dirt reads like a gringa remix of Nazario's *Enrique's Journey* and a sloppy mash-up of Urrea's entire oeuvre. His early works, *Across the Wire* and *By the Lake of Sleeping Children*, echo throughout *Dirt*. The book's cringe-inducing awkwardness reminds me of the time I walked in on my roommate dressed from head to toe in my clothes. It astonished and disturbed me to find this fellow undergrad in front of our dorm room mirror, pretending to be . . . me. Suddenly aware of my presence, she made eye contact with me through the reflection. Unsure of what to do, I left. We never discussed the event.

She returned my clothes to the closet, but her choice to wear them as a costume had changed them. My roommate and I weren't the same size. They smelled like her.

I couldn't wear them anymore.

Cummins did the same thing as my roommate but took her audacity a step further: she stepped out in public wearing her ill-fitting Mexican costume.

Dirt is a Frankenstein of a book, a clumsy and distorted spectacle, and while some white critics have compared Cummins to Steinbeck, I think a more apt comparison is to Vanilla Ice. According to the *Hollywood Reporter*, Imperative Entertainment, a production banner notorious for having teamed up with the likes of the libertarian cowboy Clint Eastwood, has acquired the rights to the "Mexican migrant drama novel."

Because my catastrophic imagination is highly active these days, I can visualize what this film might inspire. I can see Trump sitting in the White House's movie theater, his little hands reaching for popcorn as he absorbs *Dirt*'s screen adaptation. "This!" he yells. *"This is why we must invade."* I don't think Cummins intended to write a novel that would serve a Trumpian agenda, but that's the danger of becoming a messiah. You never know who will follow you into the promised land.

CREEP

One.

I spent my girlhood in a valley where softness crept after sunset.

In preparation, amber light bathed everything. Hills thirsting along the horizon turned golden. Lettuce, broccoli, cauliflower, and strawberries planted in tight rows asserted harsh, human symmetry. At the sound of gunfire, a cottontail rabbit froze. From the nearby vineyard, more gunshots. The rabbit leapt into ceanothus, disappearing into the shrub's lilac canopy.

Startled crows sailed away from the grapes, toward the blue.

I wondered if this violence would disturb the flavor of whatever wine was to be made using the fruit we could see from home. Connoisseurs brag that they can taste place in wine and while I understood that the vineyard's drink would be California-flavored, I wanted to know if it would taste of the dangers specific to here.

Recalling *Aesop's Fables*, I felt sympathy for the crows. The only birds I found more elegant were vultures. Vultures exist to remind us of our destiny. They also exist for the plain sake of being vultures.

My bedroom's tall window offered me a view of nightfall. Through dirty glass, I watched its descent. An owl hooted. I shut my water-stained curtains and changed into my nightgown. I brushed my teeth. After crawling into bed, I listened.

A bullfrog broke the ice. In minutes, an army joined him, chorusing.

Frog song isn't soothing. It's an ominous music, one I had to give myself over to so that I could lapse into dreams I prayed would be free of frogs and men. I preferred dreaming about beautiful women, fresh-baked pretzels, and dolphins.

I dreamt.

It crept.

At sunrise, my siblings and I got ready for school. Once dressed, I threw open my curtains to witness the predictable horror. Everything was gone. In its place hovered white. Staring at the low-hanging cloud fluffing against my window, I wondered how much it would slow our dad's already slow driving speed. It could take us an extra fifteen minutes to get to town, and I knew that navigating the soup would affect Dad's language. His temper flared easily, and because driving in fog elevated his anxiety, he was going to fill the station wagon with words that Mom prohibited us from repeating.

Definitely *shit.*

Definitely *dammit.*

Maybe *son of a bitch.*

If things went really wrong, *asshole.*

The fog's natural properties fascinated me. So did the stories that Dad told about it. The white floated like miles of strange breath exiled from its source. It embodied gothic verbs. It oozed. Crept. Snaked. Snuck. Its moisture tickled and licked, droplets settling on eyebrows, eyelashes, bangs, and sage. The inscrutability of the white's shape and size teased. Intangible, the soup was potentially infinite, and waking up in a house engulfed by cloud prompted chicken-or-egg questions. Are we hiding in the white or has the white hidden us?

There were things that seemed both real and not that could be experienced only in the fog. Before one saw these things, one heard them, and Dad enjoyed repeating a particular tale as he navigated country roads on fog-free Saturday afternoons. He eased us into this story with onomatopoeia suggestive of ruin and decay, the sound of his voice shaping our imaginings:

Squeak.
Squeak.
Squeak...

Squeak.
Squeak.
Squeak.

Squeak.
Squeak.
Squeak.

Hooves clop!

Lantern light pierces the haze!

A horse-drawn carriage manned by a Mexican emerges from the night!

The coachman looks as haggard as his animal, but to the traveler stranded along these back roads, the Mexican and his horse come as a relief. It's terrible to get a flat tire in the fog. The coachman offers the traveler a ride, he accepts, and they journey westward. At a eucalyptus tree bank, the coachman and the passenger part ways, the latter heading toward a truck stop. At its diner, the man orders a cup of coffee, and when he shares his rescuer's name with his waitress, he's chilled to learn that he rode alongside someone who was buried the year Benito Juárez became Mexico's twenty-sixth president: 1858.

Squeak.

Squeak.

SQUEAK!

While such legends lent necrotic romance to the fog, encountering undead Mexicans in it worried me less than other obstacles. At least people lived to recycle the story of the spectral coachman.

Drivers who swerved to avoid cattle, deer, and tractors weren't so lucky. Shrines commemorating these victims proliferated along our back roads. Foxen Canyon. Dominion. Telephone. Palmer. Santa Maria Mesa. Clark. Hands nailed a whitewashed cross to the pole by the egg farm where two young men encountered Orpheus. Nick and Tom. The fog endangered everyone who entered it, increasing the possibility that one might hit or be hit, and headlights didn't do much. They brightened the white but failed to cut it.

From our station wagon's back seat, I watched wisps move along our windows. The fog's softness was uncanny. How was it that something we couldn't hold in our hands could kill us?

How could a cushion be lethal? Isn't heaven supposed to be whiteness as far as the eye can see? This preview of paradise made me not want to go. The monotony felt purgatorial, and we weren't the only ones in it. Whether we liked it or not, we traveled through this strange weather together.

TT and I sat side by side in our ninth-grade English class. We were best friends, and on the first day of school, we staked out desks in the corner by the trash. TT and I lived to talk to each other, and we wanted to be able to whisper in peace. We resented adult intrusion.

Our English curriculum emphasized grammar and composition, but on occasion, our teacher, Mrs. M, talked about literature. As she read aloud about conflicts that shape narrative arcs, Mrs. M paced the linoleum floor. Her orthopedic shoes made suffering-mammal sounds. Man initiated every conflict that Mrs. M talked about. He ended some of them too. Man versus man. Man versus self. Man versus society. Man versus the supernatural. Man versus science. Man versus nature. By age fourteen, feminism had found me, and with my immature understanding of *The Second Sex*, I stared at Mrs. M's wrinkled brow, silently critiquing her lesson.

In another class, the History of Western Civilization, I'd asked our teacher, Mr. J, "Why do you lecture so often on mankind?" I told him that the word seemed exclusive. Many of us, myself included, were girls who'd grow up to be women. Why not mention womankind too?

An athlete wearing a letterman jacket rolled his eyes.

I didn't care. Annoyance can lead to enlightenment.

Mr. J explained that my schemas were narrow, that *mankind* and *humanity* obviously imply the presence of women because *woman* has the word *man* in her, which means that any mention of *man* also evokes *woman*. Mr. J concluded his word salad by saying, "*Mankind* is universal. *He,* the pronoun, is universal."

"Why can't *womankind* be universal?" I asked. "Shouldn't there be a universal *she*?"

Mr. J blushed. Fiddling with his tie clip, he answered, "We don't have time for this. Let's move on. This is unrelated to the German Empire."

Mr. J returned to his lecture on Otto von Bismarck but soon paused, making time to reminisce about his college days. He explained that he'd worked at a grocery store, an especially fun place for a young man in the summertime. The heat forced girls to wear fewer clothes, and when an attractive female shopper entered the market, our teacher and his male coworkers tracked her movements. As a courtesy to other male staff, one of her observers would access the public address system, using the store's speakers to announce, in coded language, the shopper's location.

"Some guys met their wives this way," Mr. J bragged.

I wondered which conflict drove this anecdote's narrative arc and hated that I'd likely be expected to classify it as man versus man.

After the umpteenth time that Mrs. M threatened to separate TT and me for talking too much, she followed through. Mrs. M ordered a front-row nerd to trade seats with me. I exhaled a dramatic sigh, grabbed my stuff, and before migrating to my new desk, I cast a sorrowful look at TT.

Mrs. M told us to turn to a page in our grammar and composition books and instructed us to diagram twenty sentences. I placed a clean sheet of paper on my desk and got to work. Unlike many of my classmates, I relished diagramming sentences. It was like autopsying prose, and though my diagrams were imperfect, I got decent scores.

I was dissecting a prepositional phrase when orthopedic shoes squealed in my direction. Mrs. M's hand intruded into my workspace. Bare fingers pressed a Post-it note to my desktop.

I *loved* passing notes in class. I'd never had a teacher give me one.

Excited, I read the message written in Mrs. M's matronly cursive.

Close your legs.

I can see your panties.

My guts churned. I pressed my knees together and looked at Mrs. M.

The lipless slit through which she'd explained conflict curled into a smile.

I wanted the earth to split open and take me, as it had taken Persephone.

Woman versus girl, 1991.

Man versus nature made no sense. Isn't man nature? Isn't that the same as man versus self? Was I stupid for my inability to parse man from dirt? TT and I went to a Catholic high school, and in religion class, we read the Old Testament. The book of Genesis stated that God built Adam from mud. That didn't read like a metaphor.

The books that Mrs. M assigned to us, Erich Maria Remarque's *All Quiet on the Western Front,* John Knowles's *A Separate Peace,* Shakespeare's *Romeo and Juliet,* Edmond Rostand's *Cyrano de Bergerac,* and Nevil Shute's *On the Beach,* rested on a white bookshelf beside my bedroom window.

Only one of these titles, *On the Beach*, prompted parental complaint. Its detractors found Shute's representation of nuclear war unfair, arguing that the book obscured the bright side of radiation, and I was pretty sure I knew whose parents had bitched. Some of my classmates' moms and dads worked at Vandenberg Air Force Base, a place where intercontinental ballistic missiles wait for their moment to shine.

We read *Romeo and Juliet* aloud in class. I liked that the story involved teenagers defying their parents. I was a teenager doing the same. At night, I slid my tall window open, climbed out, and escaped into the fog.

Nocturnal and crepuscular animals bore witness to my comings and goings.

In the dark, I sometimes rendezvoused with a pale girl, a classmate one year my senior. Hand in hand, we wandered through the countryside, marveling at bats, moonlit grapevines, and tarantulas creeping across asphalt. Near a barn molting white paint, we pressed our lips together. We thought of ourselves as *Juliet and Juliet.*

Having become a voracious reader of myth once I entered puberty, I recognized *Romeo and Juliet* as a retelling of the story of Pyramus and Thisbe. The Elizabethan tragedy also seemed a bit Mexican. Our mom, a Mexican immigrant, kept Spanish-language books on our living room shelves, and one, a novel titled *Pedro Páramo*, bore an inscription in her father's block script.

Hermosa hija: esta es una novela de las más importantes en idioma castellano. Juan, su autor, y yo, fuimos condiscipulos.

Tu papá, Ricardo

Reading *Pedro Páramo* clarified my parents' worldview, one that revolved around the inevitability of suffering. It was best to surrender to pain, and *Pedro Páramo* expressed this resignation through place, its author, Juan Rulfo, illuminating an underworld filled with ghosts talkative enough to drive Mrs. M batshit crazy. *Pedro Páramo* collects their murmurings and collages the dreams, recollections, and dialogues of the damned . . .

"Do you believe in hell, Justina?"

"Yes, Susana. And in heaven, too."

"I only believe in hell," Susana said.

In addition to TT, my other best friend was TV.

TV and I enjoyed a rich and complex relationship. It parented me, teaching me about my place in the world through an incessant parade of stereotypes.

In 1991, political theater dominated our TV. Mrs. M probably would've described the federal hearings as a case of man versus man. It wasn't. It was woman versus misogynists.

"I have no personal vendetta against Clarence Thomas," said Anita Hill, a thirty-five- year-old graduate of Yale Law School, phallic microphone aimed at her lips.

As Mom and I made meat loaf, we listened to thirteen crusty men interrogate the female lawyer. Seated before the Senate Judiciary Committee, Hill testified that the Supreme Court nominee Clarence Thomas had sexually harassed her while he was her supervisor at the Department of Education and the Equal Employment Opportunity Commission. As Hill coolly stated facts, congressmen glared.

"I felt that my job could be taken away or it could be at least threatened, that I wasn't going to be able to work, that this person who had some power in the new Administration would make it difficult for me in terms of other positions."

In religion class, a kid asked our teacher, Mr. K, "What do you think of the Anita Hill thing?"

Mr. K answered, "Anita Hill is a very attractive woman."

The kid, an ugly white boy, seemed taken aback. He said, "But . . . she's Black."

I clenched my jaw.

Mr. K said, "I know."

Without raising my hand, I blurted, "What about what she's saying about Clarence Thomas? He sexually harassed her."

"There's no such thing as sexual harassment," said Mr. K.

"There's not?"

"No, there's not. Sexual harassment victims aren't real."

"What are they, then?"

"They're women who don't want to exercise personal responsibility."

"Responsibility for what?"

Mr. K smiled. He repeated, "Anita Hill is a very attractive woman." His eyes rested on L, a cheerleader he drooled over. Kids sometimes speculated that the two of them were doing it. Those who gossiped about them said they probably had sex in the trailer where the youth ministry met. The story seemed plausible. The trailer did have a couch.

CALLER: Can you send someone to my house?

911 DISPATCHER: What's the problem there?

CALLER: My husband, or ex-husband, has just broken into my house and he's ranting and raving outside in the front yard.

911: Has he been drinking or anything?

CALLER: No. But he's crazy.

911: Did he hit you?

CALLER: No.

911: What is your name?

CALLER: Nicole Simpson.

Ex-husband versus ex-wife, 1993.

• • •

In 1994, a white Bronco dominated our TV screen.

Driven by O.J. Simpson, the vehicle led Southland cops on a slow-speed chase. Live coverage showed streets and highways lined with cheering crowds. Fans unfurled homemade banners, waving messages of love and support from bridges, overpasses, and curbs. The atmosphere of O.J.'s pursuit was festive and news cameras captured sports bar audiences watching the chase. They whooped and rooted for the former athlete. It might as well have been the Super Bowl. I knew Simpson was a retired football hero, but I wasn't sure what position he played. I didn't care. I hated sports. I held only one athletic record, the longest mile in our school's history. I walked it in thirty minutes and took pride in my accomplishment.

I knew Simpson as an entertainer. I'd seen him in TV commercials and had laughed at his slapstick performances in the *Naked Gun* movies. Simpson played Officer Nordberg and his job was to absorb abuse that in real life would've killed him. In one scene, the handsome actor sits in a wheelchair, his arm resting in a sling. After congratulating Nordberg on healing from recent injuries, a friend slaps him on the shoulder. The pressure sends Nordberg's wheelchair sailing and the contraption rattles down a long flight of stadium stairs, catching against a barrier. O.J.'s stunt double is catapulted into the air. We hear him crash into the dugout.

At school, all boys could talk about was O.J.'s innocence. They believed he was everything but a murderer, and I heard ridiculous theories about what had "really happened" to Nicole. The most absurd involved cocaine and Colombians.

I interrupted two classmates expounding on the coke theory to say, "O.J. killed Nicole. Men kill their wives all the time."

"INNOCENT UNTIL PROVEN GUILTY!" one of the boys yelled.

"What are you talking about, dumbass? You just tried and convicted a bunch of imaginary Colombians."

"Get out of here, bitch," the other boy hissed. "Go watch Lifetime—'Television for Women.'"

They chuckled as I walked away.

I was unbothered. I knew that they probably secretly watched Lifetime with their moms.

I graduated from high school in 1995 and left the valley for university.

My sister, O, and my brother, H, were next in line to endure Catholic high school.

In ninth grade, I learned about conflicts that drive narrative arcs.

In ninth grade, my brother and sister learned about femicide.

O was friends with the girl, a fifteen-year-old cheerleader who'd broken up with her seventeen-year-old boyfriend. He went to a different school, and on an autumn evening, he crept into his ex-girlfriend's house. After shooting her, he turned his weapon on himself. An ambulance carried the girl to the Catholic hospital by the egg farm. She died there. Patients in need of eyes and skin got them soon after.

School administrators staged the cheerleader's memorial in the same place where they held mass, the gym. The basketball court was where we, the student body, regularly received the body and blood of Christ. Songs by Boyz II Men and Mariah Carey played while kids wept. Classmates adorned a Christmas tree, hanging ornaments that symbolized the cheerleader's hopes and interests.

O dangled a pair of miniature ballet shoes from a branch.

She and the cheerleader had taken dance classes together.

According to one published report, the violence "shocked" local kids. This account left out that the cheerleader had told friends she meant to get a restraining order against her ex-boyfriend. He was scary. The newspaper also failed to mention that kids had said that they saw the ex-boyfriend assault the cheerleader on campus after cheerleading practice.

The principal, a priest with terrible posture, "urged prayers" for the family of the "estranged boyfriend." He ordered the student body "not to be judgmental."

The principal's commandment seemed out of character. I'd seen him behave very judgmentally. When he'd visited my religion class to lecture us on sex, he'd given us specific instructions for how to deal with homosexuals: love the sinner, hate the sin.

Why wasn't killing a fifteen-year-old girl a sin worth hating?

It seemed to me that making room for rage was the compassionate thing to do.

Without rage, how do people heal? Without rage, how does one produce dignity?

On Sundays, I attended mass at the brutalist church across the street from my university dorm. I found Catholic liturgy comforting. It was predictable and familiar while at the same time otherworldly. Its incense created a recognizable fog. Standing in line with fellow parishioners, I shuffled toward the altar. Our feet moved together. Though I'd been having trouble sustaining belief in God, I had no problem believing in God's mom. She seemed like a given.

She was the reason I was there, in church.

For many of us, Catholicism isn't about Jesus. It's about the woman who made him.

Once it was my turn to take the eucharist, I stared into the priest's beady eyes. His celibate gaze was revolting. Not wanting his fingers to brush my lips—who knows where they had been—I held out my cupped hands. Daintily, he nestled the body of Christ in them. The priest beside him offered me his chalice. I wondered where its drink had come from, where it had been made. I didn't want to taste home. I wanted nothing to do with that awful Merlot. I knew what watered those grapes and I shook my head, no.

I hurried back to my pew and knelt.

The divine heard my blasphemous thoughts.

• • •

Gunfire be damned, the crows kept coming.

O overheard girls gossiping about the cheerleader's murder. One said, "It's just like *Romeo and Juliet*."

"Take this, all of you, and drink from it: for this is the chalice of my blood, the blood of the new and eternal covenant, which will be poured out for you and for many for the forgiveness of sins.

"Do this in memory of me."

Kids treated the cheerleader's locker like a condolence card, scrawling messages on it, leaving signatures and drawings. The administration removed the door and gave the memento to the girl's family.

When O was in twelfth grade, a student group invited a guest speaker to her religion class. The group opposed capital punishment and hoped the speaker would persuade their classmates to feel the same way.

O listened to the guest describe his profession. He defended people accused of doing atrocious things and he went into enough detail to make my sister tremble.

By that time, I'd been studying at UC Berkeley for years. I came back now and then and one of those visits happened the summer of 1996, after my freshman year of university. I returned to the valley to spend vacation with my family.

On a July afternoon, I walked along a sidewalk. The sun shone.

Somebody crept behind me. They made their presence known by throwing their arms around me in a terrifying embrace. I told myself a lie. I told myself that the person gripping me must be someone I know. It must be a friend who snuck up on me. This is a pleasant surprise.

When I see who it is, we will laugh. My fear will dissolve.

I turned my head.

A strange teenager grinned. His face hovered close enough for a kiss. Vanishing from view, he burrowed under my skirt, rooting for truffles between my legs. His fingers pawed at my crotch and underwear.

The stranger raped me with his face.

I got away. I returned to university as planned. I continued to attend mass. I stopped believing in God. I never stopped believing in his mom.

In November, the same stranger crept behind a sixteen-year-old girl. This time, he brought a knife. During the assault, the girl demanded to know what the stranger wanted.

"I want you," he replied. "I want to mark your beautiful face."

She escaped.

Predictably, he escalated.

Later that month, he chased a Mexican woman who, by day, nursed cups of coffee at a Salvation Army shelter. By night, she walked city sidewalks alone.

The Mexican woman did not escape with her life. After the stranger took it, he hurried to a nearby pay phone. A 911 operator listened to him lie about an "attack" he'd "witnessed" at Oakley Park. When she asked for more details, the caller hung up. By the time the cops arrived, he'd vanished.

In December, the stranger flashed his knife at a shopgirl leaving work. He said, "Don't scream and I won't have to stab you."

She fought and ran for help.

The guest speaker was the attorney who had represented this stranger, the man charged with attempting to sodomize me, and to O's class, the lawyer repeated arguments he'd presented at trial. He explained that his client had been abused. He explained that his client suffered from traumatic brain injury.

O watched her sixteen-, seventeen-, and eighteen-year-old classmates.

Half looked sympathetic. The other half looked bored.

O felt like screaming. Instead, she shook.

The dismissal bell rang.

Students collected their belongings and emptied out of the classroom.

O approached the guest speaker. She asked, "Your client is Tommy Martinez, isn't it?"

The question shocked the lawyer. "Yes! How did you know?"

O answered, "I hope he burns in hell." She turned and walked to Spanish.

My parents find wine helpful. They buy it by the box.

The detective assigned to my case unwittingly used the title of Alice Sebold's memoir to describe my survival: *Lucky*. Like many survivors of sexual assault, I didn't feel that way.

I felt hypervigilant and I lived in a mirage, one that distorted my sense of danger. Threat seemed everywhere, which meant that it was nowhere, and when an eyelash landing on your cheek triggers the same startle response as a knife aimed at your heart, navigating human society gets very, very tricky.

*"No one knows better than I do how far heaven is, but I also know all the shortcuts. The secret is to die . . . when you want to, and not when He proposes."**

---

* Rulfo, *Pedro Páramo*.

Two.

Twenty years after I escaped the valley, its fog found me again. It crept into my life with well-rehearsed stealth, and it brought a coachman who would take me for a ride. Some people scoff when I share the story of this misadventure. They want to believe that the recollections of my horror are a fiction, a fairy tale, but the truth doesn't rely on belief. With or without faith, the truth simply is. My recollections implicate a preacher's son. His name is Q.

I open my eyes. Sunbeams pierce Q's French patio door, reminding me of where he made me sleep.

I'm flooded with rage. And annoyance.

Our argument began last night, at a restaurant. Throughout dinner, Q directed double entendres about meat at our server. When I told him, "Stop, you're being gross," his eyes flashed.

Peering across our long table, which held a plate of untouched veal marrow, Q hissed, "I'm giving that waitress the time of her life!"

"No, you're not. She's smiling because we're paying her."

After dinner, Q drove us to the house where we'd lived together. He had chosen it. I'd spent my last week there sleeping in the spare room.

I'd moved out because things had gotten weird. Q had quit touching me with everything but his eyes. I often sensed them on me and when I'd look up, I'd catch Q glaring. He nursed a quiet but potent contempt for months, and when I asked him what was wrong, he answered, "Nothing."

His icy stares persisted. I felt more than unwelcome. I felt loathed.

I pioneered new ways of asking "what's wrong?"

Q insisted, "Everything's fine, babe."

Q never uses *babe* affectionately. He always bathes the word in sarcasm.

I had an office in our house, a detached room where a psychotherapist had seen her clients. It was where I worked on an unfinished manuscript. Every day, I sat at a table, chronicling the events leading up to the attack I experienced in 1996. Sometimes, Q would stand in my office window, staring. He would say nothing. After lingering long enough to make his presence known, he'd skulk away.

One afternoon, he barged into the office and sat cross-legged on the carpet. He patted the floor in front of his bare feet. I scrambled off my chair and joined him.

"You're gonna stop asking why I'm not affectionate anymore," he said. "But if and when I decide to touch you, accept it. And no more talking about sex. Your book included. When I want to talk about sex, we'll talk about it. When I want to have sex, we'll have it."

Our chilly home became chillier. We weren't living as a romantic couple. Neither were we living as roommates. I didn't have a name for what we'd become. That made me anxious.

On a Saturday morning, I announced, "I'm moving out. I don't like this."

Q sat at the dining room table he'd built using a repurposed door. I stood nearby. Bursting into tears, he lunged at me, throwing his arms around my hips, weeping into my stomach. His performance seemed theatrical. Inorganic. I felt confused. Why was he suddenly clutching me? Why the sorrow? Was it feigned or real? Oddly, I did feel a flicker of hope. Maybe now he'd explain what was going on. Maybe now I'd have a word to describe the condition under which we were living. I nodded with encouragement.

"What happened to you, the thing that happened to you . . ."

Q described the worst parts of 1996. He knew about them because as we'd gotten to know each other, I'd told him why having sex sometimes terrified me.

"What Tommy did to you makes me sick!" Q cried. "It's disgusting! It disgusts me! It horrifies me! So . . . I can't touch you. The thought makes me sick. I don't want to touch you, because when I think about you, all I think about is RAPE!"

Q didn't say the last word the way he'd spoken the others. He howled it.

He burst into tears again and grabbed me. He cried into my belly button. I petted him. I also felt disgusted. With myself. My history as a sexual assault victim had rendered me grotesque. The living embodiment of rape itself. Q knew that one of my greatest fears was being found unlovable and unfuckable because of this. Was I experiencing a self-fulfilling prophecy? I needed a gut check.

Q's inveterate sarcasm had repelled most of my friends. But not A. I drove to their house and told them what Q had said. After some silence, A said, "He rape-shamed you. That's fucked-up."

"What should I do?"

"Leave him! Stay here. You can live here."

And so, I rented a room from A. My departure triggered a romantic campaign.

Q pursued me with tenacity, and this impassioned version of my ex-boyfriend had nothing in common with the sullen couch potato I'd shared a cold house with. This Q was repentant. This Q promised things would never "go sideways" again. This Q begged for a second chance. This Q left hand-picked flower bouquets and love letters on my car at night.

On a mission to prove that I wasn't grotesque, I said yes to Q.

We went to dinner a few times.

His aversion transformed into desire. He now wanted to have lots of adventurous sex. It felt good to incite lust. The sex was fun. Not at all conservative as it had been before. I asked Q what had changed. He said something about valuing what's been lost. I remained hesitant. I noticed clues that the old Q was still there, waiting to make an appearance. And he did. Several weeks into his pursuit, he snapped and called me a bitch for eating a potato chip he felt was rightfully his.

I'd consented to sex with Q to show him he'd been wrong. Now that I'd proven my point, I was done.

Q and I didn't have sex when we got home from the restaurant where he'd verbally abused our server. I tried to leave the house, but when I used the bathroom, Q took my purse, which had my keys, wallet, and phone, and hid it. I begged, "Please, give me my purse!" I was on the verge of tears. It was midnight. I was trapped.

"Quit it! You'll get it back in the morning."

Q climbed into bed and fell asleep. I slid off my boots but kept everything else on, a long wool coat included. I slept beside Q but remained on top of the covers.

The sun has also woken up Q. He's practically holding his breath. Listening. Waiting. He probably doesn't want to hear my voice. But he's going to.

"Hey. Let's talk about what happened last night."

"It's too early. We can talk about it later."

Later means never, and since I never want to argue with Q again, I say, "I can't do this anymore. I'm done. You and me—"

Q's fists pummel his mattress. It hurts to be knocked back by those hands. Q punched me once because he didn't like that I'd tapped him on the shoulder. He said that the tapping was rude and that my poor etiquette had invited punishment.

"Fuck you," Q hisses. That he's not screaming terrifies me. He's controlled. He doesn't want the neighbors to hear. "Get out," he whisper-shouts. "LEAVE!"

I fly off the bed. My boots rest about six feet away, by what used to be my side of the closet. I crawl to them, crouching as I slide one over my foot.

I look over my shoulder.

Q is kneeling, his face wolfish.

"You fucking cunt!" he hisses. "Are you gonna leave? That's all you do! All you do is LEAVE! That's all you're good for! LEAVING! You . . . fucking . . . CUNT."

I crawl to my other boot. Hands grasp my throat. They squeeze. Q strangles and drags me to the bed. He suspends me over the side. I can see the trail my heels made.

Breath warms my cheek, and 1996 comes to mind. Déjà vu. Enunciating each word crisply, Q says, “You will obey me.”

And so I decide to obey the only person who can save me from Q: Q.

“Sit on the bed.”

He releases my neck.

To show him that I want to live, I sit.

Just as I did in 1996, I turn my head to see who’s behind me. It’s my ex-boyfriend, the man to whom I just said, “I can’t do this anymore.” Q’s fist flies at my face but stops short of breaking my nose. He repeats these motions, demonstrating the beating that will happen if I struggle.

He flops onto his mattress.

In a childish voice, he commands, “Lie down.”

I obey.

He lifts my coat and dress and tugs down my underwear. Again, 1996.

I hear a voice, mine, demand, “What are you doing?”

Q whispers, “Trying to get you pregnant.”

As Q ejaculates, I leap off him and land on the carpet. I want to run but my legs are shaking so that I can hardly stand.

Q jumps off the bed and positions himself between me and the door.

“Please,” I beg. “I’m really hungry. I’m shaking because I’m really hungry.”

I’m trying to convince all three of us that my fear is a response to low blood sugar. The third party present in Q’s room is nuestra Santísima Muerte, Death. I want Her to go away. I don’t want to die in Q’s stupid little room. I want Her to take me in a different time and place. I want a good death. We all deserve to have one. My devotion to Santísima Muerte is why I keep a talisman in Her skeletal shape close to my pillow.

“Okay,” Q agrees. “But you have to eat with me.”

“Yes. Please. I will eat with you.” Anything to live.

Q drives us to a diner with faded menus and dusty fake flowers. He orders me a waffle and takes a picture of me. He texts it to me later. It's not extraordinary. Just a cheerless woman with a plate full of breakfast.

I'm at A's. The room I'm renting from them was supposed to be a nursery. It's painted brightly for a baby that never came.

I rest on the bed. It's nighttime in October. Thumbtacks affix to the wall two pages torn from different books. One depicts Persephone being snatched by Hades. The other, a skull painted by Georgia O'Keeffe.

I'm staring at my phone. Q is texting me. He's telling me that he's thinking of me. That he's been thinking of me.

I ask him what he's been thinking about. Maybe he'll admit what he did. Maybe he'll apologize for doing the thing pictured on the wall.

Q replies that Thanksgiving is close and that he enjoys the hours-long drive to my parents' house, where I'll be celebrating the holiday. Q has a friend who lives near the valley where I grew up. He loves visiting her. She's a vintner.

Q explains that he's entertaining fantasies that take place in that countryside. My mind's eye conjures home. Foothills. Cows grazing. Oaks twisting. Sage. Lupine. Primrose. Jimsonweed you shouldn't touch. Acorns. Barbed wire. A spider spinning her web. Q describes beating me until my blood soaks familiar soil. Red trails mark the earth. I have trouble crawling toward him. Perhaps my legs are broken. Dirt weighs me down. He stands over me as the pool beneath me expands. Seeing my blood everywhere excites him. He did that. He made it spill.

I gasp and gurgle. He muses, "You'll be begging."

I'm doing my best not to shake. This is the first time a man has described my murder and disappearance to me. This is the first time my suffering and death have been described as the source of a man's pleasure.

Q returns to texting about the holidays: "You haven't seen your parents in a while. Would you like me to drive you up?"

If I say yes, will his fantasies be made real?

If I say no, will his fantasies be made real?

If I don't answer, will his fantasies be made real?

I text, "No thank you." Dread makes a home inside of me.

Though I live with A, Q continues to treat me as if I'm his "girlfriend." I continue pretending as if I'm his "girlfriend." The price of behaving otherwise is too high.

When I tell Q that I'll be going to see my family for Thanksgiving, he gives me "permission" to drive home alone.

As I travel the coastline, my car rattles. I do what I've been trained to do in such situations. I ignore it.

When I pull into my parents' driveway, the car sputters. Dies.

A tow truck hauls it to a garage by the park where I rode my first pony.

The mechanic calls to tell my father that he's stumped. He can't find anything wrong with my car.

I drive a rental home.

Later that week, Dad calls: "The mechanic figured out what's wrong. He says he found loose screws."

I recall Q's nocturnal visits to my car. His offerings. Flowers. Love letters shoved in plastic baggies tucked under windshield wipers. Q once bragged about "fixing" the car of a guy who pissed him off.

". . . Myriam?"

"I'm still here, Dad."

I no longer live in the fog that brought Q, and with each passing day, I understand, with greater clarity, what happened inside of it. I see how the haze came to engulf me. I see its effects on the memoir I wrote in the little room that had belonged to the psychotherapist.

I wasn't conscious of it at the time, but that book became a hiding place. *Mean* was where I hid myself.

Q's terror became a part of *Mean*'s terroir. The book revivified some of the worst parts of 1996. It also created a portrait of the valley where my father taught me to read in English and Spanish and where a Holocaust survivor taught me high school French. Vache es vaca is cow. Chat es gato is cat. Côtelettes de porc es chuletas de puerco is pork chops. My French teacher Sœur J didn't teach us the word *terroir*. The term belongs to French viticultural vocabulary, and it communicates the flavor of a drink's somewhereness. The sociologist Marion Fourcade has described *terroir* as "[capturing] the correspondence between the physical and human features of a place and the character of its agricultural products," *terroir* first having appeared in Denis Morelot's 1831 treatise *Statistique de la vigne dans le départment de la Côte D'or*. The concept has been contested since the nineteenth century. Some oenophilists insist that one can absolutely savor substrate, which may contain ingredients as tangible as anise, and as intangible as envy, in every sip of wine. Terroir is why wines are named after place; its why champagne is named Champagne. Others argue that roots don't, can't, and won't absorb geologic phenomena, that plants can't metabolize and transmit place the way vintners say they can. I suggest that we work with the word metaphorically, the way Catholics are trained to work with the Bible. Terroir might be a myth but legend has the power to shape and harden reality. Imbibing myth makes us human.

Q found a way to live in my elbow. This is how.

The summer that I moved in with him, J, a lesbian stand-up comic, invited me to go skateboarding with her. When I told Q about her invitation, he turned bitchy and jealous.

"How can I trust her?" he nagged. "She's a dyke."

Assuming he was kidding, I laughed and tossed my board in the passenger seat. I met J at a skate park where we skated and skated and skated, and then we stood at the edge of a concrete bowl, a concavity built to mimic a swimming pool. J explained dropping in, how to work with, against, and through gravity so that a girl might fly along concrete walls at a 90-degree angle. Despite my fear, I gulped a deep breath and leaned forward. To my astonishment, I didn't die. As I sailed along the concrete, the air tasted extra sweet.

I scrambled back up to the lip and practiced and practiced until gravity decided to discipline me. It fed me to the concrete, my body trapping my arm, the hard surface licking skin from my knees, shins, arms, and hands. My cheek lost a little too.

With my arm swelling and my leg bleeding, I drove to a hospital. A technician x-rayed my elbow, and a doctor told me it was fine. There was no break, but it was best to keep the arm in a sling for a week.

"Do not put weight on it," the doctor ordered.

When I got home, Q glared at my injury. "What the fuck happened?"

"I fell on my arm skating."

"You shouldn't skate if you can't stay on the board."

"Everybody falls. It's part of skating."

Q pursed his lips and said, "I don't want you to hang out with J anymore."

"Huh?"

"Your arm is messed up because you did something stupid with a stupid bitch. Women like her need to be taught a lesson. Women like that should be raped."

"SHUT UP!" I screamed. "Don't talk like that! It's disgusting!"

"What your so-called friend did to you is disgusting!"

"She didn't do anything to me! She taught me to drop in! I chose to! I did this on my own!"

"Well, if you did this to yourself then *you're* the idiot."

"Stop! You did sports and you got hurt. Your knee is wrecked from football." The mention of his injury angered him even more. "Look, please, I need you to help me. The doctor told me to let my arm rest for a week. He said I'll need help doing everyday stuff."

"You think I'm going to help you? After your stupidity?"

"Yes."

"You don't deserve any help."

"You want me to act like I didn't sprain my arm?"

"Yes."

"Why?"

"To teach you a lesson."

"What lesson?"

"That you're an idiot."

"Will you stop it, please?"

Q roared, "TAKE OFF THE SLING!" Spittle landed on me.

Hours later, in the early morning, while in bed, Q taught me what it feels like for a bone to break. As the pain shot up my arm, I begged, "Please. I need to go back to the hospital. PLEASE. I'm scared I'm going to pass out. I feel dizzy."

Q drove me to the hospital I'd gone to earlier. He stayed at my side as a doctor and nurses interviewed me. None of the hospital staff behaved as if a woman with a newly broken arm visiting the emergency room at four o'clock in the morning was out of the ordinary. Maybe it's not. Maybe they see stuff like that all the time. Maybe it's routine.

When rain is coming, I feel it, and Q, in my elbow.

To look at me, there's nothing to suggest that I was a battered woman. My medical records from my time spent with Q testify to what is not visible.

Resulting lab: **RADIOLOGY**

Narrative:

HISTORY: Trauma.

TECHNIQUE: 3 views obtained.
COMPARISON: None.

FINDINGS:
There is a fracture of the lateral humeral condyle with mild displacement, associated joint effusion, soft tissue swelling. No other osseous, articular, or soft tissue abnormality is noted.

IMPRESSION:

FRACTURE OF THE MEDIAL HUMERAL EPICONYDLE WITH JOINT EFFUSION.

People often want to know how someone like Q traps women. They ask as if such captivity is an esoteric thing instead of a mundane horror, a situation so banal it's experienced by a multitude of women in the United States of America.

"How does something like that happen to someone like you?" they ask.

This question draws lines. It creates two categories of people, battered women and everybody else.

The implication is that people who studiously ask questions of people like me could never get stuck in a situation like mine, that people like me are stupid, masochistic, or insane.

At times in my life, I've acted stupidly, masochistically, and in ways that people have described as insane.

However, my ex-boyfriend stalked and routinely raped, beat, and tortured me not because I'm stupid, not because I'm a masochist, and not because I'm insane.

He did it because I'm a woman.

As Q and I walk across the backyard pavement, something gets in the way of my ankle. I trip over it.

My hand reaches for the ground. My arm absorbs the impact, saving my head, and my elbow throbs. When I stand up, Q is grinning.

"Did you trip me?"

"No!"

"Yes, you did."

"No, I didn't!"

"Yes, you did."

I stare at him. His eyes twinkle. He walks to his car, unlocks it, and holds the door open. With reluctance, I climb in.

Several days later, in the exact same spot, the same thing happens. As I get up, Q chortles.

"You tripped me."

"Don't lie: you liked it."

"No, I didn't. Please stop."

"C'mon," Q coos in a tone parents use to reassure children. He sometimes uses that voice with his students. "It's funny! Haven't you heard of slapstick?"

"I don't like being tripped."

Q sighs. "I thought you had a sense of humor."

"It's not funny."

"Soooooooooooooooooooo, you're telling me I'm not funny?"

"I'm telling you I don't care for your version of slapstick."

Q shakes his head back and forth. He says, "Well, I guess what they say about feminists is true. You people have no sense of humor."

I sit at my desk. It occupies the sunniest corner of my classroom. A magazine cover featuring Nelson Mandela hangs above the whiteboard. A postcard of Jean-Paul Sartre is taped above the light switch.

The dismissal bell has rung. A fifteen-year-old boy lingers.

He creeps toward me. I wonder what he wants to talk about. He has an A in my civics class.

"Ms. Gurba," he says. "Wanna hear a joke?"

Looking up from the keyboard, I answer, "Okay."

"Women's rights!"

"Ms. Gurba," a student says as I walk past her desk.

"Yes."

"What's that?" I'd smeared makeup along my jaw, but it seems I should've used more. Maybe I didn't blend properly.

Last night, Q disciplined me for breaking a rule. I alluded to sex while in his presence and so, to remind me that the subject is taboo, Q crept up behind me, whacked me in the head, and kicked my calves. Metal cuffs trapped my wrists. Q dragged me by their chain across the floor, to the corner.

A black trash bag awaited. I went numb. If I was going to die this way, I didn't want to feel it.

Q shoved me in the bag.

As I breathed, I listened to the plastic crinkle.

Q meticulously sorts trash, garbage, and recyclables, dropping stuff destined for the landfill or the recycling plant into three paper grocery bags, which he keeps by the kitchen door. Q cares about our planet. He votes for Democrats. He donates to liberal philanthropic causes, and he enjoys the thank-you letters he receives from organizations. He gives lonely kids rides home from school.

In the bag, I fretted about where Q might dispose of me. I worried about him doing a good job. I imagined him driving me to the countryside, as he'd described. I thought of my mother and father prevented from knowing my whereabouts. When my maternal grandmother died, my mom became distraught on the eve of her burial. She worried about her mom being cold in the tomb.

I never want Mom to worry about my remains getting cold.

"Ponte un suéter, Myriam."

I pushed away the worry and entered a trance. I found myself in an interior room, a room no one may access no matter how hard they bang on its door. My door is made of stone. Only I can open it. Only I can grant you entry.

Q yanked me from the bag and dragged me to the closet. I remained in it for I don't know how long. It's hard to tell time when you've been waiting to die in a bag. I thought about Patty Hearst. When I lived in Berkeley, I sometimes walked past the home that members of the Symbionese Liberation Army kidnapped her from. The building looked ordinary.

Q pulled me out of the closet and dragged me to the bed. I glimpsed something descend and felt it squeeze my neck. A belt. He pulled on it. He did things to my head that made it feel like it was going to pop off.

After unlocking the handcuffs and removing his belt from my neck, Q sent me to the bathroom. "Fix yourself," he said. "You look like you've been raped." At the sink, I stared at my reflection in the medicine cabinet mirror. Welts were appearing. I showered and put on a full face of makeup.

Q doesn't like to be reminded of what he's done.

"Come watch TV!" he grumbled.

I joined him in the living room and sat on the couch. He rested his head in my lap.

My student is waiting. I say, "I don't know, sweetie. I bruise easily."

I am filled with shame. I hate lying to kids. I felt betrayed when I found out Santa wasn't real. There was no need to lie about him. Just give kids gifts and call it a day.

Legal definition of kidnapping

: an act or instance of the crime of seizing, confining, inveighing, abducting, or carrying away a person by force or fraud . . .

People want to believe that if they encountered someone like Q, they'd immediately know they were in the presence of danger.

Ha.

People who hurt people can be charmers. It works in their favor. Charm disarms victims and make us feel special. Chosen.

When Q came into my life, he brought lots of sunshine. He did that strategically. He brought so much sunshine that sometimes, I couldn't see. He overwhelmed me with affection and attention. During our courtship, I boasted to friends and family about how dizzyingly romantic Q acted, and so, when he started behaving differently, I felt confused. I also felt embarrassed. Extremely embarrassed. No one likes to admit they've been duped.

Those who believe that if they encountered someone like Q they'd immediately sense danger delude themselves. It's not like you're on your first, second, third, fourth, or fifth date with a Q when they announce, "Pass the salt, you dog-faced cunt, or I'll slice you from neck to stomach!"

That part comes once they, with the help of others, have lured you into the fog.

Neither Tommy Martinez nor Q acted alone. Men like that never do. They're part of a noun-filled fog.

People.

Places.

Things.

Time is the most valuable thing that captivity drains from prisoners.

Time flows from every prisoner and into the great abyss, irrigating our substrate.

Vines drink heartily.

Coffee House Press releases the book that I wrote in the psychotherapist's room. The book chronicles my sense of being haunted by the spirit of Sophia Castro Torres, the Mexican migrant whose life was taken by the teen who raped me with his face.

Q hates the attention that *Mean*'s publication brings. When I tell him that the director of his favorite TV series complimented my book, his mood sours. He growls, "That's great, babe!" His word choice is ominous. Like Pavlov, he's conditioned me to expect behavior paired with sound. *Babe* signals that soon, his hand will reach for my head. It'll cover my whole face and then some, his thumb sliding under my chin, his fingertips digging into my scalp. Having my face squeezed makes me feel obliterated. After holding my face captive, Q usually shoves me. His actions make me feel like a non-number: zero. I am reduced to a vessel. Numbness fills me. Numbness enables me to go on.

The publication of *Mean* coincides with the rising popularity of #MeToo, the social movement founded by Tarana Burke. #MeToo invites women and girls to share stories about people who've sexually harmed us. Many of the stories shared unfold in or around the workplace.

Q first communicated his romantic interest in me through a coworker. As my department head welcomed me to a new high school campus, she said, "Q's been asking questions about you."

"What'd he ask?"

"If you were married."

The inquiry seemed bold.

During our courtship, Q tricked me. He pretended to be devoted to language. He performed a literary persona and recruited others to participate in his charade. His buddy told me, "You two are perfect for each other. He's an aspiring writer!" Q told me that the novel that made him fall in love with novels was *Lolita*. Q said that *Lolita* introduced him to the magic of prose. It introduced him to new words, like *nymphet*. He said that he would read aloud from the book to his mom. I thought that was odd. Who reads *Lolita* to their mom? Still, I told myself that we all come to literature in different ways. *Lolita* was part of Q's path.

Once I moved in, Q ditched his pretenses. In truth, books bore him. The only books he keeps in the house are from his college days.

He has a degree in advertising. He despises feminism and philosophy. The real Q gets his kicks watching football games on jumbo screens bolted to the walls of gentlemen's clubs. He collects vinyl and folds his socks to Herbie Hancock. He owns one heavy piece of art, a white sculpture in the shape of a tongue, which he says he stole from a gallery during an exhibition. He drinks every day and smokes marijuana from a filthy bong that he keeps next to a loaf of whole wheat bread.

Q prioritizes his reputation.

He wants to be liked by children, parents, and dogs.

Lately, he's been musing, "Babe, we should go gun shopping."

I don't want a gun in the house. I know what might happen if he buys one. I've started researching domestic violence, but I read about it only at work, and I never say those two words aloud, not to anyone. Saying the words aloud is too much. Speaking the words would make them real. In my classroom, I sit at my computer well after the dismissal bell has rung. As the sun sets, I read about my predicament. It has its own literature, forensic and otherwise.

I feel Malala Yousafzai's eyes on me. A portrait of her hangs by my classroom clock.

My students have left for the day. I stare at my phone. A friend has texted me a link to a review of *Mean* published by the *New York Times*. The review thrills my friend. He's excited to see my work receiving attention.

I'm not. Q doesn't like it when the spotlight is off him.

My palms sweat.

What will happen if Q sees this review? He'll probably congratulate me while planning my punishment.

When he feels small, others must pay. If I make him feel small, he charges extra.

I wonder if there's a way to prevent Q from seeing the review. Maybe I can hide his phone. He's hidden mine before. Maybe I can destroy his phone, run it over with my car. Maybe I can suggest we do a cleanse, that we not consume any media for a week. Maybe I can "accidentally" drop his phone in the toilet.

I know these thoughts are stupid.

There's no way to hide the *New York Times*.

I don't want to leave my classroom. I don't want to face Q.

I consider hiding under my desk, like George Costanza did in a *Seinfeld* episode called "The Nap."

Q loves Seinfeld. He thinks he's hysterical. Just like him.

*"Arriving as it does in the thick of the #MeToo movement of women bringing forth their stories of abuse and harassment, this book adds a necessary dimension to the discussion of the interplay of race, class and sexuality in sexual violence."**

I post the review to my social media. Q reads everything I post on social media. I hold my breath.

"Dance with me," says Q.

Because I'm my father's daughter, the words that come to mind are *oh* and *shit*.

Despite what it'll cost me, I say, "No."

In a childish voice, Q whines, "C'mon! Dance with me!"

He stands by the record player, dancing in place. He looks stupid.

He continues to urge me to join him. After about five minutes, I surrender.

I stand in front of him.

Q grins. "Do what I do!" he says.

He shakes his fist. I shake mine.

---

* Sehgal, "An Account of Surviving Sexual Assault Mixes Horror and Humor."

He moves his legs. I move mine.

He flaps his arm. I flap mine.

He takes a step back and his open hand sails at my face, smacking me across the cheek hard enough to whip my head back.

I freeze. He stares at me, waiting.

"You hit me."

Q straightens his spine and makes his hands into fists. He snaps, "I didn't hit you that hard."

"You hit me hard enough."

"I didn't hit you that hard. I know because I hit you." Q points at his cheek. "Hit me."

I shake my head. My disobedience infuriates him.

"Hit me as hard as I hit you, and if you hit me harder, I'll hit you again."

I'm not taking his bait. I don't want more broken bones.

I walk to the couch and sit.

Q stomps out of the living room and into the hallway. He opens and slams cabinet doors. Bangs things around. I wonder if I can escape.

I look at the living room door. Its dead bolts are secured. The kitchen door might be unlocked. If I tiptoe to it, I can grab my purse from the coat rack and sprint to my car.

I tiptoe to the kitchen.

I hear footsteps. From the opposite side, Q enters the room. I reach for a mason jar on the countertop. I pour a glass of water.

Sip.

Q sneers. He reaches for the biggest knife in the drying rack. He picks it up and grabs a dishrag. He aims the blade at my neck and polishes the steel while shaking his head back and forth.

I set my empty jar in the sink.

I'm not going anywhere.

(I now think of the events of that evening as my second *New York Times* book review.)

• • •

Q was the first cisgender boyfriend that I had as an adult. We met during my late thirties, when my queer marriage collapsed.

That marriage provided me with a fifteen-year refuge from cis men, and the home I made with my ex-spouse was a man-free sanctuary, a de facto lesbian separatist space, a dreary womb. When it grew too dreary, I left in search of adventure.

Q seemed fun. Extroverted. I enjoyed the distraction. I'd seen him around campus, I knew that he was interested, and when a coworker invited me to join him for happy hour at a dive bar, Q showed up. I found Q handsome and funny. I texted our mutual acquaintance as much. When the mutual acquaintance set us up on a date, I thought, *What could go wrong?*

Q excels at courtship. It's his sharpest skill.

He's much better at it than he is at telling the truth.

Q used books, as well as my friends, acquaintances, misfortunes, and naivete to ensnare me.

When Q learned I'd be traveling to Portland, he flew there first, to visit family. Q contacted a bookseller friend of mine and the two conspired to develop a scavenger hunt at Powell's City of Books. The afternoon that I arrived at the store, the bookseller chaperoned me from floor to floor, aisle to aisle, and book to book, beginning with Taschen's *Book of Symbols.* Q had hidden notes jotted with quotes, proclamations, and clues between so many pages, and the experience of finding one after another after another made me giddy.

Nobody had ever done anything so elaborate to win me over. My ex-wife had courted me with Jack in the Box.

I stood in the stacks, crying. I'm rarely moved to tears by romance, but the level of personalization and care that had been poured into this game overwhelmed me.

A wrinkled white-haired woman asked, "Why are you crying, dear?"

I explained that a man I was falling in love with had staged a scavenger hunt for me, that he'd left love notes and wildflowers in over a dozen books.

The old woman smiled. "That's special," she said. "He sounds like a keeper."

I walked on clouds those first months with Q.

I also experienced an existential crisis. I'd lived as a lesbian for nearly sixteen years. Now I was getting gay divorced and dating a cis man. People no longer stared at me when I entered a room as part of a couple, and in Q's company, men stopped ogling me the way they had in my wife's presence. Men respected that I was with a man, and I knew that this treatment stemmed from my status as an owned object, a petit curio.

My new invisibility made me feel safer in public, and during our honeymoon period, I also felt safe with Q in private, at home. That was why I told him about Tommy. That was why I shared secrets with him. The illusion of kindness drew me in. He made small, sweet gestures, like giving me the last of his favorite chocolate chip cookies. He also cooked and I took that as a good sign.

One Saturday morning, as we ate a home-cooked breakfast, Q burst into tears.

"I'm so happy!" he said. "I've been burned so many times. I didn't think that there was anyone for me. I thought I was through with women. But then *you* came!"

He sobbed.

I'd never seen a man act that way. I found it a little melodramatic, but I told myself not to be judgmental.

He's sweet, I repeated to myself, and when he invited me to live with him, I never doubted his motivations. The invitation came after our principal summoned me to his office and asked me to sign a document verifying that he'd given me a pink letter. The notice informed me of my termination. The school district was reducing its work force and I lacked the seniority that shielded other faculty, Q included, from the guillotine.

I'd given this school district eight years of my life. I didn't love working for it, but who loves work? I needed a salary and health insurance and I taught in exchange for these things. I don't romanticize teaching. I'm the daughter of two public school teachers. They taught me pragmatism.

Getting pink-slipped gave me nervous diarrhea.

"Don't worry," Q said. "You'll find a job. You're a good teacher. The kids love you. The district will probably hire you back, and if they don't, you can use this time to write!"

My wife and I had put our house on the market, and I checked out apartments for rent. I told Q that I was terrified. "I'm in my thirties and I've never lived alone," I confessed. "I don't know how to do this. It freaks me out."

"Stay with me," Q offered. "Stay with me as long as you need to." He held out his arms and embraced me. That was how Q became my landlord.

After losing my job, I resubmit my resume to the same school district that cut me. A principal calls. We schedule an interview.

I sit in his air-conditioned office. We know each other. I've worked at this school before. It's the first place I worked after getting my teaching credential. It's the first place where I got pinked. Still, I'm hopeful. I want to believe that this school district wants me. That it cares about its teachers. This principal has always been cool with me. He laughs at my jokes.

"I was shocked to see your application in the pool," he says. "When I saw it, I thought, 'What the hell is Gurba doing in here?' You're a talented teacher and we'd love to have you back. Problem is, the position we have is part-time. Would you be willing to work part-time under special contract?"

It's not that I'm unwilling. It's that I have no other options.

"Of course," I say. "I'd love to work on this campus again."

"Have you ever taught psychology?"

"No."

"Neither have I. You'll start Monday."

Go stand on the sidewalk outside your home. Look at the homes in your neighborhood. There are people being held behind those doors. You can't hear them screaming because people don't yell much in captivity. Imprisonment turns people quietly jumpy. At other times, listless. We become adept at pacing and pretending.

These prisoners, the people you call your neighbors, live in somewhat spacious prisons. We look normal. Sometimes, we smile. Sometimes, we're young. Sometimes, we're old. Sometimes, we're beautiful. Sometimes, we're smart. Sometimes, we're immigrants. Sometimes, we're white. Sometimes, we're not. Some of us have been married for a very long time. Some of us will die in captivity. Some of us will be entombed with our captors. Some women refuse to leave because we know what happens to a subset of us who do. Every day, in the United States of America, men murder approximately three women who are current or former romantic partners. Often, these murder victims are pregnant. We become acceptable sacrifices.

The morning after Q brandishes the knife, we sit at the dining room table.

I eat sourdough toast smothered in marmalade. My face is covered in makeup. I act as if everything is fine. I sip my coffee. Chew.

Q enjoys being read to. He texts me a *New York Times* article. Sweetly, he asks, "Will you read it to me?"

I pick up my phone and read the story aloud to him. When I look up, his palm flies at me, smacking me like he did the night before. Q smiles, picks up his cup and dish, and carries them to the sink, setting them in the basin. Without saying goodbye, he exits through the kitchen door.

I go to the bedroom to make the bed. Q taught me how. It's not that I didn't know how to make a bed. Q didn't like my way of doing it. He didn't like how I did any of our housekeeping and so he taught me how do the chores "properly." When Q taught me about the bed, I'd just finished arranging the comforter.

"Babe!" he barked. "That's not how you do it."

Holding a pillow, he skipped around the bed. It's strange to see a grown man skip, but I couldn't consider that for long. Everything was gone. I lay on my back. I became still as Q suffocated me. Just as quickly, I was able to breathe again. Grabbing my wrist, Q yanked me off the bed. The room was a blur.

"The stripes," said Q, "go the other way."

Through the blur, I watched him correct my mistake.

"Okay?"

I nodded. That was one of the first times Q used violence, and his weapon confused me. Q used something soft to harm. He showed me how a pillow could be deadly. He was acting as if he hadn't done anything weird, like asphyxiating a girlfriend was a normal thing to do.

He was whistling.

"Why did you think it was okay to put a pillow over my face?"

"I was just playin'! Guys are playful! You've never dated guys. You don't know how we are. It's called roughhousing. Look it up."

I looked at Q with shock.

"Babe," he said. "You lack experience."

I told myself to give Q the benefit of the doubt. I remembered what the old woman at the bookstore had said, "He's a keeper."

Smoothing the comforter, I make sure that its stripes run parallel with the bed's head and foot. White blotches stain the coverlet. Cum.

Once my chore is done, I drive to work. I prepare to lecture teenagers about the human brain. Their frontal lobes are still developing.

• • •

"You're talking like someone who wants to get hit," says Q.

He hates when I use long words, and I made the mistake of saying *extemporaneously*.

I feel his shoes against my legs. He kicks, kicks, kicks, kicks. I'm careful not to move.

Q is grinning. I've seen that smile before. It's the same smile Tommy was wearing when I turned around and saw him.

The next day, my leg swells. Q notices.

"What happened to your leg?" he asks.

I'm scared of how to answer. I'm scared that if I tell the truth, he'll kick me again.

"I don't know."

Q cocks his head to one side. In a very concerned tone, he says, "You should have a doctor take a look at that," and walks away.

I drive myself to a clinic.

PATIENT: Myriam Gurba Visit Type: Urgent Care Visit Date: 12/29/2017 11:50 AM
DATE OF BIRTH: 05/14/1977 Historian: Self. Provider: XXXX XXX MD

This 40 year old female presents for musculoskeletal pain.

HISTORY OF PRESENT ILLNESS:
1. musculoskeletal pain
ONSET: 1 day ago. Severity level is moderate severe. It occurs consistently and is worsening.
LOCATION: left knee. There is no radiation. The pain is sharp. Context: there is no injury. The pain is aggravated by sitting and

walking. There are no relieving factors. Associated symptoms include swelling. Additional information: left knee swelling below kneecap, occurred at rest yesterday, today worsening, denies any falls.

ASSESSMENT/PLAN:

1. Acute pain of left knee (M25.562)

Rest, ice, elevate, Ibu

Q behaves as if I'm his confessor. He tells me stories about hurting people. Usually, his admissions begin as part of a casually told anecdote that takes an alarming turn. For instance, Q told me that he dated a woman who shared with him that she had rape fantasies. Q said that he decided to make her fantasies come true but said that he didn't enjoy helping, that what he did felt too much like a real rape. Q also complains about teaching high school. He says that the female students make it hard for him to focus on his job. He tells me that he's friends with male faculty members who have the same struggle, that they're always thinking about "perving out" on chosen girls.

I convince myself that it's good that Q rapes me. This way, he won't rape other people. This way, he won't rape the girls he can't stop thinking about, the girls he imagines in certain "positions."

Q reminds me that his favorite book is *Lolita*. He tells me that my body would be more attractive if I were still a teenager. He asks to see pictures of me at fourteen. I don't know if this is true or not but he told me that he once propped a camcorder in his closet and filmed a girl while they had sex.

"When I watched the video," says Q, "she seemed scared." He looks amused.

I ask, "How old was she?"

"Legal."

"Did you ask to film her?"

Q laughs. "Of course not."

"Why'd she look scared?"

"Maybe she thought I was doing weird stuff to her."

Q does weird stuff to feet.

Q complains a lot about a woman he once lived with. He calls her Crazy V and says that when she moved out, she wrecked his TV. He says that he once went to a party where a group of men tried beating him up. These men knew V. Q escaped.

I ask, "Why did they want to kick your ass?"

"They said I beat up V."

"Did you?"

"Yes. But . . . she deserved it."

I know I have to "break up" with Q but it's hard. The last time I tried, Death showed up. When I consider another escape, I feel the memory of his hands squeezing my throat. I knew about phantom limbs but hadn't realized that they could be somebody else's. The memory of Q's hands functions as an invisible dog collar.

I sit at the table, typing a lesson plan. Q watches.

"Aw, look at Brave work!" he says. Brave was his dog. Brave has been dead for years, but Q revived him, nicknaming me "the new Brave."

Q declares, "It's just like watching a dog play the piano!"

That's one of his favorite jokes. He took it from *Mad Men*, one of his favorite shows. The other is *Game of Thrones*.

As I walk across the living room, I feel Q's foot in my lower back. My head whips and the blows continue. He shoves me into the bedroom and pushes me down on the bed. He looks like he hates me. I look down, at his crotch. His penis is pudding. Soft. His fist comes at my face.

When I was a kid, there was a lady I saw on the news a lot. She was part of a murder trial. It seemed like the whole country hated her. Her name was Hedda Nussbaum. Her face looked like it had been through a lot. People accused of her being a bad person because she didn't stop her boyfriend, a lawyer named Joel, from killing a little girl that lived with the two of them. I remember being confused about why the little girl lived with them. I remember being frightened of Hedda's face. Joel had made Hedda's face the way it was.

When Q hits my face, I think of Hedda.

I tell Q that I want to see a chiropractor. My back and leg pain are getting worse.

Q calls a chiropractor and makes appointments for the both of us, scheduling them on the same day. After he hangs up, he says, "I adore doing things with you as a couple."

The chiropractor sends me to have an MRI.

Patient Name: Gurba, Myriam Accession#: XXXXXXXXXX

MR#: XXXXXXXXXX REFERRING PHYSICIAN: XXXXXXX, XXXXXXXXX

SEX: F Age: 40 years

At L4-5, a trace bulge is seen with predominant left foraminal component measuring 1-2 mm.

At L5-S1, a diffuse disc bulge is identified with the left paracentral broad-based protrusion extending 8 mm posteriorly.

For the past week, I've been driving around with a suitcase in my trunk.

After work, I drive to A's. We sit in their living room.

"May I please have my room back?" I ask.

"Of course. You're always welcome here, dude."

A's girlfriend refers me to a victim advocate. I call her and make an appointment to discuss my escape plan. I go to her office. It's gray and soothing. She sits in an armchair. I sit on a love seat. I explain that I fear separation violence. Q is a strangler, and the romantic captives of men who strangle are at elevated risk for murder. We aren't strangled to death, however. First, stranglers squeeze as a show of power. Later, they often shoot to kill. For strangulation survivors, the risk of femicide increases by 750 percent.

I say, "I'm tired. I'm tired of being punished all the time. At this point, I'd rather be killed for trying to leave again than for making the bed wrong."

The advocate validates my concerns. She says, "Q doesn't need a face-to-face goodbye. What you've planned is for your safety. You understand this situation better than anyone else. You're the expert."

The text message I send to Q is terse. I tell him that our relationship is over. In the hopes that niceness will make him leave me alone, I add something about cherishing our time together. That part is fiction.

I send the message at night, while Q is on campus, working.

On my way to A's, I realize I forgot my toiletry bag. It has my albuterol inhaler. Foolishly, I return to retrieve it.

I make a U-turn. I get the bag and climb back into my car. My headlights illuminate Q.

He stands in the gutter, beside the curb. He throws his hands up in the air.

I pull away. Look in the rearview mirror.

Q's car appears behind mine. He flashes his headlights.

I turn and turn and turn to try to lose him.

My phone won't stop ringing. Q tries to pull up beside me. My phone chimes over and over.

As I turn at a red light, I look at my phone.

Q's messages cycle between cruel, bitter, desperate, and panicked.

"C'mon. You're better than this."

"After three years, this is how it ends?"

"Please talk to me. Please. I'll meet you anywhere. We can meet at a parking lot. We can meet anywhere you want."

"What have you been telling people?"

I call home. Dad answers.

"Hello?"

"Q is chasing me. I'm in my car. He's in his car. I'm really scared. He kicked the shit out of me around Christmas and I'm afraid he's . . .

I DON'T KNOW WHAT TO DO!

He's texting me! He won't stop texting me.

I'm scared.

I'M SCARED."

"Don't get out of the car. Don't be alone with him.

Shit.

Honey, shit.

Shit.

Shit.

Shit."

When my father frets, he utters *shit* in staccato.

"I'm calling A. If anything happens to me, you know who did it."

I hang up.

I call A.

"What's up?"

"I sent Q the text. He's chasing me in the car. I can't get rid of him. I don't know what to do. I'm low on gas."

"Come here. NOW. Pull into the driveway. When you get out of your car, run as fast as you can to the front door. Z will be waiting for you. We'll take care of you."

I follow A's instructions.

Q remains close.

After parking in the driveway, I sprint up the walk and jump onto the porch. Z throws open the front door. I rush in and Z locks us inside. I collapse. I can't stand. I'm shaking. My teeth are chattering.

Z sits beside me. She pets me.

I'm the most terrified I've ever been.

Z and I listen to the argument outdoors.

"Let me talk to her. She's my girlfriend."

"She's not your girlfriend."

"You can watch! You can listen! You can be in the room when I talk to her. I'll let you listen. I'll let you stay in the room!"

"You're not coming into my house."

"I need to talk to her."

"You're a fucking creep. Get out of here."

Q laughs. "WHAT DID SHE TELL YOU?" he screams.

"That you're a creep."

Q laughs again.

We hear a door slam shut. A car peels away.

The front door opens. A enters. They look paler than usual. They ask, "Do you want us to call the police?"

A Mexican and a Chicano raised me. They cultivated my distrust of cops and the cops themselves helped. When I was ten, my godmother, cousins, and I witnessed an armed kidnapping in Guadalajara. Men in plain clothes surrounded two women in a sedan. The men carried machine guns. They beat the car with them. They threatened murder.

From a street corner, a uniformed cop watched. He was their lookout.

"No," I say to A. "I just want Q to leave me alone."

"He's really scary," says A.

I nod at the understatement.

*"That corpse weighed heavily on the soul of everyone present. It lay on a dais in the center of the church, surrounded with new candles and flowers; a father stood there, alone, waiting for the mass to end."**

---

* Rulfo, *Pedro Páramo.*

• • •

I lie in bed, trying to relax. I imagine Q outside the house, crouched beneath the window. When I begin to drift to sleep, memories flood me. I think of things Q did to me. I feel those things in my hands, an arthritic trauma.

He slammed my head against a table. He whacked me with his shoes and kicked me. He pressed his thumbs into my eyes. But the memory that keeps me up is what he did to the arm I use to write.

It happened when he sat beside me on the couch.

He was in a pissy mood. I'd gone to New York for a few days. Q didn't like to be left without an audience. And he was going to show me just how bitter he was about that.

Like a gentleman, Q reached for my right hand, taking it between his hands. He looked me in the eye, gripped my thumb, and slowly pulled it back, making it pop. He repeated this move for each of my fingers, pausing at my pinkie. He pulled it back so far that I thought it might break.

When the finger torture was done, Q patted the back of my hand. He returned it to me, stood, and walked to the kitchen.

Three.

It is difficult to know when one has exited the fog. There are no signposts and one exits gradually. The noncolor is dense, then thin, and then, if one is very fortunate, not at all.

While in the fog, I read constantly. Books gave me a place to hide, and writing my own further enabled my fugitivity, letting me escape to home reimagined. With words and punctuation, I reconstructed the valley where I was born. I hid from Q in that place made of words. That fugitive cave offered breathing room. More than a thing, language is a place, and language afforded me somewhere to love. I didn't love Q. I dreaded, pitied, and superficially obeyed him, and the spaces we occupied together were thick with dread, pity, and Death. Q made loving him impossible, and yet, I had love to give. Almost everyone has love to give. Because Q disrupted my ability to love my fellow human beings, isolating me from those I care about most, I gave my heart to language.

Every letter with which I built my literary valley was embroidered with love.

I lived in *Mean* in a way that I couldn't live anywhere else. *Mean* became a land Q couldn't invade. He couldn't grab my ideas and throw them across the room. He couldn't snatch my imagination and crumple it. He couldn't urinate on my memories.

Mean's world occupied an interior terrain that sprouted, blossomed, and grew thorns.

In my literary valley, I could express any string of words.

In my literary valley, I could extemporize.

In my literary valley, I could invite spirits.

In my literary valley, I could banish them.

In my literary valley, I exorcise.

In my literary valley, I fill my chalice.

In my literary valley, I play with my own blood and the blood of others.

In my literary valley, I call the shots.

In my literary valley, I become a philosopher queen.

While I was trapped with Q, two German philosophers kept me company, Hannah Arendt and Martin Heidegger. Q referred to the former as "that aren't bitch," and I read and reread specific passages from her slim polemic *On Violence*.

The volume lived on my nightstand.

Once I freed myself from Q, many of Arendt's passages came into sharper focus. Once liberated, I came to fully understand and embrace this assertion: "Only when there is reason to suspect that conditions could be changed and are not, does rage arise."

Once free, I saw the world through a red lens. I was warmed by molten rage. Long buried inside me, this lava no longer required containment. For three years, I had endured constant degradation, living under ever-present threats of rape, injury, and femicide. Now I was preoccupied with thoughts of punishment and revenge.

I fantasized about turning Q's body into a broadside, his skin announcing the injuries he had caused me. I visualized the word *rape* scabbing across his forehead. I daydreamed Kafka: ". . . there are two kinds of needles arranged in multiple patterns. Each long needle has a short one beside it. The long needle does the writing, and the short needle sprays a jet of water to wash away the blood and keep the inscription clear. Blood and water together are then conducted here though small runnels into this main runnel and down a waste pipe into the pit."

During my three years with Q, he'd spoken the words *I'm sorry* on a few occasions. His regime had required me to accept his hollow apologies and to perform forgiveness. Now that I had agency, I was free to hate Q. Love and hate were, at last, my choices to make.

The fog seems scary but it's just water, thousands and thousands of gallons of water floating in space.

"It's always tempting to believe," wrote Adam Hochschild, "that a bad system is the fault of one bad man."

It's true.

The villain is a seductive, and reductive, trope. The villain tempts us to make the story his, and it might seem as if this bricolage is Q's, or Tommy's, but it's not. The fog inspired and breathed this construction, this collection of words and symbols, into existence.

Tommy and Q creep through this place.

But they do not dwell here.

• • •

Every man who rapes, smacks, whips, trips, spits on, gouges, abducts, strangles, and otherwise degrades, dehumanizes, and destroys women is kin to someone. Every badly behaved man is a father or a brother or a son or an uncle or a cousin or a brother-in-law or a godfather or a stepfather or a grandfather or a great-grandfather or a friend or a best friend or a prom date or a next-door neighbor or a favorite teacher. Embedded within these systems of family, friendship, and community, these creepy men may appear harmless, their evil obscured by a benign collective presence, a fog of sorts. This softness swaddles and protect them. This fog abets.

Do you dwell in the fog? Would you admit it if you did?

"Father, we want you to bless him!"

"No," he said, shaking his head emphatically. "I won't give my blessing. He was an evil man, and he shall not enter the Kingdom of Heaven. God will not smile on me if I intercede for him."

*As he spoke, he clasped his hands tightly, hoping to conceal their trembling. To no avail.**

Have you walked through the valley of the shadow of death?
Have you feared evil?
What has comforted you?
Has anyone prepared a table for you in the presence of your enemies?
Has anyone anointed your head with oil?
Does your cup overflow?
Have mercy and goodness followed you?
In whose house do you dwell?
From whose house have you fled?

---

* Rulfo, *Pedro Páramo.*

• • •

Definition of *perfunctory*

: characterized by routine or superficiality : MECHANICAL

: a perfunctory smile

: lacking interest or enthusiasm

The director of human resources invites me to meet with her. Because her email doesn't go into detail about the purpose of our meeting, I'm disinclined to go alone.

In the lobby of a labyrinthine building, my advocate meets me. An assistant escorts us to a suite. The director greets us, her manicured hands gesturing for us to join her at a blond conference table. Metal filing cabinets surround us. I wonder how many bones they hold.

Fluorescent lighting does the director's skin no favors. Her hair looks good. She wears business casual and speaks softly in legalese. My lawyer sent her a copy of the restraining order granted by a domestic violence court judge. My lawyer also sent her a copy of my declaration of abuse, a five-page document I submitted to the court detailing some of Q's worst behaviors. This document includes descriptions of rape. It includes Q's description of his fantasy of driving me to the countryside to kill me. Among the pieces of evidence that I submitted to the court were Q's text messages. One of the messages describes necrophilia.

"We are here to support you in any way we can," says the director. "It is also necessary that I remain neutral, and I must admit . . . I have a very hard time believing your story about Q. He is very well-liked." She folds her claws together.

Though I'm relieved to have a witness present, I feel my soul constrict. The purpose of this meeting is becoming apparent. Nevertheless, I explain to the director that I'm not Q's first victim. I explain to her that allowing him to be around women and kids puts people at risk. I ask her when he'll be removed from his position.

Straightening her spine, she answers, "If Q is convicted of felony assault, then yes, we will remove him." Of course, Q through his attorney denied all the allegations, and in addition, the police declined to press any charges against him.

Q engaged in so many behaviors defined as felonious by the law. One of these behaviors is rape. Fewer than 1 percent of rapes lead to felony conviction.

I now understand the purpose of this meeting.

"Is there anything else we can do for you, Ms. Gurba?"

"I'm afraid," I tell the director. "I'm afraid Q is going to hurt somebody."

"You have nothing to worry about," she says.

"How do you know?"

"Because Q gave me his word!"

I want to laugh. Shriek. Flip the table. Slap someone. Open the file cabinets and drag the skeletons out.

Instead, I speak.

"Q has made a lot of promises. He's broken every one of them."

A once-popular teacher comes to mind. On his teaching application, he admitted to having pled guilty to misdemeanor charges, to having beaten up his girlfriend, to having "inflicted some serious injuries."

The injuries? A broken jaw and detached retina.

When the once-popular teacher began inflicting injuries on a new victim, a Mexican girl he met on a high school campus, a school administrator asked him to stop. After giving his word that he'd stop hurting the girl, the once-popular teacher used his hands to take the victim's life. Next, he took his own.

When Q would get mad or frustrated, he would "joke" about ending our lives the same way.

A spokesman defended the district's decision to employ the murderer. He told reporters "that applicants convicted of misdemeanors could be hired if the crimes had no bearing on their fitness to teach."

Call me crazy but I believe that inflicting "some serious injuries" on an ex-girlfriend may have some bearing on a man's pedagogical fitness.

"Is there anything else we can do for you, Ms. Gurba?"

"Yes. There's a pair of handcuffs Q bought as a stage prop. He used them to rape me. Please retrieve those. Kids shouldn't be playing with them."

The director picks up a pen and, as if handcuffs are easily forgettable, writes what I've said on a yellow legal pad.

"How will I know that you've recovered and removed the handcuffs?"

"You have my word that they'll be removed."

On countless occasions, and in multiple languages, the people of this institution have referred to us using the word *family*. We are not coworkers. We are family.

Families often sacrifice their own. I learned that in high school. I took an entire class on the Old Testament.

A book and a life are works of art. Making art isn't inherently cathartic. Instead, it can be a protective cocoon.

Fog is a place.

Family is a place.

Evil is a place.

A book is a place.

A hole is a place.

Zero is a place.

A valley is a place.

A vineyard is a place.

Once again, I am glad to be alive.

Once again, I am glad to be here.

Once again, I am glad you are here. To witness.

Let's imagine ourselves back in the vineyard. This time, there are no gunshots. This time, the crows are allowed to do as they please. This time, we sink to our knees and thank those who protected us. We thank those who wrote fable and myth. We thank those who honor the spirits of women. We bring our face close to the soil, close enough to smell California. We inhale the earth. She smells so delicious that we want it in our mouths. If we press our tongue to the richness, who, what, when, and where will we taste?

We will taste a world.

SOURCES

TELL

Alatorre, Antonio. "La Persona de Juan Rulfo." *Revista Canadiense de Estudios Hispánicos* 22, no. 2 (1998).

Barker, Gabby. "I Didn't See Maradona's Hand, But I Contributed to the Goal of the Century." *Sportsfinding*, December 6, 2020. https://sportsfinding.com/ali-bennaceur-i-didnt-see-maradonas-hand-but-i-contributed-to-the-goal-of-the-century/72693/.

"Burroughs 101." *This American Life*. National Public Radio. Chicago, January 30, 2015.

Burroughs, William S. *Junky*. New York: Penguin Books, 1977.

———. *Queer*. New York: Penguin Books, 2010.

Cockburn, Alexander. "Harvard and Murder: The Case of Carlos Salinas." *The Nation*, May 29, 1995.

Cronenberg, David, dir. *Naked Lunch*. Recorded Picture Company, 1991.

De Aguilar, Alberto E. "Jugando a la Guerra Tres Niñitos 'Fusilaron' a una Sirvienta." *Excélsior*, December 18, 1951.

"The Doane Stuart School's Beat Generation Connection." The Doane Stuart School. https://www.doanestuart.org/the-doane-stuart-schools-beat-generation-connection/.

Eschner, Kat. "How America's First Adding Machine Is Connected to 'Naked Lunch.'" *Smithsonian Magazine*, August 21, 2017. https://www.smithsonianmag.com/smart-news/how-americas-first-adding-machine-connected-naked-lunch-180964534/.

Grauerholz, James. "The Death of Joan Vollmer Burroughs: What Really Happened?" American Studies Department, University of Kansas, January 7, 2002. Prepared for the Fifth Congress of the Americas at Universidad de las Americas/Puebla, October 8, 2001.

Indiana, Gary. "The Naked Lunch Report." *Village Voice*, October 31, 1991.

Johnson, Joyce. *Minor Characters: A Young Woman's Coming-of-Age in the Beat Orbit of Jack Kerouac*. New York: Penguin Books, July 1, 1999.

Johnson, Kirk. "A Witness Tells of Finding Body in Park Slaying." *New York Times*, January 8, 1988.

Kahlo, Frida. *The Suicide of Dorothy Hale*. 1938.

Lennig, Arthur. *The Immortal Count: The Life and Films of Bela Lugosi*. Lexington: University Press of Kentucky, August 2010.

Leyser, Yony, dir. *William S. Burroughs: A Man Within*. Interviews with Laurie Anderson, Amiri Baraka, Jello Biafra, Genesis Breyer P-Orridge, David Cronenberg, Iggy Pop, Patti Smith, Sonic Youth, Gus Van Sant, and John Waters. BulletProof Film Inc. and Yonilizer Productions, 2010.

Oppenheimer, Andres. *Bordering on Chaos: Guerrillas, Stockbrokers, Politicians, and Mexico's Road to Prosperity*. New York: Little, Brown & Company, 1997.

"Quiso Demostrar Su Puntería y Mató a Su Mujer. Crimen de un Norteamericano Durante Escandalosa Juerga." *La Prensa*, September 7, 1951.

Serrano Ríos, Ricardo. "El Seminarista Rulfo." *Excélsior*, January 29, 1986.

Taubman, Bryna. *The Preppy Murder Trial*. New York: Saint Martin's Press, 1988.

Wittgenstein, Ludwig. *Philosophical Investigations*. Oxford, UK: Basil Blackwell Ltd, 1986.

CUCUY

"Anton LaVey Performs Satanic Baptism for His Daughter." Bay Area Television Archive. J. Paul Leonard Library. San Francisco State University. KPIX-TV news footage, May 23, 1967. https://diva.sfsu.edu/collections/sfbatv/bundles/238406.

Arax, Mark, and Eric Malnic. "Ballistics Tests Tie Slaying in S.F. to 'Valley Intruder.'" *Los Angeles Times*, August 24, 1985.

Carlo, Philip. *The Night Stalker: The Life and Crimes of Richard Ramirez*. New York: Citadel Press Books, 1996.

Carter, Emily. "Night Stalker Richard Ramirez Was on Death Row at San Quentin When Metallica Filmed Their St. Anger Video." *Kerrang!*, February 4, 2021. https://www.kerrang.com/night-stalker-richard-ramirez

-was-on-death-row-at-san-quentin-when-metallica-filmed-their-st-anger-video.

Cillan Cillan, Francisco. "El Coco y el Miedo en el Niño." Biblioteca Virtual Miguel de Cervantes, 2008. https://www.cervantesvirtual.com/obra/el-coco-y-el-miedo-en-el-nino/.

Concordia Cemetery (website). http://www.concordiacemetery.org/about.html.

Gorney, Cynthia. "The Terrible Puzzle of McMartin Pre-School." *Washington Post,* May 17, 1983.

Goya y Lucientes, Francisco de. *Los Caprichos.* 1799. University of Glasgow Library, Special Collections Department, August 2006. https://www.gla.ac.uk/myglasgow/library/files/special/exhibns/month/aug2006.html.

"Man Found Guilty of 13 'Night Stalker' Murders." *New York Times,* September 21, 1989.

Moore, Timothy W., and Clark Lohr. *Mirandized Nation: The Inside Story of Ernesto Miranda and the Phoenix Police Department.* Phoenix Sleuth LLC, 2015.

"People v. Ramirez." Stanford Law School, Robert Crown Library, Supreme Court of California Resources. https://scocal.stanford.edu/opinion/people-v-ramirez-33683.

Picasso, Pablo. *El Loco.* 1904.

———. *Guernica.* 1937.

Stuart, Gary L. *Miranda: The Story of America's Right to Remain Silent.* Tucson: University of Arizona Press, 2004.

LOCAS

Alexander, Michelle. *The New Jim Crow: Mass Incarceration in the Age of Colorblindness.* New York: The New Press, 2020.

Arbelo Cruz, Fabiola. "Racial Inequities in Treatments of Addictive Disorders." Yale School of Medicine, October 1, 2021. https://medicine.yale.edu/news-article/racial-inequities-in-treatments-of-addictive-disorders/.

Barstow, David, and Alejandra Xanic von Bertrab. "How Wal-Mart Used Payoffs to Get Its Way in Mexico." *New York Times,* December 17, 2012.

Black, Conrad. *A Life in Full: Richard M. Nixon.* New York: Public Affairs, 2007.

Bosch, Hieronymus. *Hell.* 1504.

Boyle, Gregory J. "LAPD Must Drop CRASH in Order to Regain Public's Trust." *Los Angeles Times*, September 27, 1999.

Bugliosi, Vincent. *Helter Skelter: The True Story of the Manson Murders.* New York: W.W. Norton & Co., 1974.

"California: Zoot Suit War." *Time*, June 21, 1943. https://content.time.com/time/subscriber/article/0,33009,766730,00.html.

"Chowchilla Prisons, California." The Center for Land Use Interpretation. https://clui.org/ludb/site/chowchilla-prisons.

Davies, Lawrence E. "Seek Basic Causes of Zoot Suit Fray." *New York Times*, June 11, 1943.

Davis, Mike, and John Wiener. *Set the Night on Fire: LA in the Sixties.* New York: Verso Books, 2021.

Day, Brian. "Four Suspects Held for Bogus Gift Cards, Loaded Weapons at Walmart in Glendora." *San Gabriel Valley Tribune*, January 17, 2013. https://www.sgvtribune.com/2013/01/17/four-suspects-held-for-bogus-gift-cards-loaded-weapons-at-walmart-in-glendora/.

Donner, Richard, dir. *The Twilight Zone.* Season 5, episode 3, "Nightmare at 20,000 Feet." Written by Richard Matheson. Aired 1963 on CBS.

"The Drug War, Mass Incarceration and Race." United Nations Office on Drugs and Crime. Drug Policy Alliance. June 2015. https://www.unodc.org/documents/ungass2016/Contributions/Civil/DrugPolicyAlliance/DPA_Fact_Sheet_Drug_War_Mass_Incarceration_and_Race_June2015.pdf.

Ellroy, James. *LA Confidential.* New York: Grand Central Publishing, 1997.

Escobar, Edward J. "Bloody Christmas and the Irony of Police Professionalism: The Los Angeles Police Department, Mexican Americans, and Police Reform in the 1950s." *Pacific Historical Review* 72, no. 2 (May 2003). https://doi.org/10.1525/phr.2003.72.2.171.

———. "The Unintended Consequences of the Carceral State: Chicana/o Political Mobilization in Post-World War II America." *Journal of American History* 102, no. 1 (June 2015).

Fregoso Torres, Jorge Enrique, and Jorge Alberto Trujillo Bretón. *La Penitenciaría de Escobedo: Por Temor y Orgullo*. Guadalajara: Editorial Universidad de Guadalajara, October 8, 2020.

Gerber, Robin. *Barbie Forever: Her Inspiration, History, and Legacy.* New York: Epic Ink, 2019.

"Hispanic Prisoners in the United States." The Sentencing Project. Prison Policy Initiative. https://static.prisonpolicy.org/scans/sp/1051.pdf.

Kim, Victoria. "Court Program Helps Women Turn Their Lives Around." *Los Angeles Times*, October 19, 2010.

Kirk, Michael, dir. *Frontline*. "LAPD Blues." Written by Peter J. Boyer and Michael Kirk. Aired May 15, 2001, on PBS.

"List of Works." Barragan Foundation. 2023. https://www.barragan-foundation.org/works/list.

Muerez, Cara. "Hispanic Americans Suicide Rates Are Rising." *U.S. News and World Report*, August 18, 2022.

Obergón Pagán, Eduardo. *Murder at the Sleepy Lagoon: Zoot Suits, Race and Riot in Wartime L.A.* Chapel Hill: University of North Carolina Press, 2003.

"The Sleepy Lagoon Case." Sleepy Lagoon Defense Committee (Formerly the Citizen's Committee for the Defense of Mexican-American Youth). Los Angeles, California 1943. Online Archive of California. https://oac.cdlib.org/view?docId=hb7779p4zc&query=&brand=oac4.

"Talking Points and Data Briefing on Suicide Prevention for Latina Youth." Each Mind Matters Resource Center, 2018. https://emmresourcecenter.org/system/files/2018-08/Talking%20Points%20and%20Data%20Briefing%20on%20Suicide%20Prevention%20for%20Latina%20Youth-2.pdf.

Wilson Gilmore, Ruth. *Golden Gulag: Prisons, Surplus, Crisis, and Opposition in Globalizing California*. Berkeley: University of California Press, 2007.

Zuñiga, Javier. "Amnesty International's Findings and Recommendations Relating to Valley State Prison (California)." Amnesty International, April 1999. https://www.amnesty.org/es/wp-content/uploads/2021/06/amr510531999en.pdf.

MITOTE

Ceballos Ramos, Enrique, and Raymundo Padilla. *Historiando a Juan Rulfo*. Santiago: Editorial Tierra de Letras, 2022.

Chumacero, Alí. "El 'Pedro Páramo' de Juan Rulfo." *Revista de la Universidad de México*, April 1955. https://www.revistadelauniversidad.mx/articles/eedc09a9-83a6-46b5-978a-2250c105e2a2/el-pedro-paramo-de-juan-rulfo.

Dickens, Charles. *A Christmas Carol.* New York: Bantam Classics, 1986.

"Epoca Revolucionaria." Local (unnamed) priest's report on Villa Guerrero, undated (but likely the late 1930s), from the Archivo Histórico del Arzobispado de Guadalajara, Sección: Gobierno, Serie: Parroquias, Villa Guerrero, caja 1, expediente 23, courtesy of Nathaniel Morris.

Jones, J. A. "Tepecano House Types." *Kiva* 27, no. 4 (1962).

Llanos Valdes, Adolfo. Registro Civil. El Salitre, Jalisco, Mexico, 1915.

Miller, Marjorie. "Some Still See Decaying Display as Piece of Revolutionary History: A Farewell to Arm? Controversy Grows over a Hero in Mexico." *Los Angeles Times*, September 11, 1989.

Morris, Nathaniel. *Soldiers, Saints, and Shamans: Indigenous Communities and the Revolutionary State in Mexico's Grand Nayar, 1910–1940.* Tucson: University of Arizona Press, 2022.

Presley, James. "Mexican Views on Rural Education, 1900–1910." *The Americas* 20, no. 1 (1963).

Rohter, Larry. "A Mexican Relic Is Buried at Last." *New York Times*, December 10, 1989.

Rulfo, Juan. *Pedro Páramo*. Barcelona: RM, 2005.

———. *Pedro Páramo*. Translated by Margaret Sayers Peden. New York: Grove Press, 1994.

de Saavedra Guzman, Antonio. *El Peregrino Indiano*. Madrid: 1599.

Sanchez González, Agustín. *El General en la Bombilla: Una Espléndida Crónica Sobre la Lucha por el Poder, Que Culminó Con el Asesinato de Alvara Obregón*. México, D.F.: Editorial Planeta Mexicana, 1993.

Schoenhals, Louise. "Mexico Experiments in Rural and Primary Education: 1921–1930." *Hispanic American Historical Review*, February 1, 1964.

Shadow, Robert Dennis. *Tierra, Trabajo, y Ganado en la Región Norte de Jalisco: Una Historia Agraria de Villa Guerrero Jalisco (1600–1980)*. El Colegio de Michoacán, Universidad de Guadalajara, 2002.

Shadow, Robert D., and María J. Rodríguez-Shadow. "Religión, Economía y Política En La Rebelión Cristera: El Caso de Los Gobiernistas de Villa Guerrero, Jalisco." *Historia Mexicana*, vol. 43, no. 4, 1994, pp. 657–99.

Steinbeck, John. *Grapes of Wrath*. New York: Penguin Classics, 2006.

Talavera, Juan Carlos. "A un Siglo del Nacimiento de Edmundo Valadés." *Excélsior*, February 22, 2015.

"Toral and Nun Go on Trial for Murder of General Obregon." *New York Times*, November 3, 1928.

"Toral Is Executed for Obregon Killing." *New York Times*, February 10, 1929.
Villaseñor Villaseñor, Ramiro. *Juan Rulfo Biobibliografia*. Guadalajara, Jalisco, México: Gobierno de Jalisco, Secretaría General, Unidad Editorial, 1986.

THE WHITE ONION

Acuña, Rodolfo. *Occupied America: The Chicano's Struggle Toward Liberation*. San Francisco: Canfield Press, 1972.
Anderson, Fred, and Andrew Clayton. *The Dominion of War: Empire and Liberty in North American, 1500–2000*. New York: Penguin Books, 2005.
"Assassination Attempts, September 1975." Gerald R. Ford Presidential Library & Museum. https://www.fordlibrarymuseum.gov/avproj/assassinations.asp.
Bailey, Thomas A., and David M. Kennedy. *The American Pageant*. Lexington, Massachusetts: D.C. Heath and Company, 1987.
Beltrán, Cristina. *Cruelty as Citizenship: How Migrant Suffering Sustains White Democracy*. University of Minnesota Press, 2020.
Blay, Yaba. *One Drop: Shifting the Lens on Race*. Boston: Beacon Press, 2021.
Bloom, Stephen G. "Lesson of a Lifetime." *Smithsonian Magazine*, September 2005. https://www.smithsonianmag.com/science-nature/lesson-of-a-lifetime-72754306/.
Blurton, Heather. *Cannibalism in High Medieval English Literature*. New York: Palgrave Macmillan, 2007.
Bonilla-Silva, Eduardo. "The Invisible Weight of Whiteness: The Racial Grammar of Everyday Life in Contemporary America." *Michigan Sociological Review* 26 (2012).
Burton, Tim, dir. *Pee-wee's Big Adventure*. Performances by Paul Reubens and Elizabeth Daily. Warner Bros., 1985.
Collins, Patricia Hill. *Black Feminist Thought: Knowledge, Consciousness, and the Politics of Empowerment*. New York: Routledge Classics, 2008.
Contreras, Shirley. "G. Allan Hancock Has a Colorful History." *Santa Maria Times*, October 1, 2017. Updated January 15, 2021. https://santamariatimes.com/lifestyles/columnist/shirley_contreras/g-allan-hancock-has-a-colorful-history/article_b72077c5-f3fd-5746-8f73-1e46823aa581.html.

Córdova, Jeanne. *When We Were Outlaws*. Midway, FL: Spinsters Ink, 2011.

"County of Santa Barbara, California, Agricultural Production Report 2021." County of Santa Barbara Agriculture/Weights & Measures Department, 2021. https://content.civicplus.com/api/assets/d84d16ed-052c-4c6d-a329-e676ef39ead7?cache=1800.

Curtis, Bryan. "Machete Stirs Immigration Debates: 'Mexploitation' at the Movies." *Daily Beast*, August 31, 2010. https://www.thedailybeast.com/machete-stirs-immigration-debates-mexploitation-at-the-movies.

Daugherty, Tracy. *The Last Love Song: A Biography of Joan Didion*. New York: St. Martin's Press, 2016.

Didion, Joan. *Run River*. New York: Vintage International, 1994.

———. *Slouching Towards Bethlehem*. New York: Farrar, Straus and Giroux, 2008.

———. *Where I Was From*. New York: Vintage International, 2003.

———. *The White Album*. New York: Farrar, Straus and Giroux, 2009.

———. *The Year of Magical Thinking*. New York: Vintage International, 2007.

Fernández-Armesto, Felipe. *Our America: A Hispanic History of the United States*. New York: W.W. Norton & Company, 2014.

Fields, Barbara J., and Karen E. Fields. *Racecraft: The Soul of Inequality in American Life*. London: Verso, 2014.

Fife, Austin E., and Terry E. Stevenson. "Santa Ana Wind." *Western Folklore* 17, no. 4 (1958).

Flower, Enola. *A Child's History of California*. California State Department of Education, 1949.

"Free Swim Lessons Given in Wake of Recent Tragedy." *Santa Maria Times*, June 3, 1990.

Galvez, Arturo. Registro Civil de Sayula, Jalisco, Mexico, 1918.

Gast, John. *American Progress*. 1872.

Greene, Graham. *The Power and the Glory*. New York: Penguin Classics, 2015.

Houghton, Eliza P. Donner. *The Expedition of the Donner Party and Its Tragic Fate*. Chicago: A.C. McClurg & Co., 1911.

"H-2A Temporary Agricultural Worker Program." U.S. Department of Homeland Security. Updated December 21, 2022. https://www.dhs.gov/h-2a-temporary-agricultural-worker-program.

"Injuries, Illnesses and Deaths in Agriculture, 2015–19." TED: The

Economics Daily. U.S. Bureau of Labor Statistics, Department of Labor, September 22, 2021. https://www.bls.gov/opub/ted/2021/injuries-illnesses-and-deaths-in-agriculture-2015-19.htm.

Jiménez, Tomás R. "Mexican Immigrant Replenishment and the Continuing Significance of Ethnicity and Race." *American Journal of Sociology* 113, no. 6 (2008).

Laskey, Anne. *I. Magnin, Beverly Hills.* TESSA Digital Collections of the Los Angeles Public Library, 1978. https://tessa2.lapl.org/digital/collection/photos/id/116011.

Luketic, Robert, dir. *Legally Blonde.* MGM Distribution Co., 2001.

"Manson Trial Proceeds Despite Nixon Comments." *New York Times,* August 4, 1970.

Morse, Nancy. "Parents of Basin Drown Victims Sue." *Santa Maria Times,* July 30, 1991.

Otwell, Rachel. "Illinois Won't Return Santa Ana's Leg to Mexico." WNIJ News. Northern Public Radio, November 14, 2016. https://www.northernpublicradio.org/news/2016-11-14/illinois-wont-return-santa-anas-wooden-leg-to-mexico.

Rolls Press/Popperfoto. *Linda Kasabian Arrives in Court.* Getty Images, August 13, 1970. https://www.gettyimages.com/detail/news-photo/linda-kasabian-star-witness-in-the-sharon-tate-and-labianca-news-photo/640917815.

Ruiz v. City of Santa Maria. United States Court of Appeals, Ninth Circuit. No. 96-56564, November 5, 1998. https://caselaw.findlaw.com/us-9th-circuit/1274678.html.

Schallhorn, Kaitlyn. "J&G Berry Farms Strike Ends." *Santa Barbara News-Press,* May 7, 2022. https://newspress.com/jg-berry-farms-strike-ends/.

"'Sheep Dog Cowboy' Star for National Horse Show." *Santa Maria Times,* July 4, 1970.

Siner, Ken. "The Wetback Season Has Opened." *Santa Maria Times,* June 19, 1957.

Susman, Gary. "Winona Ryder Stole for Role, Saks Employee Testifies." *Entertainment Weekly,* April 8, 2010. https://ew.com/article/2010/04/08/winona-ryder-stole-role-saks-employee-testifies/.

"This Week in History: Ozzy Osbourne Arrested for Urinating on the Alamo Cenotaph." *My San Antonio,* February 15, 2022. https://

www.mysanantonio.com/entertainment/article/San-Antonio-Ozzy-Osbourne-pee-Alamo-Cenotaph-16920580.php.

Trejo, Danny, with Donal Logue. *Trejo: My Life of Crime, Redemption, and Hollywood.* New York: Atria Books, 2021.

Wilson Gilmore, Ruth. *Golden Gulag: Prisons, Surplus, Crisis, and Opposition in Globalizing California.* Berkeley: University of California Press, 2007.

NAVAJAZO

Alcántar, Luis. "La Culpa la Tuvo Cupido." *¡Pásala!*, February 10, 2020. https://www.pressreader.com/mexico/pasala/20200210/281706911682679.

Berkowitz, Eric. *The Boundaries of Desire: A Century of Good Sex, Bad Laws, and Changing Identities.* Berkeley, CA: Counterpoint, 2015.

Chozick, Amy. "You Know the Lorena Bobbitt Story. But Not All of It." *New York Times*, January 30, 2019.

"El Crudo Relato del Asesino de Ingrid Escamilla." *La Prensa*, February 11, 2020. https://www.laprensa.hn/mundo/relato-asesino-ingrid-escamilla-mexico-francisco-robledo-CDlp1355986.

Donner, Regine. "Oral History Interview with Regine Donner." By Joan Ringelheim. The Jeff and Toby Herr Oral History Archive. United States Holocaust Memorial Museum. April 4, 2002. https://collections.ushmm.org/search/catalog/irn519930.

Finn, Natalie. "What You Didn't Know About the Still Shocking Story of John and Lorena Bobbitt." *Entertainment Weekly*, February 15, 2019. Updated May 25, 2020. https://www.eonline.com/news/1011312/what-you-didn-t-know-about-the-story-of-john-and-lorena-bobbitt-and-why-the-details-are-more-cringe-worthy-than-ever.

García, Imelda. "El Asesinato de Ingrid Escamilla, el Feminicidio Que Conmocionó a México." *Al Día Dallas*, February 12, 2020. https://www.dallasnews.com/espanol/al-dia/dallas-fort-worth/2020/02/12/el-asesinato-de-ingrid-escamilla-el-feminicidio-que-conmociono-a-mexico/.

Goya y Lucientes, Francisco de. *Saturn.* 1820–1823. Museo del Prado.

Guillén, Nicolás. "Chévere." 1962.

Herrera, Hayden. *A Biography of Frida Kahlo.* New York: Harper Perennial, 2002.

Kahlo, Frida. *Unos Cuantos Piquetitos*. 1935.

Masters, Kim. "Lorena Bobbitt: Sex, Lies, and an 8-Inch Carving Knife." *Vanity Fair*, November 1, 1993.

Mata Othón, Atalo. "Ingrid y Su Asesino Tenían una Relación 'Extraña': Vecinos." *Excélsior*, November 2, 2020.

Miller, Bill, and Marylou Tousignant. "Bobbitt Liked Rough Sex, Jury Told." *Washington Post*, January 12, 1994.

Miller, Henry. *Crazy Cock*. New York: Grove Weidenfeld, 1991.

Pershing, Linda. "'His Wife Seized His Prize and Cut It to Size': Folk and Popular Commentary on Lorena Bobbitt." *NWSA Journal* 8, no. 3 (1996).

Ross, Michael. "Lorena Bobbitt Testifies on Abuse Claims." *Los Angeles Times*, January 13, 1994.

Sicardo, Joseph. *Saint Rita of Cascia: Saint of the Impossible*. Charlotte, NC: TAN Books, 1993.

Suñer, Maite. "Castradoras." *Marie Claire España*, March 1994.

Van Rijn, Rembrandt. *Lucretia*. 1664. National Gallery of Art.

WATERLOO

Capote, Truman. *In Cold Blood*. New York: Vintage International, 2001. First published 1965 by Random House (New York).

Lauerman, Kerry. "The Man Who Loves to Hate." *Mother Jones*, March/April 1999.

Lengel, Allan. "Thousands Mourn Student's Death." *Washington Post*, October 15, 1998.

Rothman, Lily. "Read the 'Yep, I'm Gay' Ellen DeGeneres Interview from 1997." *Time*, April 13, 2022. Updated April 14, 2022. https://time.com/4728994/ellen-degeneres-1997-coming-out-cover/.

Shepard, Judy. *The Meaning of Matthew: My Son's Murder in Laramie, and a World Transformed*. New York: Plume, May 25, 2010.

Stevens, George, dir. *The Greatest Story Ever Told*. Performances by Max von Sydow, Telly Savalas, and John Wayne. United Artists, 1965.

White, Karen. "Estrada Pleads Guilty to Murder." *Santa Maria Times*, April 11, 2000.

Wyeth, Andrew. "Christina's World." 1948. The Museum of Modern Art.

SLIMED

Alter, Alexandra, Corina Knoll, and Karen Zraik. "He Was Convicted of Raping Alice Sebold. Then the Case Unraveled." *New York Times*, December 15, 2021.

Buthelezi, Mbongiseni, Natalie Melas, and David Damrosch. *The Princeton Sourcebook on Comparative Literature: From the Enlightenment to the Global Present.* Princeton, NJ: Princeton University Press, 2009.

Dahl, Roald. *James and the Giant Peach.* New York: Puffin Books, 2000. First published 1961 by Alfred A. Knopf, Inc.

Despentes, Virginie. *King Kong Theory.* Translated by Frank Wynne. New York: FSG Originals, 2021.

Dione, Melanie. "The Infuriating Failure of Alice Sebold's Apology." Bitch Media, December 9, 2021. https://www.bitchmedia.org/article/alice-sebold-apology-failure.

Golder, Yves. "Margaret Thatcher in *Spitting Image.*" *French Journal of British Studies* XXIV-4 (2019). https://doi.org/10.4000/rfcb.4891.

Ito, Shiori. *Black Box.* Translated by Allison Markin Powell. New York: The Feminist Press at the City University of New York, 2021.

Johnson, Chantal V. *Post-traumatic.* New York: Little, Brown and Company, 2022.

LaMotte, Sandee. "Sexual Assault Linked to Later Brain Damage in Women, Study Finds." CNN, September 22, 2021. https://www.cnn.com/2021/09/22/health/sexual-assault-brain-damage-wellness/index.html.

Landau, Judith, and Jack Saul. "Facilitating Family and Community Resilience in Response to Major Disaster." In *Living Beyond Loss*, 2nd ed., edited by Froma Walsh and Monica McGoldrick. New York: W. W. Norton & Company, 2004.

Marsh, Moira. *Practically Joking.* Boulder: Utah State University Press, 2015.

Martin, Steve. *Born Standing Up.* New York: Scribner, 2007.

Nelson, Maggie. *The Red Parts: Autobiography of a Trial.* Minneapolis: Graywolf Press, 2016. First published 2007 by Free Press (New York).

Oz, Frank, dir. *The Muppets Take Manhattan.* Tri-Star Pictures, 1984.

Palahniuk, Chuck. *Fight Club.* New York: W.W. Norton, 2005.

People v. Tommy Jesse Martinez. Supreme Court of California, No. S074624, August 30, 2005. https://www.courts.ca.gov/documents

/s074624_-_people_v._tommy_jesse_martinez_-_appellant%27s_opening_brief.pdf.
Sebold, Alice. *Lucky*. New York: Scribner, 1999.
———. *The Lovely Bones*. New York: Little, Brown and Company, 2002.
Stark, Evan. *Coercive Control*. Oxford: Oxford University Press, 2009.
You Can't Do That On Television. "April Fools' Prank." NickRewind (YouTube channel). https://www.youtube.com/watch?v=ezHeVkITwxw&t=1s.

ITCHY

Arendt, Hannah. *The Origins of Totalitarianism*. Orlando: Harcourt Inc, 1976.
Gund, Catherine, and Daresha Kyi, dir. *Chavela*. Aubin Pictures, 2017.
Dorado Romo, David. *Ringside Seat to a Revolution: An Underground Cultural History of El Paso and Juárez: 1893–1923*. Cinco Puntos Press, 2005.
Gines, Kathryn T. *Hannah Arendt and the Negro Question*. Bloomington: Indiana University Press, 2014.
González, Gilbert G. *Labor and Community: Mexican Citrus Worker Villages in a Southern California County 1900–1950*. Urbana: University of Illinois Press, 1994.
"A History of Mexican Americans in California: Historic Sites; Westminster School/Seventeenth Street School." National Park Services. https://www.nps.gov/parkhistory/online_books/5views/5views5h99.htm.
Hitler, Adolf. *Mein Kampf*. Translated by Ralph Manheim. New York: Houghton Mifflin, 1999.
Hlushchenko, Dilfuza. "This Day—September 3, 1941 Zyklon B Used as Weapon of Mass Destruction for the First Time." Museum "Jewish Memory and Holocaust in Ukraine," March 9, 2020. https://www.jmhum.org/en/news-list/689-this-day-september-3-1941-zyklon-b-used-as-a-weapon-of-mass-destruction-for-the-first-time.
"James Edward Allison (Architect)." Pacific Coast Architecture Database. https://pcad.lib.washington.edu/person/356/.
Kafka, Franz. *The Complete Stories*. New York: Schocken Books, 1971.
Kakel, III, Carroll P. *The American West and the Nazi East: A Comparative and Interpretive Perspective*. New York: Palgrave Macmillan, 2011.
"'La Luna Grande' de Chavela Vargas es para García Lorca." *El Universo*,

April 14, 2012. https://www.eluniverso.com/2012/04/14/1/1380/la-luna-grande-chavela-vargas-garcia-lorca.html/.

Madrid, E. Michael. "The Unheralded History of the Lemon Grove Desegregation Case." *Multicultural Education*, Spring 2008. https://files.eric.ed.gov/fulltext/EJ793848.pdf.

Mendez et al. v. Westminster School District of Orange County et al. U.S. District Court for the Southern District of California. 64 F. Supp. 544 (S.D. Cal. 1946). Civil Action No. 4292, February 18, 1946. https://law.justia.com/cases/federal/district-courts/FSupp/64/544/1952972/.

Mendez et al. v. Westminster. United States District Court, Southern District of California, Central Division. No. 4292-M. Civil. July 5, 1945. https://mendezetalvwestminster.com/court-documents/.

Miller, Reid. "A Lesson in Moral Spectatorship." *Critical Inquiry* 34, no. 4, (2008).

Munemitsu, Janice. *The Kindness of Color: The Story of Two Families and* Mendez, et al. v Westminster, *the 1947 Desegregation of California Public Schools.* Janice Munemitsu, 2021.

O'Sullivan, John. "Annexation." *The United States Magazine and Democratic Review* 17, no. 1 (July–August 1845).

"Prosecutor Asks Acquittal of Nazi Who Supplied Gas to Kill Jews." Jewish Telegraphic Agency. *Daily News Bulletin*, May 27, 1955. https://www.jta.org/archive/prosecutor-asks-acquittal-of-nazi-who-supplied-gas-to-kill-jews.

Raffles, Hugh. *Insectopedia*. New York: Vintage Books, 2011.

Reisler, Mark. "Always the Laborer, Never the Citizen: Anglo Perceptions of the Mexican Immigrant During the 1920s." *Pacific Historical Review* 45, no. 2 (1976).

Reyna, Carlos. "Chavela Vargas en la Intimidad." *Gatopardo*, March 8, 2018. https://gatopardo.com/arte-y-cultura/chavela-vargas-documental/.

Ruiz, Vicki L. *From Out of the Shadows: Mexican Women in Twentieth-Century America*. Oxford: Oxford University Press, 1998.

Smith, Woodruff D. "Friedrich Ratzel and the Origins of Lebensraum." *German Studies Review*, 3, no. 1 (1980): 51–68. https://doi.org/10.2307/1429483. Accessed November 28, 2022.

Spring, Joel. *Deculturalization and the Struggle for Equality: A Brief History of the Education of Dominated Cultures in the United States*. New York: McGraw-Hill Education, 2012.

Stern, Alexandra Minna. "Buildings, Boundaries, and Blood: Medicalization and Nation-Building on the U.S.-Mexico Border, 1910–1930." *The Hispanic American Historical Review* 79, no. 1 (1999).

Terrell, Jazzie. "Resistance: Forced Fumigation and Gasoline Baths at the Texas-Mexico Border." University of Arizona, 2020. http://doi.org/10.13140/RG.2.2.22775.24485.

U.S. Commission on Civil Rights. Meeting transcript. October 21, 2016. https://www.usccr.gov/files/calendar/trnscrpt/Unedited-Commission-Business-Meeting-Transcript-10-21-16.pdf.

Young-Bruehl, Elisabeth. *Hannah Arendt: For Love of the World*. New Haven: Yale University Press, 2004.

Zinsser, Hans. *Rats, Lice and History*. London: Routledge, 2007.

PENDEJA, YOU AIN'T STEINBECK

"Author Bio." Reyna Grande (website). http://reynagrande.com/bio/.

Chee, Alexander. "How to Unlearn Everything." *Vulture*, October 30, 2019. https://www.vulture.com/2019/10/author-alexander-chee-on-his-advice-to-writers.html.

Cummins, Jeanine. *American Dirt*. New York: Flatiron Books, 2020.

———. "Murder Isn't Black or White." *New York Times*, December 31, 2015.

———. *A Rip in Heaven*. New York: Berkley Books, 2004.

Grande, Reyna. *Across a Hundred Mountains*. New York: Washington Square Press, 2007.

———. "On Imposter Syndrome." Reyna Grande (website). http://reynagrande.com/on-impostor-syndrome/.

Kit, Borys. "Migrant Border Crossing Movie 'American Dirt' in the Works From 'Blood Diamond' Writer." *Hollywood Reporter*, January 15, 2019. https://www.hollywoodreporter.com/news/general-news/migrant-border-crossing-movie-american-dirt-works-1176263/.

Paz, Octavio. *The Labyrinth of Solitude*. New York: Grove Press, 1994.

Sontag, Susan. *Against Interpretation and Other Essays*. New York: Farrar, Straus and Giroux, 2013.

Urrea, Luis Alberto. *Across the Wire: Life and Hard Times on the Mexican Border*. New York: Anchor, 1993.

———. *By the Lake of Sleeping Children: The Secret Life of the Mexican Border*. New York: Anchor, 1996.

CREEP

Aesop. *Aesop's Fables*. Edited by Jack Zipes. New York: Signet, 2004.

De Beauvoir, Simone. *The Second Sex*. New York: Vintage, 2012.

Fourcade, Marion. "The Vile and the Noble: On the Relation between Natural and Social Classifications in the French Wine World." The Sociological Quarterly 53, no. 4 (Fall 2012).

Hochschild, Adam. *King Leopold's Ghost: A Story of Greed, Terror, and Heroism in Colonial Africa*. New York: Mariner Books, 1999.

Kafka, Franz. "In the Penal Colony." *The Complete Stories*. New York: Schocken Books, 1971.

"Nicole's 911 Call of 1993." The Simpson Trial Transcripts (website). http://simpson.walraven.org/911-1993.html.

"Professor Hill: I Have No Personal Vendetta against Clarence Thomas." *Washington Post*, October 12, 1991. https://www.washingtonpost.com/archive/politics/1991/10/12/professor-hill-i-have-no-personal-vendetta-against-clarence-thomas/213dc8d5-22d0-4ed4-97ce-b11699e6e004/.

Rulfo, Juan. *Pedro Páramo*. Translated by Margaret Sayers Peden. New York: Grove Press, 1994.

Sehgal, Parul. "An Account of Surviving Sexual Assault Mixes Horror and Humor." *New York Times*, December 19, 2017.

Shakespeare, William. *Romeo and Juliet*. New York: Simon & Schuster, 2004.

Shute, Nevil. *On the Beach*. New York: Vintage International, 2010.

Zucker, David, dir. *The Naked Gun: From the Files of Police Squad!* With performances by Leslie Nielson and O.J. Simpson. Paramount Pictures, 1988.

ACKNOWLEDGMENTS

Creep couldn't have happened without the support and encouragement of many. I'm grateful to my parents and brother and sister for being my family. I'm grateful to my Abuelito and Abuelita for teaching me about art. I don't have an MFA, but I did have the experience of belonging to las Guayabas, a Latina literary collective that taught me how to be in community with other writers, and for that, I'm immensely fortunate. I'd like to toss some kisses toward heaven, in the hopes that my Guayaba mentor in fearlessness, tatiana de la tierra, catches them. Wendy, Griselda, Loma, Desiree, Danielle, Mari, Randa, Lisa, your friendship is gold. Olga, without your insights, I could not have brought my Abuelito's story to the page. Lauren and Amy, thank you for your editorial guidance. Nathaniel Morris, I appreciate the time you took to entertain my questions about Villa Guerrero. Lee, Haley, Sylvia, and Tiombe, all of you saved my life. I owe you everything. Rayhané, you sold this book. Thank you. To the students who have taught me so much, I'm honored to have worked with you. Sophia, you are always in my prayers. GC, you are my heart. And to everyone who got in the way of this book happening, fuck you.

ABOUT THE AUTHOR

Myriam Gurba lives in southern California and will probably never leave. She is the author of four books and is trying to bang out two more. Her writing has been widely anthologized and has been published by the *New York Times*, the *Los Angeles Times*, the *Believer*, and the *Paris Review*.

Avid Reader Press, an imprint of Simon & Schuster, is built on the idea that the most rewarding publishing has three common denominators: great books, published with intense focus, in true partnership. Thank you to the Avid Reader Press colleagues who collaborated on *Creep*, as well as to the hundreds of professionals in the Simon & Schuster advertising, audio, communications, design, ebook, finance, human resources, legal, marketing, operations, production, sales, supply chain, subsidiary rights, and warehouse departments whose invaluable support and expertise benefit every one of our titles.

Editorial
Lauren Wein, *VP and Editorial Director*
Amy Guay, *Assistant Editor*

Jacket Design
Alison Forner, *Senior Art Director*
Clay Smith, *Senior Designer*
Sydney Newman, *Art Associate*

Marketing
Emily Lewis, *Marketing Manager*

Production
Allison Green, *Managing Editor*
Jessica Chin, *Manager Copyediting*
Alicia Brancato, *Production Manager*
Paul Dippolito, *Interior Text Designer*
Ritika Karnik, *Desktop Compositor*
Cait Lamborne, *Ebook Developer*

Publicity
Alexandra Primiani, *Associate Director of Publicity*
Eva Kerins, *Publicity Assistant*

Subsidiary Rights
Paul O'Halloran, *VP and Director of Subsidiary Rights*

BOOK CLUB FAVORITES
READER'S GUIDE

CREEP

MYRIAM GURBA

This reading group guide for Creep *includes an introduction, discussion questions, ideas for enhancing your book club, and a Q&A with author Myriam Gurba. The suggested questions are intended to help your reading group find new and interesting angles and topics for your discussion. We hope that these ideas will enrich your conversation and increase your enjoyment of the book.*

INTRODUCTION

Oppression isn't an event—it's an environment. So declares *Creep*, a radical and unflinching essay collection that indicts the creeps skulking in our neighborhoods and collective consciousness, as well as the systems that allow them to live among us. In eleven essays, Myriam Gurba redefines accountability by analyzing the creeps in our newspaper headlines, politics, and homes, as well as how rhetoric, propaganda, and institutions serve creepy causes. Braiding together stories of literature's shining stars, rape jokes, and moments both hilarious ad harrowing from her own life, Gurba exposes our societal devotion to toxic traditions and the people who perpetuate them, all in prose that is in turn gleeful, blunt, poetic, and darkly funny.

TOPICS & QUESTIONS FOR DISCUSSION

1. Reflect on Gurba's writing style in *Creep*—its perspective, rhythm, and tone. What words would you use to describe it? Do you notice any differences across or within pieces?

2. Which is your favorite essay, and why?

3. Think about Gurba's treatment of William S. Burroughs, Richard Ramirez, Desiree, Lorena Gallo, and her own experiences with assault and abuse. How does *Creep* reframe how we typically see true crime narratives depicted? What does Gurba's approach give readers?

4. How does the California of *Creep* differ from the California of popular media? Are there any specific lines about California that you felt were especially evocative?

5. The first line of "Mitote" is "Before destroying my idols, I lay flowers at their feet" (page 89). How does this relate to Gurba's relationship with her grandfather, and *Creep*'s project overall?

6. How would you describe Gurba's sense of humor? How does it impact your reading of the book, especially the more difficult topics? Where there any moments of humor that you found especially surprising?

7. We get many glimpses of Gurba's childhood throughout *Creep*—from the opening "morbid games" she plays with Renee Jr. in "Tell" (page 1), to her relationship with Desiree in "Locas," and her experience at Orcutt Junior High School in "Navajazo" (page 158). How do these anecdotes demonstrate and shape Gurba's worldview? Can you identify similar moments of realization or indignation in your own life?

8. Think about the major relationships Gurba dramatizes in *Creep*—for example, with Desiree, her Abeulito, and her girlfriend Sam. Which did you find the most emotionally or narratively compelling? Why do you think that is?

9. In the titular essay, Gurba reflects on the murder of her sister's fifteen-year-old friend by her seventeen-year-old ex-boyfriend. "Without rage, how do people heal? Without rage, how does one produce dignity?" Gurba wonders (page 273). What role does anger have in Gurba's conception of a better world? What other instances of generative anger are there in *Creep*?

10. "Creep" is the collection's longest essay. What emotions did it bring up for you? Why do you think Gurba chose to conclude with this essay?

ENHANCE YOUR BOOK CLUB

1. Choose a few events that *Creep* explores—for example, the *San Gabriel Valley Tribune* article that reports Desiree's involvement in gift card fraud (page 5), or Ingrid Escamilla Vargas' murder (page 175)—and write a new newspaper headline in the spirit of reconfiguring dominant narratives.

2. In "The White Onion," Gurba writes, "These days, I find what Didion doesn't show more interesting than what she tells. Literary criticism, along with history, hands me a scalpel, enabling me to slice open the stomachs of those subjects made visible by her prose" (page 152). Select a Joan Didion work that appears in *Creep*—*Run, River*; "Guaymas, Sonora," "The White Album," or *Where I Was From*—and read it for your next book club. In your discussion, analyze Didion's silences, and compare and contrast her California with that of Gurba's in *Creep*.

3. Select one piece from *Creep* and read it closely together—research the references Gurba makes, pay close attention to the rhetorical devices she employs, and discuss how the essay connects and what it contributes to the collection as a whole.

A CONVERSATION WITH MYRIAM GURBA

What did you bring from your experience writing *Mean* to your experience writing *Creep*? On a craft and research level, how were the processes similar and different?

Creep is an unorthodox sequel to my true crime memoir *Mean*. While *Mean* chronicles my experience of surviving stranger-perpetrated sexual assault, *Creep* closely examines the impact of intimate partner violence. Typically, a sequel follows the same form and genre as its predecessor, but I deviated from both of those when I set out to write *Creep*. Instead, I used the personal essay, in combination with history and cultural criticism, to continue the literary and political project initiated by *Mean*. Specifically, I wanted to introduce readers to the dangerous conditions under which I wrote *Mean*.

Stylistically, *Mean* and *Creep* share key similarities. For instance, the texture of *Mean* was created through collaging. I collected personal ephemera and inserted it into the narrative so that readers could experience contemporary artifacts that might create an illusion of intimacy, of the audience being granted access into my private world. Some examples of ephemera from *Mean* include my university class schedules, excerpts of essays I wrote while completing my bachelor's degree, and some poetry written by my attacker. Collaging also happens in *Creep*. Rather than narrate the physical injuries my abuser inflicted on me, I insert medicals records into the text. These records function as literary x-rays, allowing the reader to see past the charade of normalcy in which I had to participate for self-preservation. These medical records inventory the physical harm which I sustained but was prohibited from discussing by my abuser.

I enjoy doing research and learned from missteps I made while writing *Mean*. I tried not to reproduce those mistakes when writing *Creep*. One of the lessons I learned from *Mean* is that when researching femicide, I must protect myself from the effects of vicarious trauma. I worked hard to insulate myself from such injury while working on *Creep*. One method that I used was to limit the amount of time I spent with certain materials. Once my gut would tell me that more time spent with research materials was going to be harmful, I stepped away from the work and engaged in a restorative activity. Baking was one of these restorative activities and while writing *Creep*, I baked my ass off. I have mastered the apple pie, and my scones are exquisite.

What does the epigraph mean to you? Why did you choose it?

The epigraph is a nod to *The Plain in Flames*, a short story collection published by Mexican author Juan Rulfo, my grandfather's frenemy. I chose the lines because I appreciate their moral ambiguity.

How did you decide on the order of the essays?

I very deliberately placed the collection's title essay at the end of the book. The graphic violence described by "Creep" challenges readers, and had it led the collection, some readers might have had an even harder time stomaching it. Cumulatively, the essays create a fog of sorts, one through which I, the narrator, lead the reader. Once the audience arrives at "Creep," they are immersed in my world and will likely have a harder time turning away from the violence that they encounter on the page.

Methodologically speaking, how does queerness function in *Creep*?

Creep appropriates stylistic and structural tics found in Juan Rulfo's *Pedro Páramo*, a gothic novel set in a fictional Mexican ghost town and narrated by the dead. Some critics have accused Rulfo's fractal masterpiece of having no core and I love that! *Creep* also lacks a core and I believe that that is the core of the book's queerness. *Creep* has no singular thesis. Instead, its core is dynamic. It shape-shifts, adapts, appropriates, rebels, and is reborn as needed.

Was there a particular moment or scene that was especially pleasurable to write? Is there a line, section, or chapter of which you're especially proud?

I really enjoyed writing this line in the acknowledgements section, "And to everyone who got in the way of this book happening, fuck you."

What is the relationship between humor and heaviness in *Creep* (and in life)?

In order to live, Joan Didion told stories. In order to live, I tell jokes. Humor protects me from pain both on and off the page and I encourage survivors of gender-based violence to use humor in their recovery. Laughing at rapists and turning *them* into the butt of jokes is a quick and effective way of restoring one's dignity. I meditate on the distinctions between survivor-generated humor versus perpetrator-generated humor in the essay "Slimed." I'm particularly fascinated by the notion of rape as a misogynist practical joke.

What does it feel like to write about your childhood? Your ancestors?

I enjoy writing about my childhood. I had A LOT of fun as a kid. I also had outrageously high self-esteem despite a decade of terrible haircuts. I feel compelled to write as much as I possibly can about my ancestors because doing so is part of my spiritual practice. I engage in ancestor veneration, but I don't approach the practice as idealization. At times, ancestor veneration veers into the sphere of reckoning. I am especially interested in correcting absences. My family descends from various populations, including nations indigenous to what is now called Mexico. We also descend from enslaved Africans trafficked in the Americas. My practice of ancestor veneration spurs me to research, reconstruct, and write our histories as a form of spiritual resistance, an antidote to the amnesia imposed by settler colonialism. "Mitote," an essay that functions as an anti-tribute to my maternal grandfather, was written in this vein. I love my grandfather, but he could also be a real asshole.

Near the very end of the book, you write "A book and a life are works of art. Making art isn't inherently cathartic. Instead, it can be a protective cocoon." How does this relate to your experience developing and writing *Creep*?
When *Mean* published, I was asked the same stale question over and over again. Was the experience of writing about sexual assault "cathartic?" The question made me want punch the people asking it in the mouth. When I was working on *Mean,* I didn't give a fuck about catharsis; I was trying to stay alive. I was living with a man whom I feared might kill me. One of the few places where I could hide from my abuser was my imagination. My art was another place. While writing *Mean* was protective, it was never purgative. Perhaps writing about trauma is cathartic for some but there are many of us who seek healing using other modalities. Also, catharsis is supposed to be the reader's reward, not the artist's. Aristotle taught that catharsis is aroused in the audience of those watching a tragedy. It does not belong to the author of the tragedy. I wish that the myth of artmaking as catharsis would die.

What do you hope readers take away from reading *Creep*?
The desire to buy everything I ever have or will write. Just kidding! Honestly, I hope that readers experience some entertainment or amusement. I do write to entertain. I can't help it. I also hope that those who want or need edification experience it. My greatest hope is that readers are spurred to participate in social movements that combat the forms of violence condemned by the book. Awareness is useless without action.